The Krampus and the Old, Dark Christmas:
Roots and Rebirth of the Folkloric Devil
by Al Ridenour

©2016 Al Ridenour
ISBN 9781627310345

Feral House
1240 W. Sims Way Suite 124
Port Townsend, WA 98368
www.FeralHouse.com

Design by Sean Tejaratchi

Bibliography and other supplemental material:
http://krampuslosangeles.com/book/

Printed in China.

THE
KRAMPUS
AND THE OLD, DARK CHRISTMAS
ROOTS AND REBIRTH OF THE FOLKLORIC DEVIL

BY

AL RIDENOUR

FERAL HOUSE

SIGNIFICANT TOWNS & LANDMARKS

1. **Bad Mitterndorf**
   Nicholas play, *Schabmänner*

2. **Bad Gastein**
   Classic Krampus and house visits

3. **Bavarian Forest**
   Rauhnacht folklore and events

4. **Berchtesgaden**
   Nicholas procession/play.

5. **Breitenbach am Inn**
   Perchten

6. **Frau-Holle-Teich**
   Frau Holle mythology/site

7. **Altenmarkt**
   Perchtenlauf

8. **Hörselberg**
   Subterranean home of Holle

9. **Kirchseeon**
   Perchten event

10. **Kyffhauser-Berg**
    Alternate mountain home of Holle

11. **Lienz, Osttirol**
    Site of Nicholas play deaths

12. **Lucerne**
    "Night Folk," Wild Hunter Türst

13. **Öblarn**
    Nicholas-Krampus play

14. **Prags**
    Early Nicholas play

15. **Prettau**
    Early folk/Nicholas plays

16. **Rauris**
    Birdlike *Schnabelperchten*

17. **Mt. Schlern**
    Witchcraft site

18. **Sonthofen**
    Wild Barbaras and Klausen

19. **Tegernsee**
    Medieval Christmas play

20. **Thuringian Forest**
    Frau Holle and Wild Hunt

21. **Urnäsch**
    Silvesterchlausen

22. **Waldkirchen**
    Rauhnacht event

23. **Wassertrüdingen**
    St. Martin's Nußmärtel.

24. **Weißenbach**
    Nicholas play, "graphite devils"

ALPS

BOHEMIA
(Czech, historic)

CZECH REPUBLIC

SLOVAKIA

UPPER
AUSTRIA

LOWER
AUSTRIA

Vienna ✶

Salzburg ✶

AUSTRIA

4

STYRIA

BURGEN-
LAND

1

7 24 13

ZBURG

STYRIA

16

2

Graz ✶

HUNGARY

CARINTHIA

FRIULI

SLOVENIA

CROATIA

TABLE OF CONTENTS

Introduction

THE DEAD OF WINTER

"It was the Yuletide, that men call Christmas though they know in their hearts it is older than Bethlehem and Babylon, older than Memphis and mankind."
— H.P. Lovecraft, "The Festival"

In his 1925 short story, Lovecraft describes a "Yule-rite, older than man and fated to survive him," a vision prompted by a trip to Marblehead, Massachusetts a few years earlier, where he perceived, "in a flash all the past of New England—all the past of Old England—all the past of Anglo-Saxondom and the Western World." His recent study of folklore combines with this vision in "The Festival," describing the "survival of some clan of pre-Aryan sorcerers who preserved primitive rites like those of the witch-cult." Lovecraft reports that at the time he had been reading Margaret Murray's *The Witch-Cult in Western Europe*, and while Murray's theories have since been discounted, the author's intuitions about the holiday's connection to witchcraft and an older, darker world are in fact sound. It's an intuition I believe we all share in some measure.

Christmas requires the darkness. Every child understands that it's only at midnight the Christmas mystery unfolds. The holiday we've spun from sugarplums and annual TV specials can't exist without those dark edges where imagination blooms. Not by chance it aligns with the long, black night of the solstice and Nature's last breath. Skeletal trees or howling winds aren't required. Even those who've grown up with the hum of Christmas air-conditioning have felt the uncanny as they await that curious night traveler traversing skies in archaic costume and prophet's beard.

A Christmas Carol, illustration by Arthur Rackham (1915). *British Library, London.*

Come late November, the child's world of consensual reality begins to dissolve—magic elves crouch and spy in suburban homes, still-moist pines are suddenly hauled indoors, and parents whisper and sleepwalk through rituals they can't explain. Tradition lies heavy as if overseen by long-departed ancestors.

In the 20th century, the Krampus has arrived in English-speaking lands like a thing long awaited. This menacing old-world companion to St. Nicholas shocks us with his brutal threats of punishment for naughty children, but somehow, also, he seems inevitable. In a secular society where the craving for the Other is more commonly satisfied through horror and fantasy than the midnight mass, this monstrous character seems custom-made to provide a thrill of holiday awe. It doesn't hurt that he comes from the German-speaking world. Christmas in America, and a lesser extent in the UK, has long shown bias toward the German. Our Christmas tree, Santa Claus, "Silent Night," card exchanges, and even the libretto of *The Nutcracker* are all unashamedly Germanic.

Even the friction between the savage Krampus and our notion of the holiday as cozy domestic idyll is slowly working in the beast's favor. For Americans who came of age in the rebellious punk-rock era, the Krampus now cuts a handsome figure. Somewhat myopically perceived as the "anti-Santa," he seems to express the requisite countercultural contempt for the Coca-Cola guzzling, bloated patriarch of all that is consumerist and parental. As Dead Kennedys fans succumb to reproductive urges, hanging up that family Krampus ornament purchased at an alternative craft fair becomes an increasingly important token of a fading rebellion. Slowly, or perhaps more quickly than we expect, the advance guard of American parenting is breaking ground for the Krampus alongside Grandma's visit, the Christmas dinner, and other enduring family traditions.

Before the Krampus, the counterculture had no real figurehead for its holiday revolution. While neo-pagans of the 1960s gleefully dug out Christmas' non-Christian roots, for Americans of the punk-rock generation, it was left to the arrival of slasher-Santa movies of the 1970s to really do some violence to the seasonal status quo. Growing out of 1974's *Silent Night, Bloody Night* and *Black Christmas* (and the more finely-tuned psychodrama of 1980's *Christmas Evil*) an entire cinematic genre of holiday horror was born.

What is significant here is the American idea of holiday horror beginning as something subversive, a knife-wielding intrusion from outside attacking the holiday ideal of domestic bliss. In Europe, we now see another tack taken, and the traditional folklore of Christmas has become integral to more recent horror films like Finland's *Rare Exports* and Holland's *Sint* ("Saint") with their Krampus-like and St. Nicholas-inspired figures coming from within the holiday traditions. The 2010 release date of the two films notably corresponds with the recent international uptick of interest in the traditions discussed in this book.

It is, of course, not the shock of radical new juxtapositions or subversive frisson Europeans experience in the Krampus, as he's been around in one form another since the 18th century. While English-speakers may correctly surmise that the tradition is one of some antiquity and even rather pagan, it comes as a surprise that this fearsome devil is hardly an isolated example of yuletide horrors. The Krampus springs from a deep-rooted European understanding of Christmas as a time of supernatural mayhem.

Literature is perhaps where we English-speakers best intuit the connection of our holiday to the darkness of the dying year. The longer nights are perfect for fireside retellings of what Christopher Marlowe and his contemporaries called "winter tales" as in his 1595 play *The Jew of Malta*:

> *Now I remember those old women's words*
> *Who in my wealth would tell me winter's tales*
> *And speak of spirits and ghosts that glide by night.*

A couple decades later, Prince Mamillius of Shakespeare's *The Winter's Tale* defines the genre: "A sad tale's best for winter; I have one / Of sprites and goblins."

It was left to the Victorians to revive the holiday horror story as a bona fide tradition. In 1891, British travel-writer and humorist Jerome K. Jerome introduced an anthology of Christmas ghost stories, explaining, "Whenever five or six English-speaking people meet round a fire on Christmas Eve, they start telling each other ghost stories. Nothing satisfies us on Christmas Eve but to hear each other tell authentic anecdotes about specters." Henry James even employs the then-common telling of holiday ghost stories as framing device for his 1898 gothic novella *Turn of the Screw*. But it is Charles Dickens' *A Christmas Carol* that most famously embodies the phenomenon.

Most Americans will be surprised that Dickens' tale of chain-dragging, shrouded specters is but one of his efforts in the field. Published in 1837, *The Pickwick Papers* also notably contains "The Story of the Goblins Who Stole a Sexton," in which a mean-spirited gravedigger is dragged underground on Christmas Eve by a goblin. Much like Ebenezer Scrooge, his adventure leaves him a changed man. Also set during the holidays is Dickens' 1848's story "The Haunted Man and the Ghost's Bargain, A Fancy for Christmas-Time" and 1851's "The Last Words of the Old Year." Others of his many ghost stories, while not explicitly set during the holidays, were issued in collections marketed as Christmas reading.

Though no longer occupying the central place it once did, the tradition of the holiday spook story has been supported into the 21st century by British radio and television. In 1971, BBC One inaugurated an annual tradition with the series "A Ghost Story for Christmas." Running through 1978, it was resurrected by BBC

Welsh *Mari Lwyd.* *Photo by R. fiend (2011), (CC BY-SA 3.0).*

Four with episodes in 2005, 2006, 2010, and 2013 featuring both original screenplays and traditional tales including those by Edwardian ghost-story master M.R. James.

However, outside cosmopolitan Britain and traditions maintained by the BBC, one also finds vestiges of an older, darker holiday closer to the world of the Krampus. The Christmas devil of Alpine Europe belongs to the wider family of Europe's costumed mumming traditions, one particularly strong in Britain at Christmastime. These often-slapstick folk plays enacted throughout the island, with their common theme of death and resurrection, were once believed to represent vestigial forms of ancient fertility rites akin to those described in Murray's *The Witch-Cult in Western Europe*. While these notions are now largely discredited, there remains in these traditions something somehow undeniably witchy.

A case in point: the Welsh tradition of the *Mari Lywd* ("grey mare"), a ghoulish horse skull paraded on a pole by men shrouded in a sheet. Once common throughout Wales, but now preserved only in certain regions of the southeast, this nightmarish creature parades through nocturnal streets, hovering at windows and thumping on doors in the weeks between Christmas and late January.

Also flying in the face of the "peace and goodwill" of the modern Christmas is the strange Irish custom of Wren Day (December 26) in which "wrenboys" dressed in shaggy straw costumes or ragged clothes capture or kill a bird and display the miserable thing on a decorated pole. The custom is said to offer symbolic retribution against a seductive Celtic goddess who would drown men in the sea, one only assailable on St. Stephen's day when she would transform herself into a small and helpless wren.

Even in the US, in the backwoods settlements of Pennsylvania, and here and there throughout the Midwest, there once existed a rough and threatening Christmas figure known as the Belsnickel. Introduced by German immigrants in the early 1800s and persisting in certain areas into the 1930s, this frightening character appeared throughout the Christmas season toting a whip and dressed in ragged clothes or furs. Raising a ruckus in public streets and often entering private homes without the owner's leave, the Belsnickel would terrify adults and scatter sweets for children, chasing them with his whip as they went for the bait.

These are but a few examples of an older, more dangerous Christmas with ties to the Krampus phenomenon. Slumbering for many decades, customs such as these and the darker notion of holiday-making they represent shows signs of return as a younger generation of both European and now American returns to the street with their horned masks, fur suits, and noisy bells. Having acquainted ourselves with a few examples of holiday ghosts, ruffians, and bugaboos from a more familiar English-speaking world, we may now be better prepared to undertake a journey to the snow-swept Alps where the Krampus himself arose.

Chapter One

GRUSS VOM KRAMPUS, THE DARK COMPANION

From Alps to Internet

Heading into the Austrian state of Carinthia from Northeast Italy, the Eastern Alps startle you with their approach. There are no rolling foothills to warn you of what is to come. They leap into sight, jutting up brutally, like a craggy wall encircling a clouded kingdom of snow and stone. As my train climbed higher and was enclosed within those walls, I felt I had entered a sort of magic circle.

I had never seen a Krampus, but this Alpine climb seemed a fittingly dramatic overture to that experience. I was traveling from Venice to Austria's Gastein Valley, a region known for preserving the Krampus tradition in its oldest form. Just outside the Austrian border, I passed through Italy's Friuli region, one where 17th-century Inquisitors struggled against the *benandanti*, a secretive visionary cult accused of witchcraft. Later I would learn that this cult was one of the many threads connected to the mythology of the Krampus.

Racing through rugged precipices, it was all too easy to imagine some goat-footed creature uniquely adapted to haunt the villages below. In 48 hours, I would see young men donning animal hides and horns to play out a tradition with roots in the 18th century. I was a world away from my laptop and the Internet images that had sent me on the journey. In this dramatic landscape, I felt on the verge of a mythic encounter, but the truth is, like any English-speaker, the bulk of my knowledge and enthusiasm was fueled by Wikipedia, blogs, and Austrian tourism websites.

Krampus card, (ca.1920-30), Austria.

As any older out-of-touch individual will assure you, the Internet exists to destroy attention spans, literacy, taste, morals, and manners, that is—to do the Devil's work. Perhaps it's true, and who's to say till the last LOLcat is counted, but one devil that has definitely expanded his reach online is the Krampus.

Beginning in the early 2000s, many English-speaking web users began stumbling upon strangely arresting pictures said to have something to do with an odd European Christmas custom. Mostly these were scans of pre-WWI postcards featuring what appeared to be a bishop accompanied by a chained, furry devil. The creature went by the name "Krampus" and this peculiar word appeared in the German phrase "*Gruß vom Krampus*" ("Greetings from the Krampus") emblazoned on the cards. Then there were the children—shackled and tethered on chains, caught in a basket carried on the creature's back, or menaced by switches clutched in that devilish claw. It was the kids that threw us. If this was something to do with Christmas, it was light-years from the cloying celebration of childhood wonder marketed today. These jarring images were increasingly forwarded and reposted, studied with morbid curiosity, and eventually, in some quarters, gleefully embraced as a sort of countercultural holiday meme. Many of these images were channeled into pop consciousness by Chicago author and art curator Monte Beauchamp, who in 2004 published the first of several graphic compilations of *Krampuskarten*.

A decade or so later, the Krampus is more familiar. The St. Nicholas depicted in bishop's costume is clearly not the American Santa Claus but his decidedly less jolly ancestor. Like his American counterpart, he rewards good children with gifts, but here the similarity ends. He not only withholds gifts from the unruly but sees to it that miscreants are punished. This ugly duty, however, is below his ecclesiastic dignity and falls therefore to the Krampus, who either punishes them on the spot or carts them off in a basket to later be rent limb from limb, tossed into a pit or lake, or eaten. So goes the story.

The Krampus Arrives in America

Somewhere around the same time, perhaps a bit later, another sort of image depicting the Krampus also began appearing on English-language websites. While the postcard images clearly reflected an artistic style and mode of child-rearing indicative of a bygone era, we now had photographs of dozens if not hundreds of people impressively costumed as the creature and massing on clearly contemporary European streets. This, we learned, was also the Krampus—as he lives today. The parade-like happening depicted we learned to call a *Krampuslauf*

Moorpass from Maishofen, Austria, visit Hollywood Boulevard. *Photo © Vern Evans Photo.*

or "Krampus run" (despite the leisurely pace better described as "walking.") Apparently, these had been going on for years, if not decades, but no one had bothered to tell Americans what we'd been missing.

Seeing the Edwardian-era graphics fleshed out in stunning modern costumes only fanned flames of interest outside the creature's homeland. Americans were particularly eager to realize they could actually dress up as these devils, many of them not that different from the fantasy figures, Middle-Earth Orcs, or other monsters Hollywood had taught us to love. By 2011, National Public Radio and other media outlets were reporting that enthusiasts in Philadelphia were holding a homegrown version of the Krampus run. Within a few years, dozens of American cities were hosting runs and discovering the joy of extending the Halloween lifestyle into December. Today there are ongoing Krampus activities in Portland, Columbia, SC, Pittsburg, Bloomington, IN, and Dallas, to name a few. The event in Bloomington has grown to draw more spectators than any other American Krampus event, with an estimated 31,100 spectators attending in 2015.

By 2013, my friend Al Guerrero had founded the group Krampus Los Angeles, and since then we have co-produced a series of events including not only a Krampus run, but also costume lectures, films, productions of a 19th-century Austrian Krampus play in original translation, and participation with European groups. In 2014, we were joined in our *Krampuslauf* by three members of the Alt Gnigler Troupe from Salzburg, and in 20015, the entire 15-person Moor Troupe from the town of Maishofen, Austria, made a historic trek with us down Hollywood Boulevard. As there seems to be growing interest among European groups in visiting, we hope to continue and expand on this sort of exchange.

Around the time many of the homegrown troupes were springing up, the Krampus was appearing more frequently in American comics, graphic novels, and animated shorts. Particularly popular was the 2012 book *Krampus the Yule Lord* by fantasy artist Gerald Brom. Increasingly the devil appeared on T-shirts, mugs, and in the artisanal clutter of a hundred online Etsy shops. He began making walk-ons on US television shows, eventually in 2013 taking over entire episodes of shows like NBC's *Grimm* and *Lost Girl*, aired on Syfy.

The Krampus was also becoming a popular star of straight-to-video features, including 2013's *Krampus: The Christmas Devil* and *Night of the Krampus*. 2015 brought the particularly silly *Krampus: The Reckoning* and the anthology film, *A Christmas Horror Story*, starring William Shatner. All of these, however, pale in comparison to the advertising juggernaut Universal unleashed upon millions of Americans with its 2015 horror-comedy *Krampus* by director Michael Dougherty. Several more Krampus features, including one from Jim Henson Studios, are in production as I write this.

American Misconceptions

America's recent love affair with the Krampus, like any infatuation perhaps, tends to distort the object of its interest. Brom's *Krampus the Yule Lord* provided a specious backstory for the figure spun from Nordic mythology and presented him as an enemy of Santa Claus. Unfortunately the Nordic connection concocted by Brom has sometimes been accepted as fact and even repeated in a 2013 *National Geographic* article "Who Is Krampus? Explaining the Horrific Christmas Devil." As will later be discussed, the folklore may occasionally hint at a connection to Scandinavian tradition, but Brom's presentation of the Krampus as the son of the divine Loki is pure fantasy. The Krampus' furious opposition to St. Nick, an important theme in Brom's book, has also been perpetuated in the comic series *Krampus!* by Brian Joines and Dean Kotz and elsewhere by those eager to see the figure viciously opposed to the Santa Claus of their childhood. This Americanized symbol of youthful rebellion has little to do with the Krampus' traditional role working collaboratively with the saint.

Though perhaps not exactly pleased with his chained subjugation to Nicholas, the Krampus known in Europe is more than happy in his role as dutiful punisher.

There is also the Protestant confusion between St. Nicholas and Santa Claus and the date with which the Krampus is associated. Europe's Krampus makes his appearance with the historical bishop venerated as St. Nicholas. He appears on St. Nicholas Eve and Day (December 5–6). American Krampus stories, however, tend to bring in the red-and-white-clad fellow from old Coca-Cola ads, and set the story on Christmas. The urge to assimilate the European devil with Santa Claus and his traditions seems somehow to be a weakness of our genes.

The 2015 Universal movie *Krampus*, if nothing else, will remain as lasting memorial to the Krampus-as-Evil-Santa misconception. Dougherty's beast squeezes down chimneys, drives a sleigh pulled by a sort of monstrous reindeer, and is assisted by elves, who ironically look more like the Krampus than the character himself, as some appear to be outfitted with genuine Krampus masks. The monster's character design seals the deal, visualizing the Krampus as an oversized hump-backed being in a red fur-trimmed robe, white-bearded, and with ghoulish but human face resembling a rather exhausted Santa Claus.

One last misconception involves the provenance of the Krampus. While often understood as German, which he can be, he is really more distinctly Austrian. Though the custom is strongest in western Austria, throughout the country, you'll generate lively discussion if you bring up the Krampus. In Germany, however, the tradition is only really practiced in the south. A northern Berlin urbanite, for instance, would almost certainly be familiar with the Krampus but merely as a curious custom belonging to the rustic south. Austria and Bavaria are the real strongholds of the Krampus tradition. They are culturally related and distinct from the rest of Germany, and share similar dialects often fairly incomprehensible to those in northern German states.

Krampuskarten

Austria's cultural dominance during the expansion of the Austro-Hungarian Empire, and the phenomenon of Krampus cards popular into the Empire's waning pre-war years, were factors in the diffusion of the tradition. Two years after the founding of the Empire in 1867, Austria's mail system became the first to facilitate the delivery of postcards, and by the late 1880s, the *Krampuskarten* had begun to appear. This introduced the notion of the Krampus to regions beyond the creature's Alpine homeland.

The Krampus cards were necessarily created by artists more likely to reside

Krampus cards. Opposite: Poland, ca. 1910-1930. This page: Germany/Austria, ca 1920.

in metropolitan areas far from the beast's indigenous home in isolated mountain valleys. If villagers were dressing in animal hides and horns, there was no anthropologist collecting photos to serve as reference, so the imagery for the cards likely derived from traditional Catholic depictions of the devil or the pagan figure of Pan. The latter would have been particularly influential during this period as *fin de siècle* artists doted on this embodiment of pagan ideals and its associated notions of orgiastic excess. The era's mania for Pan is evidenced by its countless sculptures, prints, and paintings, the title of *Pan* as an important Symbolist art and literary journal published in Berlin, and even in the figure of the pipe-playing god appearing in and gracing the cover of Kenneth Grahame's 1908 *Wind in the Willows*.

The perplexingly different guises presented by the Krampus cards versus the traditional costumes has been confusing for Americans more recently trying to puzzle out the tradition. (Anyone who's struggled to contrive a costume converting the lower body to match the goat-footed image on the cards should breathe a sigh of relief knowing that those depictions, while older than *Krampuslauf* photos, are not necessarily a more "authentic" representation of the Krampus.)

While some superficial knowledge of the Krampus circulated to regions beyond the Alps in the *Krampuskarten* era, these areas are not where the tradition struck deep roots and developed. The phenomenon of *Krampuskarten* is in fact rather tangential to the real story of the Krampus. The vitality of the tradition lies not in its wide diffusion but in its isolated growth within a sort of cultural hothouse enforced by Alpine topography. As with the many distinct dialects and traditional costumes that characterize different nearby valley communities, the historic obstacles involved in traversing the Alps focused and preserved Krampus customs in their highly localized form. Those of us raised in the homogeneity of American melting-pot culture have trouble understanding this regionalism, which affects every aspect of the tradition, even the name by which the creature goes.

The Krampus By Any Other Name

"Krampus" is not really an individual's name but a class of entity, e.g., "vampire" not "Dracula." For this reason, and in accordance with German usage, I maintain the article "the" before the word unlike some English sources. For the curious—since it's often asked—the correct plural for Krampus in German would not be the faux-Latinate "Krampi" but *Krampusse*. For simplicity, however, I'll be pluralizing as "Krampuses." Additionally, I follow the convention of capitalizing all German nouns, so capitalization here needn't designate a proper noun.

"Krampus" is understood to derive from the Middle German *"Kralle"* ("claw") or from the Bavarian *"Krampn"* referring to something lifeless, dried out, or shriveled, the latter pointing to a connection between the Krampus and the spirits of the dead to be later discussed. "Krampus," as we'll see, is not really the name preferred in more traditional regions for the beast. This word gained wide usage in the late 19th and 20th century with the circulation of Krampus cards, and has only recently become the international standard thanks to recent print and online use.

In the Bavarian foothills and the area around Salzburg, the preferred term is actually *Kramperl*. In East Tyrol, and in older manuscripts, *Klaubauf* is the preferred term. Tyroleans and others may also simply refer to him as the *Tuifl* (dialect for "devil"), and around Salzburg similarly *Toifi*. Or sometimes, believing that the devil's name is unlucky to speak aloud, a circumlocution describing rather than naming might be used, like *Ganggerl* or *Gankerl* (probably from *"Gang"* or "gait"), a name which may also derive from the distinctive lope or hopping gait performers adopt. In strongly traditionalist areas, these regional words are preferred, but here too, with each generation, the more universal "Krampus" seems to be gaining in usage.

Along with regionalism, the Protestant/Catholic divide has been a historic factor in diversifying the tradition. In Protestant lands, as Nicholas was transformed from ecclesiastic figure to secular gift-giver, he continued to be accompanied by a number of different characters that have come to be known generically as "dark companions."

Knecht Ruprecht

In Germany, the most well known "dark companion" is Knecht Ruprecht ("Servant Ruprecht"). The character today is typically dressed in dark hooded robe accented with fur, wears a dark, bushy beard, carries switches, and totes a large sack (once used to carry off naughty children, but now to hold gifts). Other than differences in appearance, Knecht Ruprecht distinguishes himself from the Krampus as a solitary companion of St. Nicholas, never appearing in multiples or en masse as in the *Krampuslauf*. Ruprecht does not himself, like the Krampus, use switches on misbehaving children, but instead only makes a gift of them to the unruly child or his parents as a reminder of punishment due.

Occasionally, Knecht Ruprecht's face may be blackened with ashes or he may even carry a bag of ashes with which to thump the unruly and leave a telltale mark (just as in some areas of the Tyrol, the Krampus smears victims with a mixture of lard and ashes.) The blackened face, which here does not carry the baggage of

Knecht Ruprecht by Berthold Woltze (1829-1896).

American racism, probably once served as a simple way to make the face frighteningly unrecognizable. It may also have been associated with the sooty visage of the local blacksmith who worked in a fiery environment itself evocative of the Devil. Blackened faces are a common way of obscuring the faces of Christmas mummers throughout Europe, and in the case of English tradition, the performers' anonymity was said to be essential to the magical luck imparted by visiting mummers. Other theories suggest that faces were blackened because these figures represented the dead traveling in the winter nights. Under their masks, *Krampuslauf* participants today still blacken their faces, obscuring not only the visible area around the eyes, but also often blackening the entire face whether visible or not.

The identity of Knecht Ruprecht, as explored in Jacob Grimm's *Deutsche Mythologie* (1835), more likely begins with mentions of a 17th century figure in Nuremberg Christmas processions. The name chosen for Nicholas' servant would have been stereotypical. "Heinrich and Ruprecht," he writes, "were once common names for serving-men, as Hans and Claus are now," and Grimm further suggests that "Ruprecht" could have had demonic associations, remarking that Rüpel, Riepel, and Rubel were cited in witchcraft trials as names of a "little demon" companion or feline familiar of those being tried. The English Robin Goodfellow, a demonized pagan figure sometimes called "Puck," he writes, may also be related, as "Robin" is a French or Anglicized cousin of "Ruprecht."

Distaste in contemporary Germany for the more vicious punishing role assumed by the Krampus tends to now emphasize Knecht Ruprecht's role as gift-bearing servant over that of punisher, though this is not strictly a modern development. In some regions (Germany's North-eastern Saxony, and others), Ruprecht traditionally assumes the duty of handing out children's gifts, and this friendlier guise is today suggested in the television show, *The Simpsons*, where the family dog's name, "Santa's Little Helper" is rendered in the German as "Knecht Ruprecht."

The *Christkind* and the *Weihnachtsmann*

Luther also suggested that gift-giving customs be celebrated on Christmas (rather than St. Nicholas Day, New Year, or other occasions) and the role of gift-giver assigned to the "Holy Christ." With time, this came to be understood as the child of Mary and Joseph, the *Christkind* or *Christkindl* ("Christ Child"). When it came to impersonating this figure, a child rather than infant would be the practical choice, and this led to the rather odd custom of the role falling to a teenage female, who in earlier times might be to be regarded as more "pure" or "child-

Nürnberg *Christkind*, 2015-2016. *Photo © Christine Dierenbach/Stadt Nürnberg.*

like." While certainly confounding, maybe even a tad blasphemous, to English-speakers, this peculiar gender-bending figure is familiar throughout Germany. In the form of an annually-crowned and angelically-garbed adolescent girl s/he presides over the centuries-old Christkindl Market of Nuremberg, where thousands make seasonal visits to shop for Christmas trinkets or enjoy mulled wine and gingerbread. The tradition of the *Christkind* bringing gifts on Christmas Eve was also later taken up by German and Austrian Catholics as a second gift-giving occasion in addition to St. Nicholas Day.

Today the figure of the *Christkind* is well on its way to being edged out by a more modern figure, the *Weihnachtsmann* ("Christmas Man") now virtually indistinguishable from the modern American Santa Claus. The slow overshadowing in Catholic regions, of the *Christkind* by the *Weihnachtsmann*, has locally become a hot-button issue understood, perhaps a bit unfairly, as one of American cultural imperialism. While certainly influenced by America's 19th-century Santa Claus or the UK's Father Christmas, the *Weihnachtsmann* also drew on homegrown traditions of rustic, fur-clad gift-givers related to the *Ruprecht-Nicholas* hybrids discussed. One oft-cited source for the character is actually the work of Austrian artist Moritz von Schwind for a Bavarian publication, Munich's popular *Bilderbogen*, which in 1847 featured illustrations of a holiday gift-giver simply identified as "Herr Winter." Influence ran both ways, however, and America's Santa Claus tradition also embodied elements of the continental "dark companion" and European mumming traditions as will be discussed in a later chapter.

Père Fouettard, Hans Trapp, and Schmutzli

Germany's Knecht Ruprecht also has local variants in neighboring countries under German cultural influence. In the Alsace (the once-German region of France) and across the Rhine in the Palatinate, Knecht Ruprecht blends into Père Fouettard ("Father Whip") or Hans Trapp. Both characters are of similar appearance and perform roles identical to Ruprecht, but Hans Trapp (also Hans von Trapp or Hans Troth) actually happens to be associated with a historical knight and nobleman, Hans von Trotha, whose story is worth relating.

In the late 1400s, von Trotha engaged in a dispute over lands with the abbot of a nearby Benedictine monastery. During the feud, the noble dammed a river to cut off water to monastic lands in question, eventually tearing down the dam and causing devastating floods in the nearby town of Weissenburg. As result of this and further hostilities, von Trotha was summoned to Rome by Pope Alexander VI.

The knight refused to appear, writing to the Borgia Pope and accusing him of vague indecencies. In turn, he was excommunicated and henceforth referred to in local legend as the "Black Knight." Folklore associated him with the Devil, dark arts, and even cannibalism, and he was incorporated as villain into a legend associated with a nearby spring. The waters of the Jungfernsprung ("virgin's leap") in the Rhineland town of Dahn were said to have miraculously appeared where a maiden landed after a jump from a cliff. Pursued by would-be rapist von Trotha, she leapt from the cliff, but survived, thanks to the miraculous effect of ballooning skirts.

In Switzerland, where Père Fouettard is known in French regions, German-speakers refer to a character known as Schmutzli. His appearance is much like Ruprecht's, though unlike the solitary German companion, Schmutzli may appear in groups of two or three as well as individually. Originally going by the name *Butzli*, sometime in the early 1900s, the name morphed into its current form, which folk etymology derives from "*Schmutz*" or "grime" (referring to the figure's often ash-smeared face).

Zwarte Piet

In the Low Countries, Zwarte Piet ("Black Peter") fills the role. Appearing either singly or in multiples, traditionally toting a whip and bag, and dressed in garb of a Renaissance courtier, Zwarte Piet also notoriously wears blackface and curly wig. Unlike the sooty appearance of Ruprecht or Schmutzli, Black Peter is explicitly a "Blackamoor," and is a literary creation, owing little in his appearance to the Church's dark Devil or local folklore. Though not explicitly identified as Zwarte Piet, the character's first appearance comes in 1850 in "*Sint Nikolaas en zijn Knecht*" ("Saint Nicholas and His Servant") by schoolteacher Jan Schenkman. In the book, St. Nicholas and servant arrive in Holland via steamboat having begun their journey, for reasons not entirely clear, in Spain. Re-enactment of this seafaring arrival in Amsterdam has become an ongoing part of the Zwarte Piet tradition with Dutch television annually broadcasting the event now featuring an entire crew of Petes of varying ranks: Hoofdpiet (Head Pete), Rijmpiet (Rhyming Pete), etc.

Understandably, the racially charged figure today is the object of countless angry editorials, cautious defenses, finger-pointing, and demonstrations. Various revisionist attempts seek to ameliorate the damage. Ignoring the character's pointedly curly wig, it's been suggested that prior to his service to St. Nicholas, Pete had been a chimney sweep, a job that permanently darkened his skin. Another defense points to a legend associated with St. Nicholas in which the saint frees

Cover of *St. Nicholas and his Servant* by Jan Schenkman (ca. 1900-1909).
The National Library of the Netherlands, The Hague.

a slave from the "Emperor of Babylon" and returns him to his home, though no explanation is provided for Pete's subsequent servitude with Nicholas. Increasingly Pete is portrayed more as a companion or "friend" of the saint than slave, and is given the task of handing out gifts rather than brandishing a whip. For several decades, alternative Petes made up in a variety of colors other than black have also been trotted out, but this compromise has not really caught on, providing little to satisfy either defenders or detractors of the tradition.

Frightful Stories for Better Children

Whether shaped by literary, folkloric, or ecclesiastic elements, the idea of a threatening figure paired with the giving of rewards clearly meets a pragmatic need felt by parents worldwide. A bogeyman (more analytically described in German as a *Kinderschreckfigur*, i.e, "child terror figure") can ensure that children say their prayers, mind their manners, or go to sleep on time. It is likely the Krampus or other "dark companions" began as just such amorphous and changeable buga-boos—something spoken of but never actually seen. Evolving perhaps from a vague and shadowy bogeyman, like the *Schwarzer Mann* ("black man" in a racially neutral sense), the figure was only visualized with any specificity once the cus-tom of impersonating the figure was adopted. His face might naturally be black-ened and further obscured with a dark, false beard. Outfitted in whatever "rough" dark clothes that might be at hand, he would be handed a whip and bag as attri-butes of his punishing function. In more Catholic lands, where church iconogra-phy was stronger, the Krampus' appearance came to more closely approximate the Devil's, and if a costume were to be created it would naturally come from the re-sources readily available to Alpine farmers—goat horns, and animal hides.

The Krampus assumed his modern form in mid-19th century, when a mode of childrearing the Germans call the *Zuckerbrot und Peitsche* ("sugar-bread and whip") was in full force. Like St. Nicholas Day, Christmas was fully exploited with this edu-cational strategy in mind. Children's Christmas gifts—which only at this point in history transformed from small tokens like gingerbread, oranges, or sweets to the more durable keepsakes we know today—needed to be edifying or pedagogical. Bibles and books that guided the child's behavior were therefore popular choices.

Appearing in 1854, and whimsically illustrated by its author, Heinrich Hoff-mann, *Der Struwwelpeter* ("Ungroomed Peter") takes its name from its monstrous title character sporting wildly unkempt hair and grotesquely long nails. In its pag-es, children who play with matches, refuse to eat, suck their thumbs, torment ani-mals, or commit other childish misdemeanors meet ghastly fates. Providing both cautionary examples and delicious *Schadenfreude* (delight in others' mistakes), the book is still printed today. Over the years, it has inspired an 1891 translation by Mark Twain, a 1955 film rendering the story as ballet, parodies like the WW II-era satire *Der Struwwelhitler*, a dedicated museum in Frankfurt, and a 1998 opera by British punk cabaret artists The Tiger Lillies (*Shockheaded Peter*).

Hoffmann created the volume as a Christmas gift for his three-year-old, with simple text and design specifically geared to a young reader's developmental lev-el. An angelic *Christkind* is depicted in the opening pages, and the text explicitly presents the book as a Christmas book earned by good behavior.

***Kindlifresserbrunnen* ("Child Eater Fountain"), Bern, Switzerland.**
Photo: Andrew Bossi (CC-BY-SA-2.5).

N. 8.   Der Kinderfresser.

Still, still, und werdet fromm, ihr gar zu böse Kinder,
    Springet und brüllt nit so, als wie die dumme Rinder,
Laßt euch was wehren doch, seyd nicht so ungehalten,
Folgt euren Elteren, Lehrmeister und den Alten,
    Wo nit, so komm ich gar geschwind zu euch gelauffen,
Und friß euch alle auf: Seht an den großen Hauffen,
So ich schon bey mir hab, die Säcke seyn gefüllet,
Mein Korb ist starrend voll, ein Theil trag ich verhüllet
    In meinen Hosen, und ein Theil in meinen Taschen,
Diese all hab ich geraubt, zum Fressen und zum Naschen,
    Wird mir die Zahl zu viel, daß ichs nicht kann auffressen,
So henck ich theils in Rauch, theils pfleg ich zu pressen,
So lang bis alles Blut aus Adern ist geflossen,
    Das sauf ich Maaß weiß aus mit meinen Hausgenossen,
Dem WauWau und der Bercht, vil pfleg ich klein zu backen,
Zu Knöpflein oder Würst, theils aber laß ich backen,

Als wie ein Birenknopf, zum Theil thu ich verstecken
Ins stinkend Mägdeloch, Mistgrub und bey den Hecken,
Bis mich zum Fressen mahnt mein hungeriger Magen,
Alsdann verschlingt sie auch des Kinderfressers Kragen,
So mach ichs auch euch, wann ihr wollt bös verbleiben,
Faul seyl, und nichts thun, denn nur Muthwillen treiben;
Ich steck euch in mein Sack, und beiß ab Füß und Aerme,
Händ, Ohren, Naß und Kopf, zernage das Gedärme,
Herz, Leber, Lung und Bauch, Wolt ihr mir gleich entfliehen,
So hab ich Strick genug, womit ich kann euch zu mir ziehen,
Ich frage nichts darnach, ihr mögt zu Hülfe rufen
Der Regel, Ursul, Lies, Ann, Berbel und Margrethen,
Ich nehm euch dannoch mit, frag nichts nach eurem Klagen,
Wann ihrs gleich zehenmal wollt eurer Mutter sagen,
Drum seyd gehorsam, still, gesellt euch zu den Frommen,
Daß ihr nicht dörft in Bauch des Kindleinfressers kommen.

Augspurg, bey Albrecht Schmid seel. Erben, Hauß u. Laden auf dem untern Graben.

Roots of the Kinderschreckfigur

The tradition of the German *Kinderschreckfigur* goes back much further, of course, than Hoffmann's book, or even the Krampus or Ruprecht figures. Embedded in the German language, with origins often in unknown past, are any number of spooks intended to aid in the discipline of children. Children fretting over their bedtime would not only be terrorized by the *Sandmann*, but also menaced by the *Nachtkrabb* ("Night Raven") and *Nachtbock* ("Night Goat"). The *Popelmann* and *Popelhole* drag naughty children off to swamps, while the *Wassermann* or the halffish *Hakemann* prey upon children foolishly endangering themselves near water. More all-purpose bogeymen go by a variety of other names: *Mummelratz* or *Mummelputz*, the *Butz*, *Butzemann, Butzemann,* and the previously mentioned *Schwarzer Mann*. Germans have many names for things they love.

In German-speaking Bern, Switzerland, another *Kinderschreckfigur* has been memorialized in a curious 16th-century fountain. Though the intent behind its installation is lost to time, the *Kindlifresserbrunnen* ("Child-eater fountain") depicts an ogre munching on the head of a child while holding a bag of squirming victims in reserve. While it's been theorized the scene may represent the classical motif of Saturn devouring his children, it's also suggested that the depiction might simply show a fearsome character impersonated in local Carnival festivities.

Supporting the Carnival-figure theory are images represented in broadsheets typically handed out at 16th- and 17th-century Carnival celebrations across German-speaking lands. Also making his home in Bern, artist Hans Weiditz in 1520 produced a woodcut, *Der Kinderfresser,* depicting a particularly nasty ogre gobbling a child. Like the Bern fountain, this monster is shown consuming the child headfirst and carrying several more in a sack, but Weiditz's illustration bests the statue with grisly detail: trickling blood and a pile of feces dropping from one particularly panicked infant.

About 80 years later, the subject was still popular, as demonstrated by another broadsheet by German artist Lorenz Schulltes. His *Kinderfresser* shows a similar scene staged at the door of a home where children seek safety from a cannibalistic ogre in the arms of their mother. Accompanying text drives home the didactic intent with the mother warning her children, "So if you do not want to be quiet right now, I will give you to him. Therefore be silent and still, come in the house, so that he will not find you crying outside." Still another broadsheet from a few decades later, *Der Mann mit dem Sack* ("The man with the sack"), by Bavarian artist Abraham Bach, Sr., features a menacing figure with bag stuffed full of squirming tots who is pursuing a frightened boy likewise fleeing into a doorway and the comfort of his mother.

The Child Eater, woodcut by Albrecht Schmid seel. Erben, (ca. 1750).

These child-snatchers can't help but remind us of December's "dark companions," especially as they show interest in pursuing "bad" children. In fact, there is no reason to suppose Knecht Ruprecht, as imagined in the 17th century, would have been much different than Bach's *Der Mann mit dem Sack*.

Similar in many ways to the other woodcuts, a final broadsheet from 1750, *Die Butzen-Bercht,* a woodcut by Bavarian artist Albrecht Schmidt, depicts a character specifically linked with the Krampus via the character of Frau Perchta, and the *Perchten*, elements of the Krampus genealogy to be later discussed.

Holding the distaff of a flax-spinner (a well-known symbol of Perchta), this witch-like crone terrifies children seeking mother's comfort again in the home's doorway. On her back, she carries young unfortunates stuffed into a basket of the type used by the Krampus. The name of the figure, the *Butzen-Bercht*, gives us further clues. "*Bercht*" is an alternate spelling for "Perchta" or "*Percht*." The prefix "*Butz*" is a word for "spook" or "bogeyman."

This Frau Perchta has led us back to witches, and to the *benandanti* persecuted by Italian Inquisitors and mentioned in the first paragraphs of this chapter. We are finally ready to cross that border into the Austrian Alps and encounter the Krampus as he lives today.

Die Butzen-Bercht, woodcut by Schmid seel. Erben, Augsburg (ca. 1750). Einblattdrucksammlung Gustav Freytag, Stadt- und Universitätsbibliothek, Goethe Universität, Frankfurt.

Die Butzen-Bercht.

Mum, mum, mum, wo seyd ihr Kinder, wo?
    Warum versteckt ihr euch, was fliehet ihr mich so?
Ich thu den Frommen nichts, die Bösen will ich plagen,
Und sie in Lech, Mägdloch, Hundsgraben, Mistgrub tragen.
Wollt ihr auch böse seyn, faulenzen und nichts thun,
Grumpfig und muffig seyn, als wie ein pfipffig Huhn,
Nichts lernen in der Schul, nichts nähen oder spinnen,
Nichts betten und aufstehn, so sollt ihr nicht entrinnen
Meim alten Besenstiel, der Peitschen und der Ruth,
Womit ich schlagen will euch bis aufs rothe Blut:
Ich will euch Händ und Füß kreuzweiß zusammenbinden,
Und werfen in den Koth, auch will ich euch anzünden
Euer Zöpf und Haar, das Gesicht zerkratzen, und die Nas
Abschneiden, und euch brav zerzaussen: über das
All euer Dockenwerck wegnehmen, und verbrennen,
Euer schönstes Sonntagskleid verschneiden und zertrennen,

Die Gunckel will ich so einfüllen voll mit Rotz,
Daß sie recht tropfnen soll, wann ihr als wie ein Klotz
Zu lang im Bette stackt und schnarcht, so will ich haspeln
Die Därme aus dem Bauch, und ihn hernach mit Raspeln
Und Hecheln füllen ein. Ich will euch in ein Haus
Zusammen sperren, wo ein Floh bald einer Maus,
Ein Laus bald einer Katz, in ihrer Größe gleichet,
Die Wantze einem Hund: Solch Ungeziefer schleichet
Zu Nacht in euer Bett, die Schlang soll Tisch-Gesell,
Der Wurm zur Kurzweil seyn: die Bänk und Tischgestell
Sind Küh- und Ochsendreck, Geißkugeln seyn die Speisen,
Mein Rotz ist das Getränk. Wolt ihr euch nun erweisen
Zu Haus und in der Schul, gottsfürchtig, fleißig, fromm,
So komm ich Butzbercht nit, mum, mum, mum, mum, mum;
Drum seyd gehorsam, still, gesellt euch zu den Frommen,
Daß ihr nicht dörft in Korb der Butzen-Bercht kommen.

Augsburg, bey Albrecht Schmid seel. Erben, Haus und Laden auf dem untern Graben.

Chapter Two

THE DEVIL AT THE DOOR

Meeting the Krampus

My first glimpse came through the fogged window of a taxi descending a narrow mountain road. It was the sound that alerted me, a ponderous, metallic clatter somewhere out in the dark. Our headlights caught something like a lumbering forest animal, or a pack of animals blocking the road. Through the flickering snowfall, I saw only pieces: moving hillocks of fur and bobbing horns, chains, and broom-like protuberances—bundled switches wagging in the creatures' fists. As the driver eased his car by, I glimpsed the belts hung on the back with those clattering bunches of bells, each nearly the size of a cannon ball. The beasts shambled off. One turned toward us, his mask displaying an insane lantern-jawed grimace and maw crammed with impossible teeth.

More monsters passed as we neared Bad Gastein's bustling town square where the driver deposited me. I paid and shouted a "*danke schön*" over a storm of clanking bells. Immediately I found myself jostled forward. Snow and mulled wine wafted through the air, and there were shouts and laughter as a herd of Krampus pushed into the square. They progressed with a sort of dancelike hopping motion, a choreographed tantrum that sent their bells bouncing in cascading rhythms. Spectators scrambled as more devils tumbled forward. Someone spilled wine, and I was spun into a mound of snow-damp sheepskin that smelled of wet livestock. I looked up into the monster's face. Breath steamed through his painted teeth as he growled, and I thought I caught a whiff of brandy. He rattled a chain and slashed the air with switches. I lurched back, slipping in snow, and felt the blow land on my back. I'd made contact!

Krampus mask carved by Miguel Walch, Tarrenz, Austria. *Photo © Miquel Walch Holzmasken.*

Moa Pass from Bad Gastein, Austria. *Photo © Gasteinertal.com.*

On a roughly made stage strung with lights, a microphone clunked. A young woman costumed as an angel passed the mike to a St. Nicholas in ecclesiastic garb. The saint handed off his crozier to a basket-carrying companion sporting a curious beard of dried moss. Nicholas began some rhymed verses. At his first syllable, all bells went dead. Like trained dogs, each Krampus had dropped to his knees, bowing his mask almost into the snow. The heavily accented Pongau dialect was hard to match to the citified German I'd learned from time in far-off Berlin, but I picked out phrases about the saint appearing but once a year, good deeds, rewards, bad deeds, and in more solemn tone: the consequence. At this, the devils exploded—roaring and jangling and whipping the crowd again into a stumbling whirlpool. A fat man was dumped into the snow. A young girl's cap was snatched away, and I found myself pushed alarmingly close to a grill with roasting chestnuts. Encircled by stomping, clattering devils, I couldn't stop laughing.

The rumpus rolled on in waves, one troupe leaving, another entering. Each brought its angels, mossy basket-carrier, and a different St. Nicholas, each mounting the stage and gravely reciting verse, devils bowing, devils leaping. As the routine grew familiar, I shuffled through the crowd and down hillside steps leading from the square.

Krampus mask carved by Miguel Walch, Tarrenz, Austria. *Photo © Miquel Walch Holzmasken.*

The town below was a different chaos. On roads snaking in from the mountains, cars stood jammed at odd angles where devils played or blocked intersections with their migrations. Drivers honked. Tides of bells reverberated through alleys and echoed distantly from hills. Beasts galumphing through swirling snow caught in headlights threw long shadows, howled and yowled and glowed red in brake-lights or phosphor-green or blue in the neon of shop windows. Stalled cars tried to reverse out of the bedlam, skidded, and toppled neatly ploughed snowbanks. Shaggy beasts piled around vehicles, pawing and peering in windows. Young passengers shrieked as the devils seized hold of cars and rocked them.

Krampus had broken the city, but this was not enough. Down the street, some new fury erupted. I rushed toward a fresh clamor of bells, clacking horns, and thudding bodies. Two monsters came crashing into one another, shoving and twisting like yaks vying for a mate. They circled, swayed apart, and flung themselves together again, steaming, and staggering in the whirling snow. I kept my distance, not entirely sure if this was just a game.

Rempler ("battle") between Scheibling Pass and Kühkar Pass, Gastein Valley, Austria.
Photo © Gasteinertal.com.

The *Rempler*

"It's called a *Rempler*," Matthäus Rest clarifies. "Or *Rempeln*," he says, explaining it's a colloquial word for "shove."

It's two years later and I am sitting in my Los Angeles home across from Rest, a social anthropology postgrad at UCLA. He also happens to be a native of Dorfgastein, Austria, located only a few miles from Bad Gastein where I met my first Krampus. Along with Gertraud Seiser, he is co-editing an analysis of field investigations on the Krampus, *Wild und Schön: Krampuslaufen im Salzburger Land*. Not only has he grown up with these events but his grandfather was involved in early efforts spurring the contemporary renaissance of the tradition.

The *Rempler*, Rest assures me, is indeed only a sort of game or ritualized turf war that occurs between two Krampuses from different troupes. An old protocol dictates how these battles unfold, and it begins with the costumed St. Nicholas heading each group. "They can only start once the Nicholases cross their staffs and make a little sort of speech." The noncombatants withdraw to the side, he says, to "chat and maybe exchange a little schnapps," but the Nicholases must remain watchful as it's up to them when to terminate the fight. "They have to know their Krampuses and know how much they can take. It shouldn't be too short, but it also can't be too long."

The Krampuses begin their duel with a bow then charge each other. While horns may accidentally bump, risk of injury or damage to masks usually excludes intentional head-butting or locking of horns. The *Rempler* is more about body slams and shoving. The battle continues until it seems the combatants have had enough, and a Nicholas gives the word or blows a whistle carried for the occasion. The Krampuses then bow, remove their masks and shake hands, wishing each other "*A guat's Weitergeh'n!*" ("good luck and go forward") or declare, "*Treu dem guten alten Brauch*" ("true to the good old ways"). This parting formality is regarded as vital in damping any hostilities stirred up in the process.

Do the *Rempler* ever get out of control?

"Yes, they sure do," says Rest. "Sometimes they do turn into something violent. Sometimes, week before these confrontations, participants will threaten each other. You know—'if we meet, there'll be blood!' But 95% of these encounters are very professional, in a way, really just about putting on show for those watching. If you go at it out for blood, it can always backfire, and *you* could be the one with the broken bones or broken mask."

As to the history of this practice, Rest says there are no written records documenting when it began. "My grandfather said the first time he encountered it was 1949. He had never experienced this in his town because there was no other Krampus group, and they had no one to oppose. He didn't know what was happening, just that he saw this other guy coming toward him wanting to attack. So he threw him straight to the ground, which made the other group extremely annoyed. It seemed impolite, you know."

Gastein and the Krampus

I had not known what I would find when I ran toward the sound of my first *Rempler*, or indeed exactly what I was seeing, but research previous to my trip had already pointed me toward Gastein as a place where the Krampus is particularly untamed. "This *Rempeln* is an interesting thing," Rest says, "because people always refer to it as unique to Gastein. This is the last place where we still do this. In fact, there really is no real source material suggesting it was ever done anywhere else," he says.

There are many things unique or strange about the Gastein Valley. Bad ("Bath," i.e., "Spa town") Gastein is, for instance, one of the few towns in the world

Krampus from Feuerwehrpass, Dorfgastein, Austria. *Photo © Gasteinertal.com.*

with a street named after an alchemist—Paracelsus, who visited around 1523 to study the town's ostensibly miraculous thermal springs. It's also one of the few places on earth offering naturally radioactive water as a curative, and here the opportunities are not limited to bathing and drinking. Spa visitors can also inhale radioactive steam as they crouch in "healing caves" deep below the mountains. It's hard not to view this dubious underground wonder as an extension of Gastein's rich mythology of subterranean magic, of dwarves, cursed gold, and divination local legend associated with the area's once-booming gold and silver mines. From deep within its tortured geology, Gastein seems somehow to radiate an atmosphere of the unreal. It flares out from the peaks of the Tauern mountains in electrostatic luminescence we call St. Elmo's Fire but Gasteiners refer to as *Perchtenfeuer*, "fire of the *Perchten*," a type of Alpine demon related to the Krampus.

There is a unique connection between the Krampus and the Gastein Valley. The isolating effect of Alpine geography has already been mentioned as a factor in preserving the Krampus tradition from modern influence, and while the mountains and tradition extend through Bavaria and the Austrian states of Styria, Carinthia, and Tyrol, it is the Austrian states of Tyrol, and (many would say, primarily) Salzburg that are most strongly associated with the creature. Within Salzburg, the regions of Pinzgau and Pongau are sometimes singled out, and within Pongau lies the Gastein Valley. While all these regions are important, it is more than hometown pride answering when I ask Rest where one finds the exemplary Krampus.

"Oh, Gastein, of course," he says without skipping a beat. He also mentions Krampus runs in St. Johann im Pongau (said to be attended by over a thousand devils) and the annual event in Schladming (in Styria) with numbers of participants close to that.

Where the Krampus Runs

In preparing for this book, I of course corresponded with several dozen Krampus participants for more perspective on the matter. One of the questions I asked was in what city one might find the best *Krampuslauf*. Several respondents seemed put off by the idea of naming cities. It was in the country, or in small towns and villages, they insisted, where the best runs happen. Stubbornly, I nonetheless scanned Austrian newspapers for what might be named as the biggest events but found myself lost in a sea of vague superlatives, and a sense of touristic rivalry and hype.

Graz is known for a large parade. In the city of Salzburg, there are long-established, well-attended runs in the Gnigl and Maxglan neighborhoods. Not far across the Austrian/German border Munich is also noteworthy for drawing international tourists and costumed groups from across the Krampus homelands. It takes place at the hugely popular *Christkindlmarkt* (Christmas market) on Munich's central Marienplatz.

"There is an extreme boom in … how do you say," Rest hesitates, "*Advent-tourismus*?"

"Advent (from the ecclesiastic term for the four Sundays before Christmas) and "tourism" may be words that don't really go together in English, but in Germany and Austria the major Christmas markets held during that season are a huge tourist draw. There visitors enjoy a centuries-old tradition involving shopping, nibbling, and drinking one's way through dozens, sometimes hundreds, of little stalls selling trinkets, foods, and mulled wine. Rest associates the growth of this industry with growing interest in the Krampus over the recent decades.

"When I was last in Salzburg, especially in early December, there were four different Krampus events every day. Each and every one of these Christmas Markets is not complete without at least one Krampus event each day of the weekend." But he's quick to characterize this as a less traditional, commercially driven development.

Thus far Gastein's celebrations have remained mostly untouched by such commercial or touristic forces. During "the season," Rest says, Gastein's festivities mostly attract only visitors from nearby towns or natives returning for the holiday from the bigger cities. This could change with growing interest in the phenomenon, he says, but "I don't know if it's really sexy enough to compete with the big parades." As the tradition currently diffuses and diversifies, however, Gastein provides not only an excellent window to the past, but a stable reference point from which the remainder of this chapter will proceed.

The Run versus the House Visit

Unlike other regions where the Krampus appears as an adjunct to weeks-long Christmas markets, in Gastein, the devils only appear on December 5 and 6, the eve of and traditional day dedicated to St. Nicholas. Activity on the 5th in Bad Gastein revolves around the town center, and on the 6th involves the Krampus visiting outlying farmsteads. Around 3:30pm, groups assemble to begin runs that can last as late as 11pm. As many as 100 troupes (all of them local to the valley) take part, though it should be noted that troupes in Gastein may be smaller (usually under a dozen members) than in other towns, particularly smaller than those in Haiming and Matrei in Tyrol, which only have one large citywide troupe.

The connection to St. Nicholas is much more than a formality of date. Unlike less traditional cities, where Krampus packs may roam the streets unattended by any saint, in Gastein each troupe has a costumed Nicholas as leader. And unlike other cities with large runs, where the Krampus may merely strut his stuff, brandishing switches and perhaps swatting a few adults along the way, in Gastein, the carrot-and-stick role of Nicholas and his punishing assistant is taken seriously. Children and families are actually visited in their homes where the saint assays behavior and delivers small gifts, while the Krampus puts on frightening displays.

The *Hausbesuch* ("house visit") is a hallmark of activity in Gastein. Elsewhere

Krampus, Alt Gnigler Pass, Salzburg. *Photo © Martin Zehentner .*

it exists, but is largely being supplanted by performances in public spaces or runs. In Gastein, the "run" merely consists of troupes moving from house to house, following their own individualized routes. While it's no organized parade, there is some effort by groups to at least pass through a central area, "somewhere in the center," Rest says, "maybe a square, but not always in the same place year to year.

Oberpfälzer Schlossteufeln, Regensburg, Germany. *Photo © Wunschtraum Fotografie.*

It gives the troupes a little structure," he says, "while still keeping it open. They can show up or not show up. And for the spectators, it gives them a place where they might be, for instance, more likely to see a *Rempler*."

Outside traditionalist regions, and certainly in more urban areas where families don't live within walking distances, the *Hausbesuch* is not incorporated into the general house-to-house *Krampuslauf* but is a specially arranged event, sometimes attended by a smaller portion of the entire troupe. Visits may be offered via a group's website, social media pages, or newspaper listings, and must be booked well in advance. Sometimes a church-affiliated organization will work with a Krampus group to ensure that a costumed St. Nicholas appears in homes within their parish or diocese.

For these specially ordered visits, instructions are often provided for the family. The "Himmlische Höllenteufel" ("Heavenly Hell-devils") of the greater Innsbruck area, for instance, suggest parents fill out an online spreadsheet listing various good and bad deeds as a sort of crib sheet the all-knowing Nicholas can tuck into his "golden book" when reviewing children's deeds. While officially discouraging the appearance of Krampus alongside the saint (along with threats and lists of bad behaviors), the Archdiocese of Salzburg nonetheless provides guidelines for a somewhat idealized *Hausbesuch*, featuring hymns, advent wreaths with candles, and edifying talks with children encouraging them to be "little Nicholases." More practically, they remind families to turn off radios and TVs, and silence cellphones. A final caveat from the diocese: "Please do not offer St. Nicholas alcohol." The Himmlische Höllenteufel, perhaps recalling some unpleasantness between a Krampus and frightened house-pet, request that animals be locked away. They also nix the diocese' suggestion of burning advent candles, no doubt thanks to those luxuriantly furred and flammable costumes.

In Gastein, visits are more impromptu. If at all possible, Rest says, everyone gets visited. "It seems to be very important to many of the Krampuses to put this at the center of the whole thing." This doesn't just pertain to children with families, but to any house that's passed. Some groups, he says, make it a point of honor to include those who might otherwise be missed. Much of the value and vitality of this tradition, Rest believes, lies in the intimacy and sense of community this citywide open house fosters. As illustration, he relates a story about an old woman who had been gravely ill.

"She had been bedridden for years, and when she heard the Krampuses were coming, she asked to see the St. Nicholas and for him to give her the last sacrament. I'm not sure to what extent she was all there at the time. Of course the guy playing Nicholas didn't have the oil and all that stuff, and as a practicing Catholic, he knew he had to be a priest to carry out her wish, but he played along and went up right up there, to do so. As I recall, the old woman died pretty quickly after that."

Traditional Figures of the Krampus Troupe

In most traditional regions, the Krampus troupe is called a "*Krampuspass*" or, more often, just "*Pass*." The *Pass* consists mostly of men in their late teens to early 40s. Each *Pass* usually takes the name of a neighborhood, farmstead or family name, geographic feature (e.g., mountain, gorge, or boulder), a community landmark (inn or brewery) or professional association or other club (volunteer firefighting associations seem common here). Elsewhere more modern troupes, like our "Heavenly Hell-devils" above, may ignore such conventions in favor of theatricality.

The Krampus

At least among the older residents of the Gastein region, the creature is still primarily called a *"Klaubauf," "Kramperl"* or *"Toifi"* ("devil") rather than "Krampus." No troupe would have less than four Krampuses, and more typically the number would hover around six, though more might easily be present. Based on seniority or other outstanding merit, a *Vorteufel* ("head devil") is usually appointed to be the first to enter and leave homes and otherwise help Nicholas control his pack.

The Basket Carrier

The roles in the Gastein troupes are dictated by the needs of the all-important *Hausbesuch*. A product of this is the *Körblträger* or *Körbler* ("basket carrier"), a figure increasingly rare as you leave Gastein, and almost never found outside the state of Salzburg. On his back, he wears a large basket woven of thin wooden splints in which he carries small treats for the well-behaved—not an insignificant task as the full load can weigh over 100 lbs., and the basket may be refilled one or more times throughout an evening's run. The *Körblträger* may also be called a *Guazltrager* ("sweets carrier").

Also sometimes simply called the *Waldmandl* ("forest man"), the character is decidedly rustic. Along with the basket, he has a preposterously overgrown beard, often constructed of moss. Occasionally (perhaps more in the past, judging from photos), he wears a mask with exaggerated features, but more typically what little can be seen of his face is smudged with soot. His scruffy costume consists of below-the-knee lederhosen, woolen socks and sweater, and an old huntsman's hat, likely decked with some moss, bits of evergreen or bark. He carries a gnarled walking staff and lantern, the latter out of utility rather than effect as the group may easily find themselves tromping down unlit country roads. The basket or staff can be hung a carved plaque identifying the *Pass*. His basket may also be decorated with bunches of evergreen or moss. There is room for creativity here. In Bad Gastein, I noted a *Körblträger* packing a nice array of schnapps bottles deftly stuffed between wads of moss, and in Munich, a basket was adorned by a taxidermy weasel.

The Angels

While the *Körblträger* is a rather rough, ambivalent figure, Nicholas' other helper, the *Engerl* (angel), provides children with a more comforting female presence. Often played by friends or relatives of the Krampuses, the angels typically appear alone or as a single pair, though larger troupes may have more. In Gastein, they carry small baskets filled before they enter each home, with that family's portion of treats fished from the *Körblträger*'s load. As the basket-carrier is actually a rare figure elsewhere, the angel in many places takes over any gift-bearing duties

Krampus, Alt Gnigler Pass, Salzburg. *Photo © Martin Zehentner.*

Basket carrier, Munich *Krampuslauf.* Photo © Al Ridenour.

Basket carrier with troupe sign for Bochstoa Pass, Gastein Valley, Austria. Photo © Gasteinertal.com.

Bad Gastein *Krampuspass*, Bad Gastein, Austria. *Photo © Al Ridenour.*

altogether, and in even smaller groups with no angel, a Krampus may be the one to carry a sack of gifts.

The angel generally wears a small crown and the long white gown you would expect, albeit a tad bulkier thanks to layers of warm clothes. In Gastein she wears over her gown, a short cloak colored to match St. Nicholas' vestments. Outside the valley, crowns, wings, veils, or blonde wigs may be added, and not infrequently in less tradition-bound areas, there is a nod to fashion with shorter skirts or even red- or black-wardrobed "gothic" angels.

St. Nicholas

Saint Nicholas, or "the Holy Nicholas" as it's rendered in German, goes by a variety of appellations. Sometimes he's simply "the Holy Man," "the Good Man" or "the Friend of Children" (being their patron saint). He may also just go by "Nikolo," an Austrian dialect rendering of "Nicholas." Wolfgang Böhm, a photojournalist from Graz who's also written on these traditions, described to me the casting of this all-important role, saying, "Usually the duty will fall to a tall guy with a powerful but kind voice. And Nicholas is the one who probably needs the most acting talent." An aptitude for reading situations and calming excited or frightened kids is also part of Nicholas's duties as sole director of this theatrical enterprise.

Nassfelder-Pass, Bad Gastein. *Photo © Gasteinertal.com.*

The Nicholas costume, as has been noted, resembles that of a medieval bishop, complete with miter, and crozier, i.e., "hat" and "staff." Unlike an American Santa Claus, there is never an attempt to cultivate a realistic look regarding hair, and his beard and wig are invariably theatrically and impossibly white and voluminous. In years gone by, Nicholas would also sometimes appear as a masked figure. Though this practice has largely disappeared, a few modern mask-carvers today are now extending their offerings to include these old-fashioned, intimidatingly impassive Nicholas masks.

Though he always wears a white gown, the overlaying chasuble can vary in color. Outside the region, this tends to be red, or sometimes gold, but in Gastein, green, blue, purple, and other colors are found. This is one way various troupes make themselves readily identifiable to the less trained eye. Nicholas also always carries a large Bible-like "golden book" from which he may "read" of children's good and bad deeds during his appearance as previously mentioned.

A last feature of the costume would be some sort of bag or purse in which Nicholas collects donations from families visited. Though there is never a set fee demanded, a typical donation might be in the range of $10-15, Rest says, but "in the old days, the *Pass* would get a cut of bacon or a bottle of schnapps or something like that." Even today a few households may provide some snacks or beer, making them popular stops on troupes' routes.

Rest relates one story regarding the purse, recalled from an evening at a local pub. In the 1970s, he recalls, there was a *Pass* led by a Nicholas famous for his nights spent drinking till "his hair hurt" the next morning. "For his bag for the money, he chose this white ladies' purse, and when one of the farmwives in the village saw it, she thought it so funny, she began screaming, 'Oh, ma chérie! You look like a hooker.' From that day on, they started calling that *Pass* the 'Chérie-Pass.' Nobody today can remember its real name."

The House Visit

Krampus visits are geared toward children under 10 or 12, Rest says, and though older teenagers may slip outdoors to run after the troupes, ideally the whole family, including any grandparents, aunts, and uncles, will await the visits assembled on one side of a table that will later serve as a sort of safety barrier between the children and the devils. When the troupe arrives at the house, St. Nicholas enters usually only with his basket-carrier and angels. The Krampuses will wait outside or perhaps come indoors but remain out of sight in a hallway. Nicholas greets the family, introducing himself with short poem, sometimes something handed down from days gone by, but often one written by the performer himself. Here is one, in loose translation, penned by Gasteiner Patrick Deisl.

> *God's greetings, all within this house!*
> *I'm friend to all, St. Nicholas.*
> *Have no fear, just look at me.*
> *No wild stranger here you see.*
> *My coming marks the year's near end.*
> *This Forest Man my basket tends.*
> *Deeds good and bad we must review.*
> *With ringing bells comes Krampus too,*
> *What brings him joy brings terror to you.*

After his rhymed greeting, Nicholas may hand his staff to a chosen child or one of his angels and open his golden book to review what he knows of the children's behavior. He likely has just received a few whispered cues from parents as he enters. Or the saint may simply question the children directly and follow this with a few saintly remarks and encouragements.

The final test for children awaiting gifts is a performance they've been rehearsing for weeks. "They recite poems or sing songs," says Claudia Nedwed, a troupe member from Leoben, Austria. "It's funny, though, because sometimes they completely freeze knowing the Krampuses are standing right there." In areas like Gastein, this is the critical moment anticipated for weeks. "From early November until mid-December kids are just Krampus-crazed," Rest says. "Some are extremely fascinated, others are afraid, but for that time, or least two weeks per year, teachers have to set aside their curriculum and devote much of their class time to the Krampus."

In the old days, this exercise would have involved verses memorized from the Bible or catechism, or the performance of a hymn, but today more secular material may be used, though it's usually something with a holiday theme.

As a reward for trials of the *Hausbesuch*, immediately after their performance kids receive a fist-sized "Nicholas sack" (*Nikolaus-Sackerl)* containing assorted treats, typically nuts, apples, mandarin oranges, and chocolates sometimes shaped like little Krampuses or Nicholases. Dried fruits might be added, including the particularly old-fashioned "Buck Horns" ("*Buxhörndln*"), a nickname for the vaguely horn-shaped, sweet-tasting dried pods of the carob tree, which children chew for hours. A related dried-fruit creation is the *Zwetschkenkrampus*, a little figure of the Krampus crafted from prunes. These are rather fragile, so actually more likely encountered at a Christmas Market than piled into a Krampus troupe's heavily packed basket. Cookies or *Lebkuchen* (roughly: gingerbread) may also be included and are sometimes baked fresh by the troupe itself. Small Krampus-shaped breads and cookies are also created by commercial bakers and homemakers at this time of year and may be baked as an extra special gift by particularly ambitious troupe.

The preparation of the Nicholas-sacks can be quite labor-intensive given the great number of homes visited. The Gastein-area Lafener Pass reports visiting a total of 35 homes per night while giving out a total of 200 bags. Each sack typically must be wrapped in colored cellophane and tied with string to which may be attached a bit of twig or some representation of the Krampus' switches as well as a troupe card printed with a traditional slogan and the troupe's name and image. As well as time-consuming, the preparation of the bags can be expensive, more so lately, Rest says, as there is a trend to replace the once traditional plastic with more "traditional looking" and expensive burlap.

St. Nicholas, Gruabtoifi Saalfelden, Austria. *Photo © Günther Gollner.*

All the fuss over sacks, though clearly a matter of passion, is also a matter of practicality. "Up until the 1970s," Rest says, "they didn't have any form of *Sakerl*. They just filled the whole basket with cookies and oranges and chocolate, and then there came a very rainy Krampus Day, so the whole thing turned into this awful slush, and the Nicholas pulled out a few handfuls for the children and placed them on the table, and there it was—just awful, wet slime."

The fervor of traditionalist dedication that seizes the Gastein Valley every season, however, does not extend through all regions where the Krampus is found. Elsewhere, the sacks may be prepared by the parents themselves and stashed outside the door for the troupe to hand over. Occasionally other large gifts may be substituted, but more elaborate presents are usually only given on the season's second gift-giving occasion, Christmas Eve. Extravagant gifting is not traditionally associated with St. Nicholas, and the Salzburg Archdiocese, for instance, specifically requests parents refrain from this practice and stick only with the smaller traditional tokens.

The climax of the visit, of course, comes with the appearance of the Krampuses. They are usually introduced as a sort of parting warning to children that good behavior must be maintained. Having waited out of sight thus far, the devils burst in making the greatest possible racket. Switches are brandished, but none of my sources suggested that children were routinely struck during this rumpus. Older relatives may receive a playful swat, but children, after all, are normally protected from immediate exposure by the all-important dining table. This barricade therefore often becomes the object of a sort of tug-of-war, with Krampuses playfully trying to heave it away and children and family members struggling to keep it safely between them and the monsters. Krampuses often seize victims by the earlobes, pull off sweaters, or perform other acts of mischief. In the old days, Rest says, the Krampus might also wreak havoc on the house itself: "They would charge into the farmer's kitchen, and the first thing they would do was go to the stove, and grab handfuls of ash to strew about." Today of course, he says, "they have to be much more careful about good floors, and mind that they don't scratch furniture or knock down lampshades with their horns."

The chaos, Rest says (as a former St. Nicholas himself), should be theatrically pitched so that it feels just about to go over the edge when the saint gives the signal to end it with a blast of his whistle—the only thing that can be heard over the tumult of the bells. The Nicholas must only "intervene while the Krampuses still have enough power and energy to defy the order, so he has to send the *Körblträger* to get between the fighting Krampuses. If the Krampuses always obey the Nicholas, that makes the troupe boring. There has to be a spark, a moment of defiance."

St. Nikolaus Visit, **signed by "A.D." (1850).** *Photo © Volkskundemuseum, Vienna.*

Troupe Life The *Pass* develops this ability to dramatically improvise together through the long hours spent on the runs as well as countless hours of preparation. While many of my sources said their troupe began work in earnest in October or November, others were adamant about it beginning already in the summer or spring. Christian Kropf, leader of Stechla Pass in Eggersdorf bei Graz, says it can't wait till spring. "We start in January, right after the season. We meet and think about new ideas for the next season. The runs must already be announced between January and June."

"The preparation is an event for itself for the Krampus and their support staff," says Wolfgang Böhm. "It is a social event. They talk, they kid around, and they generally have a lot of fun while preparing." Troupes usually also organize year-round outings, barbecues, sporting events, and gatherings at pubs. A number of troupes maintain dedicated clubhouses, where gear might be stored and more or less formally displayed as a sort of Krampus museum. The camaraderie nurtured by these activities lies at the heart of the *Krampuspass*. "It has always been a bonding thing," says Böhm, "That's probably the best thing about Krampus for me personally."

A positive and shared sense of purpose is vital to the group's persevering through the various organizational or production headaches as well as annoyances or run-ins with unruly spectators during appearances. Friendships also support troupe members through the physical challenges of marching in formidably heavy masks and suits for several hours at a time. The Lafener Pass, mentioned above, for instances, reports runs of over 7 miles made in costumes (including mask and bells) that weigh as much as 80 lbs.

Growing up where the custom is strong, however, these inconveniences are largely dismissed as an inevitable part of a communal rite of passage. Before he was old enough to afford the necessary gear and take part, Simon Wegleiter of Haiming, Austria, says he knew he'd one day be a Krampus. "I remember so clearly," he recalls, "how as a kid, I would make my own mask, just out of cardboard, and already in November I'd be out running up and down the streets." And it did not disappoint, when that moment finally arrived, that "first time you walk through the crowds, and see them—everyone so amazed and delighted. That is just guaranteed to give you goose bumps," he recalls.

Suiting Up   Though it's not uncommon for children to craft simple Krampus masks at schools in some areas, it's only a small (if particularly motivated or skilled) number of *Pass* members who create masks or suits themselves. Traditionally, costume elements have been obtained locally from professional artisans offering the products as a seasonal sideline: woodworkers for masks, tanners or furriers for costumes, blacksmiths for bells. Today there is also a growing number of semi-professional craftspeople specializing in these items—usually former or active Krampuses themselves. While much of their output is sold online, some of these artists offer in-person sales by appointment or during open-studio hours. There are even a handful of brick-and-mortar Krampus boutiques, like the Kärntner Krampusshop in St. Jakob im Rosental, Austria. Secondhand sale of costume elements through local newspapers or Krampus community websites is also popular.

However obtained, masks and costumes tend to adhere to high standards of craftsmanship, and the costs reflect this. A recent survey of participants in the Salzburg region found that average costs for the entire ensemble hovers around $1,700, while masks alone (especially by respected carvers) can go for over $1000. And a new suit does not represent a once-in-a-lifetime purchase.

"Some troupes have a new gear every year. And some individuals are constantly changing theirs," says Claudia Nedwed of Molochs Brut in Leoben, Austria. "The question really only is, can one afford it?" Many of those I spoke with reported feeling a necessity to change some or all of their costume every 1– 5 years, with masks being the most frequently updated. Owners of multiple masks switch them out for different appearances during the season or just display them as collectable curios. Needless to say, most of these acquisitions represent trade-ups either to a higher level of craftsmanship or for benefit of innovative features.

The desire for novelty and improvement is tempered by a pervasive respect for what is "traditional." The impressively harmonious look of each troupe's masks and costumes is evidence of this respect for collective standards. In practical terms, it's also the outcome of the tendency for each troupe to connect itself to a few favorite artisans and wear their work exclusively. In the past and in traditional areas, the troupe's preferred artists are chosen from among local craftspeople, and the resulting troupe presentation is therefore one neatly conforming to particular artistic vision. This relationship between artist and troupe goes even further, with a history of some mask-carvers even founding their own troupes or troupes being named for their carver or a distinct feature of his style.

Masks

Krampus masks are often called "*Larven*," a term also used for those traditionally worn at Carnival. The word was adopted with the spread of Carnival customs from Italy into German-speaking lands, and comes from the Latin *larva* (*larua*) meaning both "mask" and "ghost."

Gasteiners also often just call them "*Klaubaufköpfe*" ("Krampus heads"), and they are a source of great local pride. Representing as much as 40 hours of work, and carved in the preferred medium of Swiss Pine, each mask weighs between 15 and 30 pounds. Traditionalist carvers eschew or downplay the use of power tools or the delicate detailing these facilitate in favor of bold, brutish caricature. Their color palette is rudimentary—eyes and teeth: white, lips: red, skin: black. There is nothing nuanced with other hues or softened by shading, and certainly nothing airbrushed. Formerly horns were painted black with red tips, but now are left their natural color.

The classic Krampus mask hardly resembles the delicately human physiognomy of the devil of the old Krampus postcards. While there is some contemporary interest in recapturing this look, traditional masks are decidedly more brutish with their exaggerated features and oversized, gaping jaws. Their larger scale means the wearer typically looks out from slits hidden beneath eyes painted at forehead level. According to a 2010 presentation by the Mask Museum in Diedorf im Augsburg, Germany, the dangling tongue ever-present in Krampus postcards is absent in about 70% of masks. Likewise, the meager pair of stubby horns common to the cards looks nothing like the tremendous animal horns towering atop most masks, sometimes in imposing number.

Traditional Gastein-style Krampus masks have one pair of curling ram's horns at the sides and 2-4 pairs of additional goat horns on top, though elsewhere the number and type of horns is a subject of debate. Universally, however, natural horns are vastly preferred over cheaper resin replicas. Sheepskin is usually used for the hood attached to the mask in Gastein, and fur or hairs may be used on the face, as with dangling horsehair mustaches unique to the town of Bad Gastein.

Much of the style of modern Krampus masks can be traced to the work of Sepp Lang (1898–1983) from Bad Hofgastein, Rest's hometown. "He was an unemployed sculptor who had studied art in Munich," Rest says, "but when he returned from university, he realized there was an interest in more elaborate masks, and decided to start making Krampus masks in order to survive." First turning his attention to this in the 1930s, Lang would have found little in the way of artistically inspiring precedents. From what can be deduced from old photos and the scattering of old specimens preserved in museums or collections, wooden masks before this tended to be simpler, flatter, and less sculpturally expressive, or were even improvised from cloth or other less durable materials, little more really than something to conceal the wearer's face. The old masks were quickly rejected by members of Krampus troupes eager to purchase the more dramatic *Langköpfe* ("Lang-heads") and the artist found an even steadier yearlong market with spa tourists. "Many of his heads were not worn, not hollowed, but carved as souvenirs specifically for visitors," Rest says.

By the 1950s, Lang was as at the height of his career, even starting his own Krampus group, the influential Lang Pass. His work soon became a model for similarly renowned Gastein sculptors like Karl Hummel and Sepp Viehauser. More recently he has served as prototype for carver Clemens Hübsch, whose traditionalism, as touted on his website, prohibits the use of routers, power saws, materials from non-native animals, or even "modern equipment like snow-board buckles" used for mask straps elsewhere.

By the time Lang passed away, he had not only raised a new standard for carvers but had done much to enhance the reputation of Krampus customs in the Gastein Valley. "Whatever Lang masks are out there," Rest says, "they tend to be kept within the family, only passed on to close relatives, and never worn." Two Lang masks are now in Rest's family, handed down by his grandfather Jo-

The "*Bleiwang-Kopf*," classic mask carved by Sepp Lang, Gastein Valley, Austria.
Photo © Matthäus Rest.

sef Rest to the anthropologist's uncle and father. Particularly important is Lang's *Bleiwang-Kopf.* "It's the first he made in his signature style, and is still very influential." Originally traded for eight cubic meters of firewood back in 1935, the mask saw active Krampus-run duty up until 1950. The mask today is worth considerably more. "I've heard that people might spend 10,000 Euros (currently $11,000) for it," he says. "I don't know if that's an exaggeration, but I think it's possible."

As an anthropologist, Rest is particularly attentive to questions of cultural diffusion. While Sepp Lang receives great respect as a hero of Gastein's native culture, Rest believes there is also a more cosmopolitan influence in his work. Even to an untrained eye, the sculptor's flamboyant style feels strangely unparalleled in the world of European academic or folk art. Many encountering these masks for the first time find themselves reminded of the tribal arts of Africa, Polynesia, or perhaps the indigenous people of North America. Given the vogue for ethnographic art after World War I, such influences, Rest observes, would have been inescapable to Lang as a university art student in Munich at the time.

"The Lang mask owned by my grandfather," he says, "has a very specific style. I showed it to a colleague in Vienna who is an expert in African art." Did it look like anything the scholar knew? "Just glancing at it, and without missing a beat, he said, 'Cameroon ... grasslands.'"

That Furry Suit

While it does not hold the same reverential status as the mask, the fur costume worn by the Gastein Krampus is also governed by tradition. The hides of sheep are somewhat preferred, but long-haired goats are also used. Five to six animals are required for each bulky costume, which weighs up to 24 pounds. Colors of the animals range from dark brown to gray and ivory, and usually appear mixed in a single suit. Some say mismatched colors and pelts are necessary as symbols of the Krampus' diabolic nature. Each suit typically costs around $600 or more.

The relatively uniform style of Gastein costume was consolidated sometime early in the 20th century. Before that, suits, like the masks, were of a more improvisational nature, perhaps old winter coats turned out to display fur lining, or—as Rest imagines—"just some fur rags and some carpet that was sewn together for the occasion and afterwards put back to its original use."

Krampus mask from Barmstoana Perchten, Hallein, Austria. *Photo © Roland Käfer.*

Classic Bad Gastein Krampus with mustache. *Photo © Gasteinertal.com.*

Long fur coats were the earliest standardized form of costume, and this legacy, as with other aspects of the tradition, is uniquely preserved in the Gastein Valley. These coats, which extend nearly to the ankles, are particularly prevalent in the town of Bad Gastein. By the 1960s, however, there appeared a coverall-style design, which by the 1980s had become somewhat more common.

One reason the long coats are, perhaps, being phased out, Rest says, is the utility of the coverall style. "They are much better for jumping over fences and such out on country roads." And while the newer coveralls may be preferred, they would not suit just any ensemble. "The old masks, like my grandfather's, they only go together with the long coat, " he says. "So there are style subtleties. If you wear the old mask with the new suit, people would see you as something of a fraud."

Switches, Bells, Basket, and Chain

Of course no Krampus would be complete without his weapon. Switches are what come to mind for most outsiders, and certainly, these bundled birch or willow twigs are the tool of choice in the old Krampus cards. However, in practice, horsehair whips made from the tails of that animal are a bit more popular as they present fewer risks of injury.

Salzburger Alexander Haslauer, who for eight years ran the online store Krampusimperium and was well-positioned to observe trends, says, "As long as I can remember, there were always horse tails and switches, but at many, many events, switches are already forbidden because of the higher risk of injuries. There was a time when I also sold lots of cow tails, but they are the worst. They have a bone inside that makes it as hard as a policeman's nightstick. They're forbidden almost everywhere already."

Those familiar with the image of the devil from *Krampuskarten* might also assume that the basket often shown strapped to the creature's back and stuffed with naughty children is a part of the traditional costume. While these do show up, they are absolutely unheard of in the Gastein Valley, and rare in any of the more traditional regions.

In reality, a large basket might be impossible to wear thanks to the bells' placement on the lower back. Massive hand-forged bells worn on a special belt are an essential part of the Krampus costume. Certainly, these are almost never portrayed in the *Krampuskarten*, but for those who grew up in areas where the Krampus roams, their sound announces the devil's coming in an unforgettable way. Böhm recalls, "Many of my early childhood memories are Krampus-related, but one of the most vivid is driving around with my brother and my dad in the days before December 5 with windows down (even though it was freezing) carefully listening for Krampus bells and maybe seeing the first ones." The bell-belts even influence the way the Krampus walks, as a springy step is usually affected in order to maximize the racket. The weight of the huge bells, typically worn in threes and totaling up to 18 pounds, can also serve as counterweight for the heavy masks in front.

Bells worn in the Gastein Valley were inspired by those once strapped to pack-horses to alert travelers of their approach through fog-shrouded mountain passes. While today, some large livestock bells may be worn, the vast majority of bells are purpose-made for the Krampus and are usually larger than those worn day-to-day by actual livestock. The style of bell preferred in Gastein is called a *Rolle*, a hammered steel sphere 5-10 inches across with a slit for sound. Another design, not really worn in Gastein but popular elsewhere, is the colorfully named *Froschmaulschelle*" ("frog-mouth bell") resembling an oversized Swiss-style cowbell. A third also worn only outside the valley is the *Balkenglocke* ("beam-bell"), a long rectangular bell often worn with clattering lengths of chain fastened atop to provide extra noise. Chains are not really worn on belts in Gastein but tend to be carried aloft by the Krampus, stretched between the fists, and waved back and forth with each leap that rings the bells.

Modern Trends in Mask and Costume

While the elements above are all that's needed for a classic Krampus, a flood of modern accouterments has appeared, mostly marketed through websites catering to the less traditional participant. Along with clawed gloves, torches, and leather-thong whips with fancy skull grips, one finds elements for an alternatively conceived Krampus impression, something like a Viking Berserker wrapped in scraps of leather and pelts, crisscrossed with bell-jingling, rivet-studded straps, ankle bands, and wrist cuffs. Innovators also adopt exotic footwear, including elfin boots with pointed toes, platform shoes often sculpted like hooves, or even footwear contrived from actual horse-hooves. There are even sculpted latex suits with comic-book musculature for those wishing to bare a little skin in December. Needless to say, all this is viewed with some suspicion, if not outright contempt, by traditionalists. Trends, most often mentioned as undesirable by those I interviewed, included synthetic fur and horns, latex muscle-suits, and LEDs illuminating eyes in masks.

Tampering with the style of the iconic Krampus mask is particularly taboo in Gastein. "If someone appeared here wearing a non-traditional mask," Rest says, "that would mean war." He describes an interview conducted by his student field-researchers with the mayor of Dorfgastein. "Without even being asked, he told our students if anyone would wear a mask from outside the valley, we would put that thing on an outbound train. There was even a sort of implied threat to the person who would do such a thing."

The Gasteiner nomenclature Rest uses for these tradition-breaking creations is "future masks." It implies a progression away from stylized folk-art forms toward a more naturalistic modern style. These may be wooden masks carved with the latest woodshop technology but can also be resin or the relatively new and pricey aluminum masks. Latex also is used, but is today fairly déclassé. Whatever the material, they are distinguished by naturalistic detail and meticulously rendered facial muscles. A nuanced airbrush finish, glistening mouth and lips, and glass eyes complete the look, with the end result looking more like the creation of a Hollywood effects shop than anything imagined by Sepp Lang.

The term "Hollywood" is often used in discussion of this trend, and subjects I spoke with repeatedly dropped in English terms to describe the style. Just as Rest refers to "future masks" employing those same English words, others used English terms like "horror," "Halloween," "Orcs," "vampires," or "zombies" to hint at a corrupting American influence. Also mentioned sometimes as undesirable was the appearance of blood and scars on masks (presumably from scuffles within the Krampus herd?). Rest recalls this trend appearing in the 1990s and connects it with Hermann Prommegger's Metzger Masken, in Grossarl, Austria, a famous proponent of the newer style. This trend toward more frightening or gory masks, he speculates, may be compensatory. Speaking of the many restrictions recently laid on the behavior of the Krampus during the runs, he says: "One might make the argument that there has to be more virtual, more aesthetic terror, to make up for the loss of actual physical threat."

I have not spoken to any participant involved with Krampus customs not eager to emphasize the traditionalism of the activities, and many jumped to offer respectful praise of its pristine preservation of the customs in places like Gastein. But the fact remains: someone is buying this stuff. Like the rock music aficionado who speaks admiringly of scratchy old 78s by Delta bluesmen, this praise may be more a way to emphasize an understanding of and deep-rooted appreciation for more contemporary reinterpretations, e.g., lip service to Robert Johnson, paid by a fan of the Rolling Stones or Jack White.

But perhaps one needn't pick sides. Alexander Haslauer of Krampusimperium, while expressing genuine respect for the Gastein forms, also admits a fondness for the sophisticated craftsmanship of modern masks, even those LED eyes that offended some of my other sources. "People are getting more used to those," he says. "I think that will be something they'll adopt more and more."

The push to reinterpret and re-envision he sees driven by the large number of new participants and events. "Especially young people want to look different, to let their own style influence their appearance. There are so many Krampus events already, some young troupes think they need to be very special to attract more people," But he sees a slow reverse in that trend. "It's getting more and more back to the roots. I have been in this business for about 14 years now, and for some time, the trend went the direction of Hollywood style masks—maybe from 2007 to 2013—but now it looks like everyone is fed up with that shit."

Wolfgang Böhm agrees. "In recent years many groups are going back to the roots of mask-making and attempting outfits that look more like reproductions of very early costumes," he says. One indication of this back-to-basics movement, Haslauer recalls, was the increasing sale of Krampusimperium's DIY "mask kits" (roughly shaped wooden shapes offered to consumers eager to try their hand at adding the finer details). "I started myself with a kit like that," he says. "They are still getting more popular every year. I sold around 100-150 each year because more young people want to make their own mask, but often don't have the possibility of

Nontraditional mask, Immortuus Pass, Piesendorf, Austria. *Photo © Immortuus Pass.*

using tools like a chainsaw or anything like that while living in flats. Or they tried with a wooden block and couldn't get the proportions right, perhaps."

These trends discussed by Böhm and Haslauer, while not influential in Gastein, describe the tradition as it's more widely practiced. While important and of historical interest, Gastein's traditionalism does not describe the wider world of the Krampus, particularly when it comes to the *Krampuslauf*, which for Gasteiners remains secondary to the house visit and is essentially little more than a trek between those homes. Elsewhere the *Krampuslauf* has since flowered into many new and varied forms. How these events are conducted, and how the Krampus interacts with spectators along the route, are questions to be answered in the following chapter."

Nontraditional mask. Oberpfälzer Schlossteufeln, Regensburg, Germany.
Photo © Wunschtraum Fotografie.

Chapter Three

THE BEAST PURSUES HIS GAME

A Cruel Sport

Europeans seem a fairly civilized lot. So, *how can they*, we Americans ask, expose their children to the horrors of the Krampus? Reaching for a comparison, all we have is the discomfort of the American child in the lap of a department store Santa. For these delicate souls, the 1983 movie *A Christmas Story*, in its portrayal of this, presents the ultimate in psyche-shattering childhood trauma. Now add to this switches, and horns, and madly clanging bells—it boggles the mind. Really, how *can* these civilized Europeans expose their children to such cruelties?

Perhaps it's something specific to the Austrians, the Germans? Something *Teutonic*? And here the conversation veers into dark speculation about a naturally martial culture, grasping at straws amid images of jackboots, monocles, and gas chambers. Or this becomes grist for a grudge against the Church, and all the horrors of the Inquisition and fantasies of Jesuit sadism project themselves upon poor St. Nicholas and his Krampus.

Wrongheaded as any of this may be, the question still deserves an answer: to what extent is this custom hurtful to children?

When I have asked my interviewees whether children are really struck by the Krampus, I received many unequivocal answers: both "yes" and "no." But the question itself presents problems. What age do we mean by "child"? And shall we count

Krampuslauf in Stallhofen, Austria. *Photo © Wolfgang Böhm.*

instances where thrill-seeking children might be old enough to taunt the Krampus and be struck? Outsiders asking about children being hit are likely thinking of blows administered in a frightening punitive manner, but this betrays a basic misunderstanding of actual practice.

Knowing only the folkloric identity of the Krampus as punisher of children, then learning of the phenomenon of Krampus runs, they may assume that young children are pursued and swatted at these events, but this is hardly the case. During public runs, there is quite often no St. Nicholas, certainly no lists of misdeeds, or pretense of actually *punishing* individuals. Switches or horse-tails might be swung, and spectators struck, but this represents a sort of mutually understood public sport. Spectators at runs have willingly put themselves on the parade's sidelines, or even push for more challenging frontline exposure. If children are present and close enough to be struck, they have either done so at their own initiative or have been urged by well-meaning parents who likely wish to see the child conquer his own fear.

I observed one such incident at a Krampus parade in Munich, where a trembling boy was gently urged forward by parents. Those around couldn't help but notice the situation, and by the time the child stood close enough for contact, a dozen or so spectators had fixed sympathetic eyes upon the boy. As the parents spoke encouragingly to their son, an approaching Krampus crouched low and ever-so-delicately extended a clawed hand. The moment the boy touched the beast, his face exploded with pride, as did the faces of those gathered around. Strangers patted his back and chuckled, exchanging friendly words with the parents, and the boy remained on the frontlines eager for his next encounter.

I witnessed other incidents like this, and though they made a strong impression, I am unable to say children are never traumatized in these affairs. Similarly, with the house visits, where I'm told it's commonly only a matter of bluff and bluster, it seems no absolute statements can be made about a symbolic swat or two. But to understand the tradition as essentially one of corporal punishment would be gravely misguided.

Fear, however, is another matter. Though acclimation to the monster plays a role outsiders can hardly conceive, and one can peruse any number of YouTube videos showing Austrian children looking rather bored as the devils storm about during home visits, fear of the Krampus is an undeniable part of the experience for many children.

Claudia Nedwed, a performer with Molochs brut in Leoben, Austria, recalls, "I was terribly afraid of the Krampus up until the age of 16. Even when I just heard the bells! Adrenalin would shoot through my veins." Wolfgang Böhm remembers how his young cousin "would always hide somewhere in the attic" when the devils arrived and recalls "stories from people now in their 50s or 60s who talk about

Krampuslauf at Munich Christkindlmarkt. *Photo by tribp, (CC BY 2.0).*

hiding in the woodshed, or beneath the bed." Even as an adult, he says, his mother is still "terribly scared of anything Krampus-related." Occasionally in the German and Austrian media, you will hear bemused reporting on the phenomenon among adults: debilitating *Krampusangst* ("Krampus phobia") and special seasonal workshops offered to those suffering from the affliction.

European sensibilities are hardly immune to the current mood of protectiveness toward the child. Things have changed greatly since Böhm was young. "We used to go out and play in the woods after breakfast and came home for supper," he recalls. "No one cared too much about it. But today if your 6-year-old is gone for the whole day, people will probably call child services on you. That said, there are stories of the old days of Krampus that make me thankful, I'm living now—drunken hordes of vandalizing men terrorizing a village for weeks. I think, we are better off today."

Most participants I spoke with downplayed the idea of the Krampus frightening children, often choosing the word "respect" instead of "fear" as the desired response. Marius Brandner, a Bavarian mask-carver and proprietor of Brandner-Masken in Berchtesgaden, Germany, says "the Krampus should be a rough character, but one inspiring respect. Kids shouldn't be thrown into a panic; that's not the meaning of the tradition. It's different from 'horror.'" (Here again the English word, "horror.")

Edi Pauliner, a performer with the Klausenverein of Sonthofen, Germany agrees. "The events shouldn't be about fear," he responds, "but more about rescuing the old ways and bringing them into modern times. Our appearance may generate a little anxiety, but kids should be told in advance we're just people in costumes."

One form of acclimating children to the activities is to encourage them to take part at an early age. Simon Wegleiter writes of his group in Haiming, Austria, "We were the first Krampus group that provided a special run just for little Krampuses. We have boys as young as 4 taking part, with a father or brother as a companion. There are some very eager kids who already have or buy their own gear."

Mike Kratzer, a Krampus with the Moor *Pass* from Maishofen, Austria, doesn't see such a need for acclimation these days, saying he's often experienced "children not really being afraid of the Krampus because they've been hardened by films and computer games." Several I spoke with expressed mixed feelings about the devil's image becoming less potent. "I don't want children to be scared," writes Böhm, "but a *Krampuslauf* more like a petting zoo is nothing I enjoy either. A Krampus that's not scary is just a guy in a smelly fur coat."

Running across the related term "*Kutschelkrampus*" ("cuddle Krampus"), I asked Rest if this might commonly be used to express distaste for a new breed of hyper-civilized devil. It could just as well be used positively, he says, in family-friendly advertisements for Christmas markets promising parents, "no hitting, no growling, no bad words—you know, just *Where the Wild Things Are*." More common, he says, is the blurb, "Krampus to Touch!" designating an unthreatening character to be petted by children. In those non-traditional scenarios, he says, the Krampus might go so far as to publically remove his mask to reassure children, an utterly unthinkable taboo in the Gastein Valley.

In Haiming, Austria, public unmasking is also anathema. Simon Wegleiter says it could be grounds for ejection from his group and compares it to speaking while masked. "With us, no active member is allowed to speak. Why would he? A Krampus is not a human." A vast majority of those I checked with agreed, saying that only growling was allowed, or indeed encouraged. And speech is impractical. Communicating over the racket of bells and through the barrier of a thick, wooden mask is inevitably exhausting.

However, while I was in the Gastein Valley, I did notice some Krampuses speaking, albeit in a gruff stage-voice. Rest says this is another distinct trait of his region and relates it to the more intimate scale of the *Hausbesuch*, where the Krampus interacts more directly with a family. During the course of a Gastein *Hausbesuch*, the *Pass* naturally encounters situations calling for improvisation as well as spoken communication between members. In the process, the Krampus might slip in sly asides to troupe members or adults. He may also improvise bits of slapstick, Rest says, like the time a Krampus answered a home phone inopportunely ringing during the performance.

It's a trickster aspect of the character Rest finds "much more articulated in Dorfgastein than it is in these parades. It's much easier to be funny when you're in front of a kid in the living room, you know." In noisy parades, the character is seen at a distance, and his repertoire and communication is often limited to striking fearsome poses.

However, when I asked other participants whether the Krampus might also be a comic as well as imposing figure, they almost unanimously objected to the notion. Rest concedes that more urban kids "never ever see a funny Krampus; they always just see this scary monster," which is not at all what he grew up with. While the Krampus of his youth certainly provided scares and occasional smacks of the rod, a comic dimension was maintained—and seemed provocative. "There was always this aspect, maybe he's just making a joke, this ambivalence," he recalls. "I think that's so much more interesting as a character."

And returning to the question of whether kids would actually be swatted by the Krampus, now or in the past, Rest is unequivocal. "Yes! They were hit, and they still are hit." But there is social context to be considered, he insists. "There was much more physical punishment 20 or 30 years ago in Austria. So maybe the physical punishment from the Krampus was not that shocking. It was just what they would have gotten anyway. The issue would be more one of psychological fear."

The Prey   Costumed *Krampuslauf* participants must constantly read the psychology of the crowd. Stefan Hable of the Mühlviertler Rauh-Teufel Pass in Sankt Georgen, Austria, while admitting that "spreading fear is somehow entertaining," exercises "gentleness with the very little kids" and has acquired certain intuitions that help him deal with adults. "Men," he says, "tend not to act scared. They are the quiet ones, holding back and perhaps taking pictures. Females can react hysterically, and young girls, there will be a couple of those who cry when we approach."

In order to avoid any negative consequences, runners play it safe when possible, ideally choosing as "victims" spectators they know: friends, relatives, or familiar community members. But that only constitutes a small fraction of activity. Other forces are at play during the run, including a certain fate-tempting impulse that tends to deliver candidates to the frontlines. Böhm suggests, "It's not that getting hit itself is desirable … well, a bit maybe, but the possibility—that

***Krampuslauf* in Liezen, Austria.** *Photo © Wolfgang Böhm.*

little fear of getting hit, that makes the whole thing exciting. Like a roller coaster."

Hable notes this thrill-seeking among kids and youths, who "sometimes demand to be beaten" by taunting the Krampus, "almost as a sort of test of courage, showing off for their circle of friends." Commonly these thrill-seekers show up to runs in protectively layered pants.

Others specify that it's males who tend to be more aggressive and provoke the Krampus. Rest is precise on this topic. "What we found in Dorfgastein is that when it comes to actual blows, the group that gets the most are boys between 13 and 15. They are too young to themselves be active Krampuses but see all their brothers, their brother's friends, and others they know included in the troupe. Since they're left out, they have something to prove, and really kind of want to instigate the situation."

Böhm, like most participants, says it's young women who are most preferred as targets. "The Krampuses are mostly adolescent boys, so they naturally interact with girls of their age in a curious way. They will try to scare them, maybe steal their hats if they are wearing them. They'll probably try to hug them and stuff like that. In short, they will try to impress them a little. But they won't really try to hit them, or hurt them. It's a way of giving attention and maybe even impressing their love interest in a more physical way than usually accepted."

Krampuslauf at Munich Christkindlmarkt. *Photo by tribp (2013) (CC BY 2.0).*

All of this brought to my mind a particular genre of *Krampuskarten* popular in the 1960s. This second wave of cards presented the Krampus in a pseudo-erotic context and paired him with busty cartoon women who might have been lifted from the pages of a *Playboy* magazine of the time. The cards played up the eroticized theme of spanking, and the Krampus was transformed into a lustful little satyr.

When I ask Böhm about an eroticized charge to the activities, he finds this a little extreme, but concedes that taking part in a run is certainly an expression of maleness, "like participation in a football team. It's a way for males to display strength." Other participants asked whether this male-female play with switches might not be a form of flirting roundly rejected the idea. Some even sounded a bit shocked, saying any flirtation that happened was strictly confined to mingling with local females at post-run parties.

But as an anthropologist, Rest was quick to disagree, even dumbfounded. "Are you serious?" he asks. "No one admitted this? There is no question about that! That is one of the few things where I would have to get in a fight with each active Krampus saying there is no erotic meaning involved." Not that it's a straight-forward matter of individual male intent, he says. Rather, it's part of a complex ritual system where women also play an active role. Female dress for these events, for instance, seems symbolically geared to courtship, he says. "Being outside in

Moorpass Maishofen, Austria. Masks: Metzger Masken. *Photo © Moorpass Maishofen.*

the Alpine winter, you know the most sensible thing to do is to wear long-johns and skiing pants, but instead they choose skinny jeans or just leggings, dressing up as if it's a nightclub or disco, or pub—not like they'll be standing outside in the snow for several hours." And there seems even be something competitive between women as to how much attention is received. "We heard from our female students that afterward, they would compare their bruises or marks to see who earned the most," he says. "So there is definitely something going on there."

Injuries and Aggression

Whatever swats might be doled out during the run are insignificant compared to other possibilities for injury. A particular concern is the over-enthusiastic or drunken spectator in some show of bravado. "Neck injuries are pretty common," says Böhm. "Idiots grabbing the Krampus by the horns and pulling can be very dangerous for the guy in the costume." Others point out that the restricted visibility of the masks is a factor in collisions, both with spectators and between runners. Horned performers ducking under and around obstacles also places those standing by in harm's way.

"When you're leading with your horns, you really have to watch," says Claudia Ned-wed. "Performers wearing platform shoes can also tip over, and then there is the fire, pyrotechnics, flares … and burns."

Torches, bonfires, flares, and other pyrotechnics, popular in less-traditional runs a few years ago, are now prohibited at most major events, says Alexander Haslauer of Krampusimperium. "Every year the government gets stricter, so in the near future they will be almost completely be banned. Some Krampus clubs just don't care and do it anyways, but they get into trouble afterwards. Almost every year there are accidents, and as a result, it's almost impossible to find insurance for a new club nowadays."

Increasingly these incidents are scrutinized, and sometimes end with pros-ecutions and negative media coverage. Slowly but surely, all of this is changing the form of the runs. Along with restricting fire and banning the more dangerous wooden switches, Krampus runs are being confined to set times and routes. Worse still, from a traditionalist's perspective, many of these routes are now lined by mobile barriers separating runners and spectators. Only those daring to reach be-yond the barricades may be touched, and the corralled devils here often do little more than pose for photos or videos captured for social media.

While Krampus-runners speak wistfully of the old freedoms and expressed sadness over incidents causing new restrictions, they also recognize that perform-ers themselves can sometimes be blamed. "Some current runners don't under-stand the tradition itself, and participate only in order to strike out anonymously while masked," admits Marius Brandner. "Naturally, that impacts the spectators, and then it's reciprocated." As a result of such misconduct, some larger urban runs have also taken to the practice of tagging all runners with registered IDs.

Despite all this, Rest is wary about drawing any conclusions about a trend toward greater mayhem in Krampus runs. "What we have to consider is that this whole thing has blown up so extremely in the last 20 years, there are just many more Krampuses now than in the 1990s. So of course there are more incidents, more drunk or unruly Krampuses now, and more reports. The sample is just larger. Apart from Eastern Tyrol, which can get violent, when you look at the whole media rep-resentation of it, you come up with not that much—here's a broken arm, there's a twisted ankle. I'm always surprised there are not many more. And what there is—so much of it's just a matter of slipping on snow, running, maybe being a little tipsy."

Moorpass Maishofen, Austria. Masks: Metzger Masken. *Photo © Moorpass Maishofen.*

Under the Influence

Alcohol use in Krampus runs has become a major focus of media attention and is consequently a hot-button issue among runners and organizers. "At the larger events," says Böhm, "alcohol is forbidden among participants. This is a pretty big step for a people that love their liquor like Austrians. Just the beer consumption alone in Austria is the second highest per capita for all of Europe. So alcohol is a definitely a thing." While Böhm says enforcement of the bans is very strict—"have a beer before the Lauf and you're out"—alcohol is still very present at those traditional, small events, like the Krampus plays he attends in northern Styria. "The groups there usually meets at an inn before the performance for a few beers while costuming," he says, "and as the play is performed at various locations, schnapps or beer is drunk along the way. They'll gradually get more drunk, so performances later in the day … they're not necessarily better." Sometimes things can get rough, he says. "If you happen to catch one of these groups en route to one of the later performances, you'd better run! I myself got beaten pretty severely last year even though I was holding my camera. They usually don't go after photographers."

The majority of those I interviewed emphatically stressed that their *Pass* prohibited alcohol before events, though many pointed to black sheep (in other groups) ignoring such rules. "I personally want to always be 100% fit and attentive during a run, so for me alcohol isn't involved," wrote Brandner. "But honestly,

Krampus group in Bad Mitterndorf, Austria. *Photo © Wolfgang Böhm.*

I was rather in the minority here." But a few I spoke with showed a more relaxed attitude, admitting that their activities were still fueled in the traditional manner. "We consume alcohol both before and after a run," wrote Mike Kratzer. "But everyone knows their limit, and no one gets abusive or aggressive. The Krampus is playing a particular role, like an actor, and if one calms the nerves a bit with alcohol beforehand, it just tends to go better."

Show and Spectacle

While alcohol may be disappearing from the contemporary Krampus run, this is hardly the case with the growing phenomenon of the *Krampuskränzchen*, more commercial events held at bars, clubs, discos, or other venues where alcohol freely flows. The word "*Kränzchen*," (literally, "wreath") refers to a social gathering or circle of people. These events, held in the weeks before December 6, may feature live or DJ'd music and costumed performers from one or more troupes. They may be held as fundraisers for a Krampus group, but this is not always the case, and some troupes refuse to take part, believing the *Kränzchen* detract from the traditional *Krampuslauf* or house visit.

Höllenzirkus ("Hell Circus") show. *Photo © Groediger Krampusse.*

The *Krampus-Spektakel* is similarly an accretion to the tradition. Like the *Kränzchen*, it is not tied to the December 6 calendar date, and might be regarded as a form of the *Kränzchen*, though more ambitious or "spectacular." A more humble name for the same is "Krampus Show." Both are highly choreographed, circus-like versions of the Krampus run in which the troupe's appearance is enhanced with various theatrical devices: torches, bonfires, smoke machines, flash-pots, flares, fireworks (both aerial and hand-carried), or rustic wooden carts or gas vehicles ridden by the devils. While some of these elements may also appear in runs, the "show" tends to happen in a contained area rather than throughout city streets and may be structured with some overarching narrative or commentary provided by a master of ceremonies on mic, or by pre-recorded narration and music (metal or horror-film-soundtracks being preferred). Various municipalities and groups can be very competitive in attracting crowds with new gimmicks, and one can even find shows with go-go dancers, and Krampuses flying on wires and trapeze.

Quite a few sources I spoke with resented these shows and their overwrought flourishes. "I hate the loud music," says Böhm. "At some places, mostly in the south, they even play Rammstein at the runs. Nothing wrong with the music itself, but it doesn't feel right at these events."

Everywhere, commercial and touristic interests are pushing for an earlier start, particularly the local ski lodges, which constitute the greater part of Gastein's winter economy. "It's really inconvenient," Rest says, "because it's just a few days too early to work with the ski resorts, which open normally on the 8th of December or the weekend after. The tourism boards have for a long time considered this an interesting option for extending the season, but they always experience strong opposition from the Krampus groups." Extending the season after the events on the 5th and 6th is also not welcome as Krampus-runners are usually physically destroyed by the grueling schedule. "Basically," Rest says," they have to get 2 days of holiday afterward just to recuperate. Nobody shows up to work on December 7th."

"True to the Good Old Ways"

Tampering with the old ways is always controversial among Krampus participants, and many groups operate under the slogan, "*Treu dem guten alten Brauch*" ("true to the good old ways"). Another term that always comes up is "*Brauchtum.*" Usually, it is translated as "tradition," but this may not be strong enough. "Traditionalism" might come closer. Some even hint romantically that such a potent word cannot find expression in English.

Speaking of his fieldwork with participants, Rest says, "We were very intrigued by this whole thing of *Brauchtum*. But I'm also very skeptical when I hear the word because I never know what it's supposed to mean. It's very obscure. They always refer to this primordial tradition, but when you really get into it, these guys all give many different answers as to what it really is."

How deeply the tradition is rooted in history is contentious. While there are clear historical precedents and influences on current practice, many erroneous claims are made in attempts to present the custom as more deeply grounded. Modern claims to antiquity are influenced by a dubious intellectual heritage, in particular an overzealous tendency during the Third Reich to explain many cultural institutions in terms of ancient Nordic religion. While certain 17th- and 18th-century practices foreshadow and influenced contemporary customs, widely circulating theories connecting the Krampus with ancient paganism must be closely examined. What is clear, in terms of direct continuity of practice, is that even in the most traditional areas like Gastein, there is little documentation of Krampus activities before the late 19th century.

One of the earliest Gastein-area troupes was the Bleiwang-Pass, started in 1935 by Rest's grandfather, Josef Rest, and named for Sepp Lang's "Bleiwang mask," now in the anthropologist's family. Even before this, the Kötschachtal *Pass*, Rest says, "was apparently around in the 1910s and '20s, and was very important in shaping this thing. Before that the customs were almost extinct in the rest of the valley by the 19th century." The Kötschachtal *Pass*, as mentioned earlier, was the troupe that provided Rest's grandfather the memorably unfortunate introduction to the custom of the *Rempler*.

"My grandfather would say 'before we started our *Pass*, there were just a couple of these, you know, farm laborers, out in the remote country who would make their own kind of makeshift masks—you know a horn here or there—and go from house to house.' He would actually speak pretty derisively of them. What these guys were doing was apparently a far cry from what took shape in the '20s and '30s."

In Europe, a second burst of Krampus activity came after World War II. Salzburg researcher Ernestine Hutter mentions Gastein's several early *Krampuspassen* being founded in 1948 and describes the Krampus runs and house visits spreading throughout the Pinzgau and Pongau regions in the late 1960s and early 1970s. The 1980s saw the largest growth of Krampus groups in Gastein, and by the 1990s this growth had spread beyond its traditional confines to non-Alpine regions.

Women and the Tradition

Even as the tradition grows in the 21st century, its origins in an extremely Catholic milieu and the conservative impulse that has preserved it in historic form are hardly beloved by progressives. "In general, it's more of a blue-collar thing," says Böhm, "and not very popular with urban intellectual people. They dismiss it as primitive and violent, at least for the most part." One of the ways the tradition has remained obdurately "true to the good old ways" is the exclusion or sidelining of women.

Women generally do not dress as the Krampus. One rationale given is that females typically lack the stamina to wear the heavy suits, bells, and masks during the long runs. Others feel less compelled to justify this exclusion and simply point to a time-honored *Brauchtum*. "With our club, there is no female presence, and we want to keep it strictly so," says Mike Kratzer.

Female participation, however, is not limited to playing the role of the Krampus, and the absolute exclusion of females is not strictly traditional. In areas where the practice is most carefully conserved and the practice of house visits retained, female participation in the role of the angel is regarded as essential. A more modern development is the inclusion in the *Pass* of females in the role of witches.

Females also fill all manner of support roles, and devote themselves to making Nicholas gift bags, feeding visiting troupes, helping with crowd control during runs, or matters of event production relating to the *Krampuskränzchen*.

Krampus from Gruabtoifi Saalfelden, Austria. *Photo © Günther Golliner.*

Women may also assist with youth-groups associated with the *Pass*, such as the "Junior Devils" club sponsored by the Mühlviertler Rauh-Teufel in Sankt Georgen, Austria. Groups like these encourage children to make simple masks, stage their own *Kinder-Krampuslauf*, or enjoy other activities designed to groom or entertain the aspiring Krampus.

Women associated with the troupe are often, but not always, friends, sisters, aunts, and mothers of male members. Girlfriends, when they do not participate themselves, express a range of attitude toward their partner's fondness for sweaty animal hide suits. Several mentioned a feeling of pride by association, saying that playing the role of Krampus represents a great honor in the community. Stefan Hable writes, "They accept it and see it as thoroughly positive. It's like membership on a soccer team." Wolfgang Naumann, in Hallein, describes something less enthusiastic: "mixed feelings — curiosity and aversion." And Mike Kratzer describes something sounding like resigned tolerance: "My girlfriend accepts my hobby and supports it. She has to if she wants to live with me."

Outside of traditionalist strongholds, it is not at all impossible to find women also in the role of the Krampus. Though still rare, modern troupes increasingly accept female members, and some mask carvers now produce decidedly femal visages for their masks. A female performer can sometimes be more child-friendly, as Böhm recalls. "About three years ago at a run near Graz, a little girl got very

scared when a Krampus walked up to her. So the Krampus removed the mask revealing a girl of about 13. She kneeled down and told the kid, 'Hey, don't be afraid, I'm just a little girl like you.' It was very touching."

Even in Gastein, women sometimes participate in non-traditional roles. As far back as the 1970s, St. Nicholas was occasionally played by a female (in the Jaga *Pass* and Gold *Pass*). And Rest says that "if you ask around long enough, you'll find a handful of females who tell you, 'well you know, there was this Krampus totally drunk, who needed someone, so I just filled in for a half hour." Gastein, however, presents a unique problem. "Local women know that the main problem would be the *Rempler*," Rest says, "because of course here they are simply outweighed."

Reflecting on the subject, Rest chuckles at something. "It's probably just a rural myth," he says. "But there have been these rumors around for years: 'yeah, you know there is this lesbian couple, and they said they want to form an all-female Pass!"

What would happen if something like this were to occur in the tradition-bound valley? "I'd be really curious to see," he says. "I think there'd be lot of bad-mouthing and people saying this and that, but I don't think much would come of it. In the end, I think nobody would actively prevent them from doing so."

Krampus Unchained

Though Gastein is intensely traditional, unconventional practice, should it occur, would encounter no top-down resistance. There is no governing body controlling the activities of the various Krampus groups, not even a self-governing association of troupes. In other regions, groups may be required to fill out paperwork, and obtain insurance to stage public events, or be required to register individual members marching in a parade, but in Gastein, the troupes themselves exist strictly under the radar.

"There is no formal legal status for these groups at all," Rest says. "They're not official. They're not associations. In a way it's anarchic, you know—a couple 16- and 17-year-olds getting together just saying: this year we're going to do it! And that's it. They start looking around for masks and costumes."

Quite apart from issues of authoritarian control, even the most well-meaning suggestion for improvements finds no official forum for discussion. "A couple years ago in Hofgastein," Rest says, "there was a plan suggested, that it might

Krampuslauf at Munich Christkindlmarkt. *Photo by tribp (CC BY 2.0).*

somehow be beneficial if the *Krampuslauf* were to follow a particular route down a main city street. When the time came, no one showed up. Every single *Pass* chose instead to deliberately avoid that particular street. Even if they'd planned to use it, they switched plans, marching down a parallel street instead."

"I like this story," he says, "but in a way, it sounds too good to be true." That urge not to be controlled by spectator convenience, particularly the convenience of tourists, he says, would naturally appeal to "young men in an area that is so highly dependent on tourism, one where perhaps half the guys playing Krampuses work in that industry."

"No, we will not give in on this," Rest says, imaging participants' reactions. "We do everything for the tourist industry for four to five months a year, but not this thing. This is ours. We won't turn it into another attraction for the tourist cycle.

"Again, it's that compelling image of the Krampus in Gastein, " he muses, "this pure, incorruptible thing that is just there for itself and is done for itself, and for those who are part of the community. And I think, in a way, this is true."

Some of the beauty of the event, for Rest, would be lost in efforts to corral the troupes and structure the spectator experience. As experienced now, it's instead a matter of individual discovery. "It's so spread out and all happening simultaneously. You hear bells over in another street. If you are a bit schooled in the whole thing, you know the sound of the *Rempler*. You can tell it's a minute or two away. If you run now, you'll catch the last dramatic moment. Or you can be out on the street for two days and not see a single *Rempler*. You feel the year was a total bore, but then you meet somebody else the next day. He has all these reports—this and this and this happened." The event in this way is a unique personal adventure rather than the programmed mass experience of the parade, he believes. "With those parades, I just go so bored."

Rite of Passage

In this way, the experience of the Krampus for spectators is an anarchic game with many possible outcomes. For costumed participants too, the tradition allows them entrance into a playful world where normal social cause and effect don't apply. They become monsters armed with switches and bells, freed to act out, create tumult wherever they go, to even strike out (at least lightly) at friends, family, and total strangers.

"I think this liminal space is a very important thing, this breaking of the rules," Rest says. "In our everyday lives, there is less and less space for excess and overflow of a certain form of unconventional vitality." Stør Sven Dah of Wiener

Neustadt says his participation as a Krampus allows just this, the chance to "live out your imagination. You slip into another role, and can let your creativity have free reign." And this is not the ersatz fantasy of a computer game. "It's decidedly non-virtual," Rest points out. "Even the fur, the visceral aspects of it, the smell of it, the wildness. Everything."

The fact that it is persons of a certain age expected to assume this role is significant to Wolfgang Böhm. He speaks of the tradition as a sort of rite of passage, one that confirms continuity between generations, the elder generation teaching and demanding commitment of the younger, "giving them purpose at a difficult time in their lives as they become adults."

The raging Krampus perfectly embodies that emotional Sturm und Drang typical of the teenage years when most runners first don their horns. But doesn't a developmental cataclysm like this leave some traces? Don't we glimpse these depths occasionally even in the most well-adjusted, grownup lives?

Böhm himself has passed his wild years and no longer participates as a costumed Krampus, but he continues a passionate involvement with the tradition, traveling here and there photographing events, writing, and sharing what he experiences in books and online projects. The Krampus, he says, "caters to the dark, melancholic part of my personality." For him, that brooding sense of fate and destiny some plan to leave behind in adolescence is still stirred by "the season of autumn and early winter—the twilight, the slowing down and the mystical feeling that foreshadows these traditional events, the tales of mythical creatures, the forests of the mountains where they lurk, and the presence of the unknown. This all has had a strong influence on me as long as I can remember."

I know he is not alone here. He is describing a familiar thing, ever poised to return, our lost, dark Christmas.

REGIONAL VARIATIONS

Krampus customs have always been highly regionalized. While modern ease in sharing imagery and marketing of costume materials across regional borders has led to greater homogeneity, certain areas, such as those mentioned below, still proudly maintain their own unique take on the tradition.

KLAUSEN

In the Oberallgäu region of the Bavarian Alps in southernmost Germany, the *Klausen* or *Wilde Klausen* ("wild Clauses," i.e., "Wild Nicholases") play a role similar to the Krampus. They do not appear as part of Nicholas house-visits, but as part of a public run, or *Klausentreiben*, and are particularly noteworthy for their unusual costuming, called the *Häs*. While the more usual wooden masks were once used, over the years, hood-like face-coverings made of hide or fur cut with eye-holes have taken their place. Rather than the goat horns traditional to the Krampus, cow horns are more common, and in some towns, deer or elk antlers are used. Bells are worn at the front of the waist rather than the back, and clothing is a patchwork of sheep, deer, fox, or badger skins, sometimes augmented with cooler and more comfortable synthetic fur. If not inherited from an older friend or family member, the unmarried males who perform as *Klausen* usually create their own costumes, as no specialized woodworking skills are required for the mask. Tradition requires that no suit should resemble another.

The *Klausentreiben* in the town of Sonthofen is the largest and best known in the region with about 200 *Klausen* belonging to the local *Klausenverein* (club) founded in 1976. Club guidelines strictly maintain a traditionalist feel, forbidding the use of nonindigenous horns like those of the African kudu or oryx used elsewhere, and the illuminated eyes or painted blood often used in modern masks. The whole body must be covered by fur (not

Opposite and this page: Klausen in Germany's Allgäu region wear fur masks in place of wooden masks.
Photos © Klausenverein, Sonthofen.

bare leather) so that no clothing or skin is visible. Gloves must be worn to hide the hands, and shoes, if exposed, may not be colorful. The Sonthofen *Klausen*, like others in the region, use willow for their switches, but limit themselves to a single green branch rather than the bundled branches used in other towns. For safety, they have also forbidden the use of antlers.

In the nearby town of Burgberg, the style of costuming is unique among *Klausen*, and rather uniform. There, performers wear only white sheepskin suits, and on their heads immense fur hats or helmets made of the same. These are adorned with cowhorns and the pelt of a badger or fox draped decoratively over the top. Barely visible under those hats, performers' faces are bare, but covered below the nose by an oversized blonde beard made of flax.

Throughout the region, green willow is used for switches, sometimes bundled, sometimes a single, long, well-chosen rod. A favorite game among the *Klausen* is to corner en masse a more obstinate spectator, demanding that he kneel and recite an "Our Father" or face a beating.

The Oberallgäu is also home to the moss-faced "wild Barbaras" (*Bärbele*), discussed later, who appear on that saint's day, December 4. As Klausen runs begin on the following night, *Bärbele* and *Klausen* appearances may sometimes bleed over each other's traditional date, and may belong to a single organization organizing both events.

BUTTNMANDL

Around Berchtesgaden, Bavaria, near the Austrian border, a unique creature called the *Buttnmandl* is part of the Krampus tradition. His costume consists of a large star-shaped bundle of straw entirely enveloping the body and leaving visible only the arms, lower legs, and a mask covering his face. He appears as part of a troupe (here alled a *Bass*), along with a St. Nicholas, more traditional Krampus figures, and angels.

The wrapping of the performer in straw is a demanding technique guarded by the the troupe as a sort of trade secret. As there are always 12 *Buttnmandln* per *Bass*, and nearly an hour is required to create each straw suit, work begins in the morning to prepare for the troupe's appearance at dusk. Preparations are usually carried out in a barn lent for the purpose, and make use of straw hand-threshed by the performers themselves sometime in late summer.

Once all *Buttnmandln* are prepared, they exit the barn, and the farmer's wife traditionally blesses the *Buttmandln* with a sprinkling of holy water. The troupe members then recite prepatory prayers: one Our Father, a Hail Mary, and an Angelus said for deceased members of the troupe. The religious aspect of the undertakings is generally taken rather seriously, and it is expected that those who are not in attendance at mass the Sunday previous to the outing will not participate.

The *Buttnmandln* also wears one or more large bells strapped to their back, carries switches of braided willow, and disguises their faces with masks, either of the carved wooden variety or a soft fur or cloth version inevitably featuring a dangling red tongue.

On the first Sunday of Advent, St. Nicholas, his "Nicholas Wife," and straw Buttnmandl appear
in the small town of Loipl, outside Berchtesgaden, Bavaria.

The name *Buttnmandl* is sometimes understood to refer exclusively to these straw-clad performers, but may also refer to the entire troupe, which also includes devil characters called *Ganggerln* ("runners") or sometimes simply *Krampein* ("Krampuses"). These characters wear a sort of lightweight version of a more usual Krampus costume consisting of fur pelts, chains, old clothes, and limbs usually exposed, but blackened with soot. Their masks are of either type described earlier, and their bells are much smaller than the usual Krampus bells, hanging from a harness on their back as well as belts. Their lightweight costuming allows them to run ahead of the straw figures and assist with various manouvers made awkward by the more cumbersome straw suits.

Along with these characters, Nicholas is accompanied by a *Nikoloweibi* ("Nicholas wife") or two angels, depening on location. The "wife," formerly played by a costumed boy but now more often a girl, is often now replaced by the female angel characters, as has been the case in the town of Berchtes gaden since 1935. Both are tasked with carrying treats distributed by the saint. Additional switches used by the troupe are sometimes carried by a *Ruatntroger* (Rod carrier). This role offers a form of apprenticeship to boys under 16 and therefore too young to undertake the other roles.

Going from house to house, the *Bass* lets out a collective devilish roar as they near each destination. The lead Buttnmandl emits a loud blast on his cow-horn trumpet, and Nicholas leads the entire troupe indoors, including the voluminous straw figures, whose entrance must sometimes be accommodated by clearing furniture or removing doors from hinges.

Nicholas conducts the visit along the usual lines with ecclesiastic flourishes, edifying rhymes or remarks, and a review of children's behavior and prepared performances. While well-behaved children receive small treats, naughty children and older observers are set upon by the *Ganggerln*, who administer not only swats but drag occupants outdoors, throwing them in and rubbing them with snow. In snowless winters, piles of old leaves or dirt does the trick, or a dunk in a garden fountain will suffice. Because the *Ganggerln* are usually blackened with soot, they will also see that some of this is smeared on their victims. The very young, and very old are spared, but household posessions are not. Furniture will be dragged outside and deposited in the front yard if at all possible. More than mere prank-

ishness, this custom, called the "*ausramma*" ("clearing out"), is interpreted (or perhaps excused) as a clearing of evil influence from inside the house.

While blows from the *Ganggerln* are understood as punishments, those administered by the straw figures are said to bring fertility. Especially suggestive of this is the *Buttnmandl Busserl* ("kiss"), namely strokes administered to a young woman on the inner surfaces of the lower legs.

Pagan origins of the *Buttnmandllauf* are assumed, as the synchronization of the tradition to the Catholic occasion of St. Nicholas Day occurred only around 1730. Previously, it fell in the weeks of the *Rauhnächten* (later to be discussed) and until the 1950s it was still practiced on Christmas Eve in Berechtesgaden, and in other areas is fixed to other Sundays in December rather than St. Nichols Day.

The straw costumes were not always a prominent feature of the tradition. The name "*Buttnmandl*" originates with the Bavarian word "*buttn*" for "rattle," referring to the bells. Up until the 1970s, straw was used in less elaborate arrangements or combined with animal hides in costumes, and this style still sometimes appears in the community of Marktschellenberg, where only straw leggings are employed.

TYROL

The name "*Klaubauf*," used interchangeably with "Krampus" in the area around Gastein and elsewhere, in East Tyrol refers to a rather different breed of monster. Here, the

Klaubauf-style Krampus in Thurn, Austria. *Photo © Stefan Tschapeller Photography.*

demon is still associated with St. Nicholas Day and the house-visit custom, but is missing some of the classic traits of the Krampus, namely horns and switches. This lack by no means detracts from the Klaubauf's ferocity. In fact, encounters with the creature in the East Tyrolean town of Matrei are notoriously violent, so much so that the city discourages tourists from taking part in the celebrations and does not welcome news reports, video, and photography documenting the event.

Rather than light swats from a horsetail or switches, the East Tyrolean *Klaubauf* engages those brave enough to step forward in a sort of wrestling match that usually ends with the *Klaubauf's* opponent thrown to the pavement or snow, quite frequently with

his shirt torn or even ripped from his body. It is commonly understood that the *Klaubauf* mask lacks horns because these would be too dangerous in such encounters. The sport reaches its most brutal climax at midnight on St. Nicholas Day, at the *Ausläuten*, or "ringing out" of the beasts, when 300 or more of these creatures, each wearing up to six bells weighing as much as 40 pounds, come storming into Matrei's town square. Hospital emergency rooms make special preparations for the event, where as many as 100 injuries may be reported each year. In December 2013, a particularly serious accident occurred when a 15-year-old student sustained a head injury resulting in a coma.

The party responsible for causing the

injury went unidentified because costumed participants wear no registration numbers, and the *Passen* are spontaneously organized and report to no official organizing committee. While the event's organic character and utter lack of municipal control clearly presents dangers, it is also viewed as a mark of authenticity. Mayor Andreas Köll, in a November 30, 2014 issue of Austria's *Kleine Zeitung*, praised the event's grassroots nature, saying, "The *Klaubauf* run is a custom of the citizens of Matrei for the citizens of Matrei, a custom which we have not allowed to degenerate into a fire spectacle or show for tourists, a custom which is to be preserved in its originality."

The impromptu battle matches between spectators and *Kleibeife* (plural) are regarded as a form of *Ranggel*, a traditional form of wrestling in the Alps sometimes used to settle disputes or establish dominance. Since the accident in 2013, special emphasis has been laid upon a "Matrei *Klaubauf* Code of Honor" which lays out certain restrictions on these matches. Any actions resulting in injury are regarded as a violation of the code, which also stipulates that spectators can only be engaged if showing clear signs of their willingness, and that "females, children, the elderly, the frail, and visitors will not be attacked." All matches are to end with the *Klaubauf* helping his victim to his feet and a conciliatory hug. A folk etymology of the word *Klaubauf* for this reason derives the name from "*aufklauben*," which could be translated as "pick up." (The real etymology of the word, however, is not definitively established.)

Beginning around the first of December, the *Klaubauf* also takes part in traditional house-visits, which are conducted mostly along lines similar to what has been discussed. Nicholas reviews the children's performance as per usual and is accompanied by two angels as well as two "beggar" characters, the male and female "Lotter" and "Lütterin," both played by young boys, and a musician on accordion. The beggars and accordionist dance wildly through the rooms of the houses visited, occasionally provoking spectators with lewd gestures, and at the end pass the hat for money (nowadays mostly donated to some worthy cause). After the performance, the *Kleibeife* rush in with the goal of dragging occupants out of the house and tossing them in the snow. Children may be exempt from some of the rougher handling, but young women, though they may be treated somewhat differently, are favorite targets of this sport.

In traditional homes, families would gather around the dining room table to await Nicholas and his troupe. Once the *Kleibeife* invaded the home, the table presented a kind of barrier between the family, and the creatures who would attack them. The *Kleibeife*'s efforts to drag away the table itself became a sort of ritual contest, with ultimate victory on devils' part resulting in the table being completely removed from the house and set outside. Retaining the table in this tug-of-war was said to bring good luck to the household, while having it displayed in the yard was a disgrace. Modernized home interiors have almost completely eliminated this rustic game of *Tischrücken* or *Tischzoichn* ("table-pulling") but it's been retained and relocated to Matrei's city square, where in simple mock-ups of old farmhouse kitchens, grown men with something to prove hide behind a heavy wooden table that teams of *Kleibeife* try to remove.

Klaubauf-style Krampus in table-pulling game, Thurn, Austria. *Photo © Stefan Tschapeller Photography.*

In South Tyrol, or Italy's Alto Adige province, one finds another variation on the Krampus theme, the *Klosn* (Clauses) of the town of Stilfs (Italian: Stelvio). The *Klosn,* named for the occasion of their appearance on the Saturday before or after St. Nicholas day, are of two classes: the bell-wearing "donkeys" who make their initial appearance on the hills over the town, wending their way down into the village like pack animals, and the "devils" or *Kleibeife.* The "donkeys" are dressed in suits banded with colorful ribbons, lending them the appearance of walking piñatas. Their faces are hidden by what looks like a ski-mask with long, Krampus-like tongues dangling from the mouths. The "devils" wear carved wooden masks similar to the familiar Krampus and robes of much longer, and more ragged multi-colored cloth ribbons.

In Schlanders (Italian: Sildandro) about 15 miles to the east, there is another interesting take on the Krampus. There, the creature's suit has a peculiar ragged look, as it is composed of wool shorn from sheep. More notable here, however, is the instrument with which the devil pursues his prey, in this case, a *Rute* the size of a young sapling. With these oversized switches they chase the young men of the city and administer beatings that rival the ferocity of activities in Matrei.

Chapter Four

THE CHURCH BREEDS A MONSTER

A Not-So-Jolly St. Nicholas

The figure of the Krampus cannot be understood apart from that of St. Nicholas. In a sense, the harsh, punishing devil merely externalizes a shadow side of the saint. That a holy man might harbor a wrathful inner aspect is today inconceivable. To put the devil back into the saint, we must return to a figure conjured by the medieval mind and rooted in Byzantine Christianity. In that world, a foreboding gloom edged the experience of light and joy, and the holy was shrouded in dread. The sensibility was embodied in the architecture of early Christendom, where the darkness of the Church's great ecclesiastical caverns purposefully evoked the foundational *mysterium* of the faith, lending a numinous quality just as essential as the glitter of candles, mosaic, and colored glass. It is therefore fitting somehow that an understanding of our more somber St. Nicholas and his sway over gothic Europe begins with a story of his bones.

In the dark of their marble altar crypt, in the Basilica Di Nicola in Bari, Italy, the bones of the long dead saint lie weeping. For centuries now, they have been observed to exude a small but precious quantity of mysterious, allegedly sweet-smelling liquid variously referred to as "oil," "myrrh," or "manna." Despite claims by skeptics that the phenomenon must have something to do with condensation, an aura of the supernatural attaches itself to the substance, and it's treasured

St. Nicholas icon, Alexa Petrov (1294), Church of St. Nicholas Novgorod Russia.

by the faithful as a source of miraculous healing. First noted in 343, shortly after Nicholas' death, the magical power of these weeping bones was a factor driving the spread of the St. Nicholas cult to the rest of Europe.

Most readers will know that the historical saint was a bishop of the early Church. Born in the city of Patara, then part of the Roman province of Lycia, in 317 he assumed the office of archbishop in the nearby port city of Myra (Demre in modern Turkey), traveled in the Holy Land, residing briefly in a cave, was for a time imprisoned by Diocletian, was freed by Constantine, and became an important voice in shaping the Nicene Creed, Christendom's central statement of faith. Further details of his life are the domain of legend.

After Nicholas' death, rumors regarding the "manna" and miraculous healings around his tomb in Myra made the site popular with early pilgrims. For reasons both devotional and commercial, the pilgrimage site and relics attracted interest in the rival Italian ports of Venice and Bari. With Myra then under Muslim rule, a party of merchants and sailors from Bari struck first, "rescuing" the relics from the infidels in 1087. Around 1099, during the First Crusade, Venetian soldiers also entered Myra, sweeping up splinters of bone left by the Bari raiders, and smuggled these to the monastery church of San Nicolò al Lido, where they are displayed today. A finger of the saint's right hand was also brought from Bari to Saint-Nicolas-de-Port in France. In 980, a vial of the manna reached German-speaking lands, donated to the city of Worms by the wife of Emperor Otto II, the Byzantine princess Theophanu, who also built Germany's first church dedicated to Nicholas in Brauweiler, near Cologne, that same year. Here a tooth of the saint was enshrined.

Unseemly Holy Legends

Around these skeletal remains swirled a growing body of saintly legend that quickly spread through Europe. The Nicholas they described feels only tangentially related to the saint as he is popularly conceived today, and two of the tales most influential at the time contain darker, less child-friendly themes. It's child-murder and cannibalism that figure into the legend establishing Nicholas's patronage over children. Set down in the mid-1100s by the early Norman poet Wace, the story tells of three traveling schoolboys who stop to overnight at an inn kept by a scheming couple. During their sleep, the boys are killed, chopped up, and flung into a brining barrel by the innkeeper who intends to sell the youngsters as meat. In the morning, St. Nicholas arrives at the hostelry to accuse the couple of their deed. He uncovers the evidence and at once conjures from the pile of hacked flesh three intact and living schoolboys. Though unheard of in the Eastern Church and considered rather ghastly there, it is a standard element in Western medieval European iconography, where the saint is frequently depicted with a salting tub containing three naked youths rejoicing in their resurrection.

Prostitution figures into the second story of Nicholas' secret nighttime charity said to have inspired our beloved Christmas gift-giving tradition. Set down around 1260 in Jacobus de Voragine's hagiographic compilation, *The Golden Legend*, this tale presents a young Nicholas wishing to charitably rid himself of wealth inherited from his recently departed parents. The saint learns of a neighbor too poor to furnish his three virgin daughters with dowries and therefore unable to marry them off. Seeing no other way out of his bind, the father resolves to sell the girls into prostitution. To rescue the maidens, Nicholas provides the man with three bags of gold, doing so in self-effacing secrecy by throwing the bags, one each on three sequential nights, through his neighbor's open window.

Stories such as these had strong populist appeal for audiences immured in the harsh realities of medieval Europe. They not only figured prominently in church iconography but also as the subject of church plays, making Nicholas an early favorite of the medieval stage. His feast day early in Advent offered the first taste of Christmas, a season uniquely associated with theatrical pageants, plays, liturgy, and revels indulging the most extravagant fantasies of the medieval mind. It's here that St. Nicholas first emerges from history as a costumed figure bringing gifts.

The Devil in Medieval Christmas Plays

The earliest known plays about St. Nicholas come from German-speaking lands, two from an 11th-century Hildesheim manuscript and a third from a 12th-century collection in Einsiedeln, Switzerland. Such plays would naturally be presented on the saint's feast day, but might also be presented throughout the Christmas season along with Nativity stories, and also less seasonal stories of the Creation, Fall, and End Times. All of these plays, like the Nicholas-Krampus practice they prefigure, featured devils.

The Benediktbeuern Christmas play from 13th-century Bavaria contains not only scenes of devils dragging King Herod off to hell, but also a ranting appearance by the Antichrist, as well as the intrusion of Lucifer into a pastoral scene in which he mocks shepherds at the Nativity, claiming the angels' good tidings are lies. Another diabolical drama probably performed during Advent is the Bavarian "Play of Antichrist" ("*Ludus de Antichristo*"). And the Hessian Christmas Play, composed in the mid-1400s around Friedberg, Germany, presents a particularly obscene Lucifer plotting to prevent the birth of Christ with his demonic underlings, whom he promises to reward with scatological trifles including "bayberries of sheep," "goat beans," and "the stuff an old nun left in the privy prior to singing matins."

King Herod, Earthly Devil

Where Lucifer might be omitted from a Christmas play, King Herod often stood in as earthly counterpart. Medieval thespians were known to take particular delight in Herod's scenery-chewing fits, and the king's futile attempt to eliminate his Messianic rival by executing all male newborns was exploited for all the pathos and terror it could summon. The histrionic blustering of actors portraying the king became such a fixture in European minds that even in in Shakespeare's era, it's referenced in Hamlet's warning to overzealous thespians not to "out-Herod Herod."

Far from the sentimental Nativity scenes imagined today, this fascination with Herod's slaughter once again reminds us how the Christmas of centuries gone by balanced seasonal good cheer with a frisson of terror. Theatrical representations of these atrocities were not only popular with medieval audiences but often enthusiastically ghastly in execution. According to medievalist Lynette Muir, in her *The Biblical Drama of Medieval Europe,* dialogue and stage direction implies that soldiers would "proudly display their lances and swords laden with spitted corpses." Some scenes, Muir writes, present soldiers sardonically guessing infant victims' ages based on weight, and German plays even featured blood-filled wooden dolls punctured during the performances.

An early 15th-century German Christmas play from Erlau adds to the slaughter an element of ghoulish farce. This manuscript gives Herod a court jester, Lappa, who joins with soldiers in joyfully murdering the little ones, giddily promising to dye his hands in the blood, and to slaughter as many children as possible, even if there are "a hundred thousand of them." The Benediktbeuern Christmas Play rewards the wicked king's deeds with an equally grisly end as stage directions dictate: "let Herod be gnawed to pieces by worms, and leaving his throne a dead man, let him be received by the devils with much rejoicing among them."

Stage design with Hellmouth from Valenciennes Passion play. Painting by Hubert Cailleau (1577).

The Devil's Stagecraft

How Herod's worm-eaten end might've been simulated remains a matter of intriguing speculation, but we do know that in order to keep the attention of audiences unable to follow Latin dialogue, a great deal of effort was devoted to visual effects—specifically those associated with the Devil. Particularly important here was the Hellmouth, a portal to the netherworld usually made to resemble a bestial maw. A 1437 Passion play from Metz, Germany, offers a lavish example, one where the Hellmouth was praised as "very well made, for by a device it opened and closed of its own accord when the devils wanted to go in or come out of it. And this great head," it continues, "had two great steel eyes which glittered wonderfully." Description of a 1474 play from Rouen mentions that upon the Hellmouth's opening, "all the devils cry out together with the drums and other thunderings made by machines, and the cannon are shot off and flames of fire are thrown out from nostrils, the eyes, and the ears."

In a 1536 pageant, *Mystery of the Holy Acts of the Apostles* presented in Bourges, the Devil appeared in "a Hell fourteen feet long by eight feet broad in fashion of a rock crowned with a tower ever burning and belching flames, wherein Lucifer's head and body alone appeared … vomiting flames of fire unceasingly, and holding in his hands certain kinds of serpents or vipers which writhed and belched fire." And in the 15th-century *The Castle of Perseverance*, the chief demon Belial was to "have gun powder burning in pipes in his hands and in his ears and in his arse when he goeth to battle."

Elaborate stagecraft such as this could hardly exist without avid support from audiences and patrons and testifies to the strength with which diabolical figures would have been enthusiastically embraced as part of Christmas entertainments.

Nicholas in Paradise Plays

As the Church's holy day dedicated to Adam and Eve falls on December 24, "Paradise plays," depicting their temptation in Eden via the diabolical Tempter, were a common feature of the Christmas season, particularly in Germany and Austria. These plays persisted into recent times, mingling with an evolving Nicholas-Krampus tradition. The Devil's appearance was, of course, one trait in common, and a Bavarian account of a Paradise play from the 19th century from the vicinity of Mitterfels mentions a familiar-sounding Lucifer with "a long and mighty tongue" who appears with his troupe outside the door making a "monstrous racket.

Again we can take as an example Gastein, where up until the 19th century a Paradise play was presented. The play's roots, however, go much further back. The Gastein version, like many in the area, is said to have been remarkably similar to playwright Hans Sachs' *The Tragedy, Creation, Fall and Expulsion of Adam from Paradise* composed in 1548. Gastein's Paradise play would have also been different from Sachs' more urban Nuremberg production. Though it may have cribbed lines from Sachs, Gastein's roving show, presented at multiple farms over an evening, would be necessarily shorter and simpler. Rather than enact scenes, characters in plays such as these merely step forward, identify themselves, and relate their deeds in short monologue. In Gastein's Paradise play, Adam is said to have done exactly this. Nicholas, as a popular Advent saint, was also prominently featured.

Jesuit Pedagogy and Nicholas

After a few centuries, the seasonal play that came to dominate the Alpine regions was the *Nikolausspiel* ("Nicholas play"). Absorbing elements of the Paradise plays, the Nicholas plays featured divine and infernal powers in competition for the human soul. But along with this medieval concern, came a new interest in dogma and catechism. Much of this was a response by the Catholic Counter-Reformation to Protestant revolution and Humanist thought. The old mystery and miracle plays in the 14th century had transitioned from Latin to the vernacular, and with this had begun degenerating into populist buffoonery. More fitting to the new intellectual climate was the morality play. In these, allegorical figures, e.g., Death, Youth, Virtue and Vice, were presented as mouthpieces for edifying truths. The dialogues between Devils and heavenly figures in the Nicholas plays, as well as their frequent inclusion of figures such as Death and Youth, reflect this tendency.

The Nicholas plays and Krampus tradition portray the saint rewarding not only pious and compliant children but those who commit to memory scholastic lessons. Significantly, in the legend of the three murdered boys, the rescued characters are not just any boys, but invariably identified as "schoolboys" or "scholars." It is originally with this privileged class of children, those studying in the cathedral boarding schools, that St. Nicholas is first associated.

As early as the 17th century we have accounts of a Nicholas impersonator quizzing youths at a Jesuit boarding school in Innsbruck. A report from the late 1600s by the Augustinian monk Abraham a Sancta Clara of Vienna stresses this mostly academic function, describing Nicholas coming "to test the children and to examine whether they had been well instructed … in matters of faith, spelling, syllable divisions, reading, writing, arithmetic, and languages."

Nicholas Meets the *Perchten*

Gradually this practice of Nicholas rewarding good study and piety spread from environments under influence of the Church and urban aristocracy to more rural areas. Once there, the saint's character tended to be colored by existing rural folklore and customs. The Alpine regions it entered were home to a sort of folk-Catholicism mingled with an indigenous pagan folklore. Dominating this landscape were ambivalent, often-devilish mountain spirits known as the *Perchten* (singular: "*Percht*"). Masqueraders posing as these figures were part of rowdy costumed processions first explicitly mentioned in 17th-century documents. Probably quite similar to the earliest Krampus runs, the *Perchtenlauf* was regarded with suspicion by Church and

civil authorities as a custom of the peasant class, one that threatened riot and occasionally resulted in violence.

Gastein again provides an example. In the late 18th century, authorities in Gastein, like those in many regions, banned the *Perchtenlauf*, but thanks to the rugged and sparsely populated Alpine environment, bans proved difficult to enforce. In Gastein's remote Kötschachtal region, the *Perchtenlauf* survived but was eventually domesticated as St. Nicholas and his moralizing function were brought into the mix. As the *Perchtenlauf* was transformed into the *Krampuslauf* and hybridized with the Nicholas play, the wild *Percht* was reshaped as the Krampus—chained and subjugated to Nicholas, and thus brought under the control of ecclesiastic narrative and civil authority. The process, however, was mostly organic, rather than one of top-down imposition. As we've seen, Nicholas and the Krampus-like devils of traditional Church drama had for centuries already exercised great popular appeal and were therefore integrated with relative ease. Here too, *Passen* in Gastein's Kötschachtal initially held out with their *Perchten* activities, but were later brought around to the new Krampus-Nicholas modality.

Here and there the acceptance of Nicholas as figurehead for the older customs was surprisingly slow. The Tyrol was one of these regions, and Hans Schuhladen, author of the definitive volume on Nicholas plays, *Die Nikolausspiele des Alpenraumes*, lists nearly a dozen towns in that state that did not adopt the Nicholas figure into their parade customs until the 20th century. In Upper Austria's Sauwald region, Nicholas only became part of costumed village processions around 1940.

That the figure of Nicholas might be added as something of a decorative afterthought to an already robust peasant tradition is a point stressed by Viennese Krampus researcher Otto Koenig. In his extensive writings on the subject, Koenig questions the real significance of the character as one "assigned at once the most senior role and yet playing no central function." He describes Nicholas' position within these Krampus customs as rather tenuous, observing, "only when he makes his entrance during a house visit with recited doggerel, admonitions and gifts is he able to briefly dominate the children." Nicholas' status within the *Krampuspass* he finds likewise insecure: "If left alone to the boys to coordinate, there is never a Nicholas," he writes. "He is only really important where the parish priest is put in charge." Koenig also observed that it could also be difficult for the troupe to find a willing member for the saintly role, that sometimes it would fall as last resort to a female, and that during long hikes between farmhouse performances, the actor playing Nicholas is sometimes lost, or ditched like an unwanted chaperone.

Lucifer mask from Nicholas play in Stumm, Tyrol (ca. 1700-1750).
Photo by G. Watzek ©Tiroler Landesmuseen/Volkskunstmuseum.

Styrian paradise play by Alois Greil, from *Kronprinzenwerk*, vol 7 (1890).

Nicholas Play or Nicholas Parade?

The push and pull between *Perchtenlauf* and church plays is evident in the evolution of the Nicholas and Krampus customs in the late 18th and 19th century. The influence of the *Perchtenlauf* pushed toward activities that were more parade-like, while the church dramas pushed toward a narrative built on the saint's function and solemnly recited dialogue.

The results of these dual influences were Nicholas plays and Nicholas parades. Nicholas parade would typically be performed outdoors, outside homes or community gathering spots, the Nicholas play more likely indoors. Both were well adapted to rural areas, bringing performance to audiences scattered over sparsely populated areas. Lacking the institutional sponsorship of the old church plays, the Nicholas plays and parades perpetuated by the peasant class would end each performance with a solicitation of gifts, food, or drink from the householder.

While these may be useful categories, the Nicholas parade and Nicholas play obviously shade into each other. The modern *Hausbesuch*, for instance, exhibits formal elements of both, reflecting the play in some of the rhymed phras-

Cast of Nicholas play in Ennstal, Austria. (1896). *Photo by E. Eisler © Volkskundemuseum, Vienna.*

es memorized and recited by Nicholas upon entry, and reflecting the parade's mute improvisational interaction when it comes to the Krampuses' antics with the children. In the classic Nicholas play, however, the Krampus was quite loquacious, as in these lines I've adapted from several nearly identical Tyrolean plays of the 19th century:

I am Krampus! Fear my name!
Far and wide extends my fame.
I arrive when I am bidden,
And sniff out children where they're hidden.
Who is naughty? Where's my prey?
I'll tear them up without delay.
Oh, Master Nicholas, I bring sad truth
Of deeds committed by these youths.
For virtue they will seldom strive,
But sin and vice in them do thrive.
And of their idling in the streets —
So boils my rage, I cannot speak!
And daily though I do my spying
I've scarcely seen a child trying.
Good children, though, are not my task,
Only for the bad I'm asked.
For those my sack is neatly suited,
Their vexing screams and whining muted,
Off I pack them to their fates,
The spoiled little reprobates!
With brats as these one choice is fit —
To toss them in the fiery pit.

Devil mask from a Nicholas play,
late 19th century.
Photo Christa Knott
© Volkskundemuseum, Vienna.

St. Nicholas Gets Rowdy

In the era during which these two phenomena thrived and competed, many were concerned about the influence of the old *Perchtenlauf* upon the St. Nicholas festivities. An amusing example comes again from the pen of Abraham a Clara, fretting in 1729 over the activities of "Nicolai-Possen" (Passen). "There are those types who wish to present themselves as the wonder-working Bishop Nicholas," he writes, "who will borrow miter and vespers-coat from the sacristy and thus outfit themselves in good and honorable manner so that children won't be so disturbed when Nicholas gets drunk and tumbles down the stairs." He concludes by noting that householders often lose valuable silver cutlery during visits of these Nicolai-Possen, but can't know for certain if "the Nicholases, or the angels, or devils are the greatest thieves."

19th-century Nicholas play presented by Krampus Los Angeles.
Photo © Paul Koudounaris (2014).

Similarly, the Vicar of the Tyrolean town of Mayrhofen complained about riotous behavior in 1815, writing, "on the night of Advent Sunday, December 3, so many costumed Nicholas ran from one tavern to another and created such a tumult that no decent person could sleep. They binged late into the night. Around midnight Lackner's and Kramer's taverns were still serving them … These Nicholas-maskers are not even the rhymers who perform in the disgustingly farcical Nicholas plays," he writes, "but merely masked individuals seeking all night long to cause the greatest mischief possible."

Sometimes troubles went further than mere noise and drunken disorder. On December 9, 1878, the local chronicle of Lassing, Austria, reported on violence among participants, writing, "last night, twenty local farm boys dressed as 'Nicholas' went to Weißenbach bei Liezen. Here they were attacked by ruffians from Liezen, Weissbach and Woerschach, and there was such a fight that after a few days a lad from Lassing succumbed to wounds and died. Another lay sick several weeks, and only the few, who escaped quickly enough, were uninjured." The slain victim, according to a reporting relative, had been killed because he had not run about fast enough while performing a part that called for him to frantically charge the audience on a hobbyhorse.

Strange Company for a Saint

There are many examples of the Nicholas figure of church tradition so compromised by pagan custom as to be almost unrecognizable. Sometimes the bestial aspect of the Alpine *Percht* is so evident in the character's costume that the name "Nicholas" or "Klaus" wouldn't seem to apply. The "Nicholas" of Illereichen, Germany, for instance, not only wore hides but also sported cloven hooves.

The other costumed figures in a Nicholas parade were hardly those associated with the traditional saint, and extended well beyond the Nicholas, angel, Krampus, and basket-carrier grouping we've seen in Gastein. In Völkermarkt, along with the saint and the *Bartl*, there was a Grim Reaper, with flowing white robe, scythe, and clock, a crone called "Mariet" or "Margarethe Maultasch" ("Margaret Bagmouth"), who would tell the fortunes of young girls, as well as a Fool (Bajazzo) in a red, bell-decked outfit, his face painted with animal blood. Strange figures also accompany the East Tyrolean parades described by Hans Schuhladen. These include a Grim Reaper who slithers about the room in imitation of the serpent of Eden, a chimney sweep, a comical doctor and quack pharmacist, male and female Fools (Bajazz and Bajazzin), a bride and groom, and a male/female pair of elixir vendors.

This pattern of male-female pairing even extends to the traditionally celibate St. Nicholas. In Lech Valley in Tyrol, Nicholas festivities include a beautifully dressed woman, the *Klasa* (a female rendering of "Klaus"), who was charged with distributing gifts. In Upper Austria, the *Niglofrau* ("Nicholas-wife") did the same, leaving gifts in shoes set out by children. Even to this day, another female, the *Nikoloweib* (played by a young boy), is sometimes part of festivities in Bavaria's Berchtesgaden region. The same can be said of the Upper Austrian town of Windischgarsten, which preserves the female *Niglofrau* and similar archaic characters.

Carnival Influences

The peasant Nicholas celebrations so offensive to sources quoted above indeed feel more appropriate to the irreverent Carnival season than the feast of a Christian saint. This feeling was voiced in a 1744 missionary's report on Nicholas practices in East Tyrol, where the eyewitness complained, "that they misplace the entertainments of Carnival to Advent, Christmas, New Year and Epiphany, when they force their way into houses in fools' costumes or other shameless outfits, and whole hordes of young men and women are carried away and give themselves over to immoderate drink and feasting."

Nicholas traditions also reached the German-speaking lands of the Protestant North, where—without Catholic deference to saints—Nicholas was even more easily absorbed into irreverent Carnival customs. The word "Klaus," in fact, was defined in the 1767 *Bremen Lower-Saxon Dictionary* as "the costumed St. Nicholas or Carnival-fool, who scares the children on Nicholas Eve as a pagan, popish folly eliminated during the past few years in Protestant northern Germany."

Just as Carnival customs were absorbed into Nicholas practices, Nicholas was absorbed into Carnival. A report from the German city of Rottweil mentions the appearance of costumed "St. Clausen" within the ranks of a group of tradesmen celebrating Carnival in 1763. That the saint should be desacralized as just another Carnival fool was of little concern in the account, indicating that the costumes themselves were not uncommon. The real impetus for the report was that the Nicholases and followers drank until the wee hours at a local inn, pretending to conduct "confirmation services" between their sloppy rounds and thereby mocked a serious liturgical process.

Early Tyrolean Diffusion

The notion of Italy being influential on the Krampus-Nicholas tradition via Carnival customs may seem strange as that country has hardly been mentioned. Indeed, the Krampus is almost completely unknown there but for a small enclave in the country's northernmost Alpine province: South Tyrol (Italian: Alto Adige). However, some of the earliest mentions of Nicholas plays and oldest preserved scripts are found there. The Italian town of Prettau on the Austrian border is of particular importance for its role in preservation and transmission of folk-dramas dating back to the 15th century. Some of these plays, preserved orally in remote areas over hundreds of years, were collected and edited in the mid-1800s, and compiled into *The Theater-book of Stegerhof*. Among these is an important St. Nicholas play performed throughout South Tyrol up through the 1960s. The town of Prags boasts a Nicholas manuscript from 1794, and the municipality of Hainzenberg preserved Nicholas and Paradise plays with texts Schuhladen matches to examples dating back to the 1600s.

From South Tyrol, plays seem to have made their way north to Austria's Lower Inn River Valley and from there to the rest of the country. This pattern of dispersal is suggested but difficult to confirm thanks to the scarcity of written record. As plays were composed in rhyme and therefore relatively easy to memorize and orally transmit, little effort was made to commit them to writing until the 1850s and '60s.

Between Tyrol and Styria lies the state of Salzburg, where Nicholas plays are relatively unknown and may have been more aggressively absorbed into other forms, such as the *Hausbesuch*. Gastein was also influenced by cultural diffusion from South Tyrol. In 1731, fear of a Protestant uprising led Archbishop Leopold Firmian to forcibly expel all Protestants from the archbishopric of Salzburg. While many of the area's farms and workplaces stood empty, law forbade residents of the states of Salzburg or nearby Carinthia to reoccupy vacated properties as they were regarded as "not strong enough in their faith." Only Bavarians and Tyroleans were deemed fervent enough, and many from South Tyrol subsequently made their home in the valley, thereby influencing the area's Nicholas traditions.

Scenes from a Nicholas Play

Oddly, the content of the Nicholas play, as it came to be defined, only rarely portrayed traditional legends of the saint, though in North Tyrol, particularly elaborate versions would occasionally insert a Nicholas story (including an obscure tale featuring a miraculously growing beard). Most productions instead conformed to the following basic sequence of acts.

Entrance and Announcement

A troupe member enters the venue to request permission to perform and announces highlights of the play. This character may be an imperial "Quartermaster," a "Herald" in fancy white dress and feathered cap, or a Hunter, or Angel. Especially in crowded taverns or sites where room must be cleared for performers, a Krampus may scare up space, or a clown (Bajazzo) will do the task.

St. Nicholas Gifting Scene

The scene that follows with Nicholas, his entourage, and children is basically a more formal version of the *Hausbesuch* described in Gastein. However, it is usually not immediately followed by the wild rumpus of the Krampuses, a scene normally postponed to the final act.

Everyman Scene

The name, borrowed from the 15th-century play of that name, is used by Schuhladen and other researchers to describe allegorical scenes set in the peasant's world. Typical is a dialogue between Death and an initially heedless Youth, who usually escapes the Reaper by calling on the Blessed Virgin, Guardian Angel, or Nicholas. Rather than Death, Satan sometimes plays the villain as he tempts a pious hermit or pilgrim. Occasionally, the last-minute repentance is not enough, as in a Styrian version featuring drunken beggars whose manipulative and insincere repentance at Nicholas' feet is played for laughs. They recognize their sin too late and are dispatched by the Reaper's scythe.

Nicholas plays are known to have become increasingly geared toward peasant themes and low humor in the second half of the 18th century. Farmers, fishermen, foresters, or other workers were presented speaking satirically of their trade or complaining of their lot. Other vaudeville-style skits would also be inserted. Humorous portrayals of traveling salesmen, regionally stereotyped characters such as "Marco," an Italian lemon-seller, wandering knife-sharpeners, or vendors of questionable elixirs often appeared. Quack doctors were also popular, as was a slapstick skit featuring a dishonest horse-trader trying to sell a broken-down nag represented by costumed performers who would charge the crowd. Occasionally, the sick horse was treated with an enema, during which the crowd would be sprayed. In an old version from Donnersbach, the enema drives the horse mad, and in an attempt to put the animal down, his head is cut off, and the crowd sprayed with blood. Elements like these were probably on the minds of those angry clerics excoriating the productions and likely reflect borrowings from Carnival tradition.

Lucifer Sermon and Krampus Attack

The Lucifer Sermon was an essential element of nearly all Nicholas plays. In this scene, the Prince of Hell accuses mankind of weakness and propensity to sin. He also laments his lot in Hell while expressing delight in the tortures he inflicts on sinners, sometimes cataloguing torments deliciously matched to the sin, i.e., a gossip's tongue "pulled out by the roots." Lucifer is usually accompanied by some lower devils, and all, including Lucifer, are dressed in the furs and masks we associate with the Krampus. Satan may be distinguished by the addition of a crown or a pitchfork. Often he will be chained and held in check by two devilish attendants. Occasionally hurling himself against the chains and barely restrained from clawing the audience, the effect of the restraint actually emphasizes rather than minimizes the danger the raging Devil is supposed to represent. Usually, the sermon leads directly into the interlude during which the Krampuses run wild. The "attacks" on spectators continue until the Hunter, Quartermaster, or other controlling character steps in to restore order.

Existing Nicholas Plays and Parades

UNESCO Honorees: Reith im Alpbachtal and Öblarn

Though there is a scattering of Nicholas plays or parades in Tyrol, Upper Austria, and Bavaria, the bulk of surviving examples (less than a dozen) is in Styria. Tyrol, however, boasts one of the oldest, the Reith im Alpbachtal play first produced in 1690 and recognized as a world heritage treasure by UNESCO. Another sharing that honor is that performed in the Styrian mountain village of Öblarn. Now called the *Krampusspiel*, instead of *Nikolausspiel*, the bulk of the play is based upon a manuscript from 1861.

The play begins as the performers enter the square, led by a half dozen or so immense, broom-shaped characters snapping whips in precisely aligned rhythms. This mysterious figure is the *Schab*, *Strohschab*, or *Schabmann*, a name derived from an old, regional word for bundled grain left standing after harvest or straw thatch used in roofing. Completely covered by his wide straw skirt and headpieces topped by two antennae-like "horns" towering over 15 feet, the *Schab* is also associated with several other Nicholas plays in the region.

Along with the usual scenes, Öblarn's *Krampusspiel* features a variety of "wild" figures who join Lucifer and his devils in storming the crowd at the end. These creatures (discussed later) are a demon-goat called the *Habergeiß*, vegetation-covered *Grassteufel* and *Flechtenmann*, and a stag-headed figure, actually an original synthesis of various folkloric figures crafted for the modern production. There is also the Blacksmith, who appears with blackened face, leather apron, and hammer, creeping low amidst the crowd and taking advantage of their distraction to use his hammer on unsuspecting toes. Now mostly a light blow or harmless pantomime, the smith formerly was said to actually nail shoes or clothing to the floor.

Graphite devil in Sytrian Krampus play in Weißenbach bei Liezen, Austria.
Photo © Wolfgang Böhm.

Weißenbach bei Liezen

The troublesome Blacksmith also appears some 25 miles northeast of Öblarn in the Nicholas play presented in Weißenbach bei Liezen. Here, thanks to a unique look developed in 1945, the Krampuses are known as "graphite-devils" and appear with bodies and faces blackened by graphite, and wearing only bright red horns, fur vests and shorts. The play is also noteworthy in that it maintains something of the old house-to-house style of presentation, with four to six performances given by the roving troupe each St. Nicholas Eve. Once performed in private farmhouses, as interiors became less rustic and homeowners more particular about stains left by the graphite-smeared bodies, performances were relocated to inns, garages, or public squares.

Bad Mitterndorf and Tauplitz

The Bad Mitterndorf play is probably the best known of the Nicholas plays and boasts a cast of nearly 100. Ongoing annual productions began in 1896 after a period of official prohibition, but elements of the play can be traced back much further. One of the masks, the Krampus-like *Bartl*, for instance, is over 200 years old.

Sytrian Krampus play in Weißenbach bei Liezen, Austria. *Photo © Wolfgang Böhm.*

Schabmänner in Bad Mitterndorf Nicholas play, Bad Mitterndorf, Austria. *Photo © Wolfgang Böhm.*

Bad Mitterndorf Nicholas play cast in 1932. *Photo by Herr König © Bad Mitterndorf Nikologruppe.*

The Mitterndorf play also maintains the practice of roving performances, presenting the play on St. Nicholas Eve in four different locations. The traditionalism of those involved has been demonstrated by repeated refusals to reschedule or reprise performances for the convenience of TV and radio. This conservative attitude, at least in years gone by, has extended to the original ecclesiastic intent behind these dramas. In 1958, the society producing the play issued a leaflet warning: "Do not laugh at the various sermons or during questioning by the priest. You not only disrupt the performance, but endanger our children's devotion to Nicholas and their education in Christian doctrine."

The production in Tauplitz is rather similar but of a smaller scale. Props and costumes from the plays are available for viewing year round in private museums.

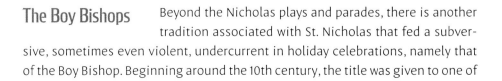

The Boy Bishops

Beyond the Nicholas plays and parades, there is another tradition associated with St. Nicholas that fed a subversive, sometimes even violent, undercurrent in holiday celebrations, namely that of the Boy Bishop. Beginning around the 10th century, the title was given to one of the choristers or students of the cathedral school elected to lead mass either on the Feast Day of St. Nicholas (because of his patronage of children) or on December 28, the Feast of the Holy Innocents, a day honoring not only the young martyrs of Herod but children in general.

The novelty of a diminutive bishop outfitted with a tiny mantel, mitre, and crozier assisted by equally diminutive chaplains drew huge crowds to the cathedrals, and services could become quite unruly. King Conrad of Germany visiting the Abbey of St. Gall near Lake Constance, Switzerland, in 911 describes a "Boy Abbot" who from his honorary seat during the mass was allowed to throw pears, apples, pancakes, or water at his fellows, mentioning also that the students on this day were accustomed to capturing their teachers or other visitors and holding them for ransom.

After the mass, the Boy Bishop and his retinue made their way through the city, demanding money and gifts along the way, ending up at a reception, where they would be generously indulged with food and drink. These processions sometimes degenerate into general riot. Writing to the bishop of Regensburg in Bavaria in 1249, Pope Innocent IV details what sounds like riots reported to him by the abbot of a nearby abbey. "Every year, while playing at appointing a bishop for themselves," he writes, "they indulge in masked shows and other mostly shameful games. Approaching the monastery each year with games of this kind and weapons in their hands, they break the doors and treat the monks and the servants of the monastery shamefully. Then they drive the horses and cattle from their stalls. These excesses," he relates, "are sometimes not accomplished without bloodshed." More than 100 years later, it seems tensions had persisted, if not escalated, as a local chronicle in 1357 notes that "a citizen of Regensburg killed . . . a canon of the cathedral church, while he was riding with his bishop, namely the bishop of the boys."

Chronicles of the Lauterberg monastery near Saale, Germany, also record a boy trampled to death during celebrations of 1137. In Salisbury, a retainer of the canon hosting a party for the Boy Bishop was beaten to death with sticks, and in 1448 parading Parisian students engaged in a battle with the night watch, after which their Boy Bishop was discovered dead in the Seine. While blood-shedding mayhem was hardly typical of the celebrations, they became troublesome enough that the tradition was in banned in most places by the 18th century.

The Feast of Fools

In cases where Boy Bishop celebrations fell on Holy Innocent's Day, they became intermingled with the even more subversive Feast of Fools, which most readers will know as an occasion for carnivalesque street parades and the election of a mock King. Though the secular side of the festivities is often emphasized, the medieval celebration is firmly connected to liturgical tradition. The Feast of Fools is generally considered to have had three or four individual feast days, all of them featuring mock elevations of ecclesiastics.

On the December 26th Feast of St. Stephen, the deacons traded positions with the priests. Priests were elevated over Bishops on St. John's Day (December 27). Students elevated, as mentioned, on Holy Innocent's, and subdeacons on the Feast of the Circumcision (January 1). Later in history, January 1 became the focus of the celebration, and likely represented an extreme in unruliness, as the subdeacons were the lowest and presumably roughest adult members of the ecclesiastic castes.

A looser understanding of the Feast even extends to include the January 14 *Asinaria Festa*, or "Feast of the Ass," a celebration of the animal that carried the Holy Family into Egypt after Christ's birth. In certain locations, a live animal would be wrangled indoors and stationed at or near the altar. The beast's entry or exit would be accompanied by the processional, the "Prose of the Ass," which scholar Neil Mackenzie, in his *The Medieval Boy Bishops*, says was "sung with a genuflection at the end, apparently to the ass, and the Mass finished with the priest dismissing the people and whinnying three times, to which the people responded with three whinnies."

At its extreme, the Feast is perhaps best described by an infamous letter written by the Faculty of Theology of Paris in 1445 in which he complains of excesses: "Priests and clerks may be seen wearing masks and monstrous visages at the hours of office. They dance in the choir dressed as women, panders or minstrels. They sing wanton songs. They eat black puddings at the horn of the altar while the celebrant is saying Mass. They play at dice there. They cense with stinking smoke from the soles of old shoes. They run and leap through the church, without a blush at their own shame. Finally they drive about the town and its theatres in shabby traps and carts, and rouse the laughter of their fellows and the bystanders in infamous performances, with indecent gesture and verses scurrilous and unchaste."

It's been suggested there's an element of polemic exaggeration here, but extremes of impiety and civil disorder are corroborated by many accounts. In 1420, the town council of Basel was troubled enough by the festivities to draft written prohibitions against "running as devils into churches or around town," stipulating that this applies no less to those dressed as goats. From Paris of 1421, we have a request from authorities that neither "the bishop of fools nor any other minister of the church" be "attacked," and that no citizen should attempt to "take by force" the bishop's "standard or his other accouterments." Nor should the bishop enter the church "escorted by his turbulent cortège." In the French town of Sens, the Archbishop was compelled in 1444 to forbid disorderly mobs, discordant singing, excessive mockery and other irregularities beyond those outlined in the rubrics. The temporary "Lord of the cloisters," he added, was not to be drenched with more than three buckets of water during Vespers on the Feast of the Circumcision, and only a single bucket would be permitted on St. John's Eve.

One churchly rationale offered for these inversions was a parallel inversion in the story of the Nativity with the birth of a mighty Messiah to lowly peasants in a humble stable. This was symbolically reinforced, in the case of the Boy Bishop, by staging the replacement of adult clergy with the boys during the singing of a particular line from the Magnificat, in which the Blessed Virgin upon hearing of her pregnancy with Jesus, is made to say, "He hath put down the mighty from their seat: and hath exalted the humble and meek." Beyond this, however, it seems that these festivities, like the Nicholas parades, represented a battleground between the Church's efforts at theatrical pedagogy, and the more mischievous, worldly instincts of those participating. Just as Otto Koenig described an unpopular St. Nicholas ditched en route during Krampus runs, the devilish spirit unleashed by the Church in the Feast of Fools outran institutional control. Frustrated by failures to regulate the celebrations, the Church finally banned the Festival altogether during the 15th century, leaving much of the secular momentum developed to channel itself into early celebrations of Carnival.

The Old Ways: Kalends and Saturnalia

Did the disruptive force that entered the medieval Feast of Fools represent vestiges of ancient paganism? Many readers here may think of the Roman Saturnalia also celebrated toward the end of December. As with the Boy Bishop or King of Fools, revelers of Rome's Saturnalia also appointed a mock ruler from among the lowly, a gesture symbolic of extreme license and social inversions that characterized the holiday. While we are accustomed to think of the Krampus in very contrary terms—that is, as an enforcer of social norms—from the side of the costumed participant, the experience is quite the opposite. A member of the *Krampuspass* embraces the role of a devil allowed taboo acts that include disturbing the peace, intimidating, striking, or otherwise manhandling his neighbor, as well as special freedoms with the opposite sex thanks to the anonymity provided by his costume.

A less familiar Roman holiday overlapping this period is the January Kalends. The first day of each month of the Julian Calendar was considered a Kalends, but that of January was considered especially important and celebrated with an additional four days of leisure and indulgence. The Kalends was also an occasion for masked processions in the guise of animals—most often described as horned beasts. Not documented in earlier classical period, this custom only appeared in historical record thanks to clerical condemnations during the Late Roman Empire. Examples are widespread throughout Europe, but it's unclear whether the practices reflected a straightforward diffusion of Roman culture or were indigenous Celtic or Germanic customs mistakenly equated by clerics with more familiar Latin concepts.

In 500, Bishop Caesarius in Arles, France, mentions Kalends activities that call to mind the Krampus' house visits, reminding his congregations that they "should not permit a little stag, a heifer, or any other kind of monster to come before your homes." Archbishop Theodore of Canterbury in his 669 inventory of required penances, *Liber Poenitentialis*, writes, "If anyone at the Kalends of January goes about as a stag or a bull; that is, making himself into a wild animal and dressing in the skin of a herd animal, and putting on the heads of beasts; those who in such wise transform themselves into the appearance of a wild animal: penance for three years because this is devilish." More than three centuries later, around 1020, the custom was still common enough in the German Rhineland, that Bishop and canonist Burchard of Worms cautions against it in his *Decretum*, asking, "Hast thou done anything like what the pagans did, and still do on the first of January, in the guise of a stag or a calf?"

Only sixty-two years after Burchard's warning, St. Nicholas' weeping bones arrived in Europe. Paradise and Nicholas plays and parades would soon follow. Could the Kalends practices be connected to or equated with the folk customs with which rural Christians later "corrupted" early Nicholas practices? While it's difficult not to view horned maskers traipsing house to house during the Christmas season, as an early form of those folk traditions, the record here is too scant to allow firm conclusions.

But Burchard goes on in the same document to describe another pagan practice, which can be more definitively connected to the Krampus. Surprisingly, perhaps, it has to do with witchcraft. He writes, "have you believed that there is any woman who can do that which some, deceived by the devil, affirm that they must do of necessity or by his command, to wit with a host of devils transformed into the likenesses of women, she who the ignorant call Holda, must ride on certain beasts during special nights and be counted as members of the company of demons."

This Germanic goddess Holda and her horde of devils brings us to a fascinating web of historical connections weaving together the medieval witchcraft appeasement rituals for the dead, and the myth of the Wild Hunt, all of which were once associated with the haunted season of Christmas.

Chapter Five

FRAU PERCHTA, WITCHES, AND GHOSTS

Witch and Goddess, Benevolent Monster

Opening this book, you knew you would read about the devils, but now we'll see how witches too figure into our dark holiday.

The witch in question—though she's also called a goddess—is a figure known primarily in Austria and Bavaria as Frau Perchta. Her name, as you might have guessed, associates her with the *Perchten*, Alpine spirits already mentioned as prototype for the Krampus. She goes by Pehrta, Berchte, Berta, and a myriad of other related or regional names. In Germany, north of Bavaria, her counterpart is Holda (also Holle, Hulda), identified from the 11th century onward by concerned churchmen like Burchard of Worms as the leader of an infernal horde. Martin Luther seemed to know her as a grotesque mumming figure, referencing in one of his sermons a weird "fraw Hulda," characterized by a long snout, rags and "straw armor." To this day, Alpine folklore paints Perchta as a monstrous being, eating, tearing asunder, or disemboweling those who displease her.

She is also a beautiful otherworldly matron whose name evokes purity and light.

Like the *Perchten*, Perchta is a creature of dualities, and makes her rounds on appointed winter nights to both reward and punish according to deed. The customs associated with her are largely those reimagined by the Church in the traditions of the Krampus and Nicholas. She is, in this sense, the egg from which it all hatches.

Witch with Alterbach Teufeln, Salzburg. *Photo © Christoph Haubner Fotografie.*

Who Are the *Perchten?*

Before discussing witches, I should briefly explain these *Perchten* you've been hearing about. This class of spirits is divided into two species, the good or "beautiful" *Schönperchten*, and the bad or "ugly" *Shiachpercht*, the latter being the model, naturally, for the Krampus. Just as the Krampus has experienced a modern revival, the *Perchten* too are very much alive in contemporary Austria and southern Germany. There are probably hundreds of *Perchten* groups and dozens of dedicated *Perchten* runs. With increasing frequency, *Perchten* swell the ranks of events promoted as Krampus-runs.

The modern *Perchten* group or *Perchten* run is almost exclusively the domain of the *Schiachperchten*. The beneficent *Schönpercht* usually today only receives attention as a historical footnote, so when I speak of *Perchten* without identifying them as either "schön" or "schiach" readers may assume the latter. This duplicates typical usage in German literature and media. While there is a handful of towns with more traditionalist events at which costumed *Schönpercht*en do appear, most of these only date to the 1930s or '40s. One exception to this is Gastein, where a continuous *Perchten* tradition can be traced to the early 1800s.

Visually, however, the modern *Percht* is mostly indistinguishable from the Krampus, wearing the same furs, horned mask, and bells. He caries an instrument with which to strike passersby, sometimes switches but more commonly the horse-tail whip. As a pagan figure, the blows he administers are not regarded as punishments for un-Christian behavior, but more loosely interpreted as "bringing luck," "driving out evil," and the like. While it's questionable, many sources insist horse-tail whips are the preferred instrument of the *Percht*. Even more often, the number of horns on the mask will be cited as a defining feature, with two signifying Krampus and four or more indicating *Percht*.

This matter with the horns is a preoccupation of instant experts, a beloved factoid in popular media introductions to the *Perchten*, and within the participant community, the stick with which to beat rivals supposedly ignorant of or betraying the tradition. However, for an anthropologist like Rest, who has grown up in traditionalist Gastein, "it is a totally a nonsensical discussion—who is *Percht* and who is Krampus." As detailed, Gastein's history with the Krampus is one of fluid and organic evolution, and even the *Perchten* and Krampus were actually undifferentiated.

"Here, the mask does not make a difference," Rest says. "Those masks used for the *Perchten* parades are the same used for the Krampus. Only people who are not schooled in the old tradition have this idea of a material difference between the two things. But to us it's totally contextual."

Perchta and Epiphany

The context to which Rest refers is specifically calendric. While the Krampus is strictly associated with St. Nicholas Day, the *Perchten* are most strongly associated with Epiphany, on January 6. In fact, Perchta's name, in its many variations, is usually understood as a corruption of the Old High German term for Epiphany, "*giberahta naht*," meaning, the "night of shining forth or manifestation." Here the reference is to Christ's manifestation to the world as represented in his "discovery" by the Magi or the disclosure of His divine nature during baptism in the Jordan. It is also possible the word "*Giberahta*" alone may be the source, making Perchta something like "the Shining One." Lovely as this sounds, it is unfortunately speculative, as none of the early texts otherwise identify Perchta specifically as "shining" but do specifically portray her as tied to the days around Epiphany.

Perchta and Holda are also sometimes associated with the Ember Days. Like the seasonal Quarter Days celebrated by modern Neopagans, the Ember Days are four sets of fast-days marked by the Church. Of these, Perchta is almost exclusively associated with the Winter Ember Days falling on the Wednesday, Friday, and Saturday after the December 13 Feast of Saint Lucy. In the Austrian state of Carinthia and in adjacent Slovenia, once part of the Austro-Hungarian Empire, Perchta was sometimes called Quatemberca (a Germanicized contraction of *quattuor temporum*, "quarter time"). She was also called Frau Faste (Lady of the Fast).

Because of Perchta's strong textual connection to Church holidays, some have therefore suggested that the figure—at least originally—was simply a personification of a Christian feast, similar to Father Christmas embodying that holiday, making her the equivalent of "Lady Epiphany." Some go even further, speculating that she may simply be an aspect of the Blessed Virgin as "Our Lady of Epiphany." But practices associated with Perchta have a long history of attracting the outrage of Catholic clerics. Even if corrupted in practice by peasant superstition, it seems unlikely that the figure central to these practices would have provoked such harsh criticism.

The calendric personification theory did not satisfy Jacob Grimm, and in his impressively exhaustive *Deutsche Mythologie,* he rejects the notion, pointing to Perchta's virtual identity to the more clearly pagan figure Holda. Perchta, for Grimm, therefore would simply be regarded as a localized name for Holda. While not identical on all points, the confluence between these two mythical figures is strong enough that modern scholars often treat the two beings as a single entity, hyphenating "Holda-Perchta" for ease of discussion.

In brief, those common traits describe a supernatural being primarily associated with the end of the year (Perchta exclusively so). Both are particularly involved with females and children, with spinning, weaving, and domestic order. Both are also known for nocturnal travels with hosts of unquiet spirits the Church regarded as damned souls or demons. Both figures can bestow blessings or invoke terror, with Perchta being more known for a frightening aspect and punitive acts. As further evidence of Holda and Perchta's identity, Grimm points to similar, lesser known, folkloric figures in whom the names combine, such as Berchthold and Hildaberta.

Celtic or Germanic Goddesses?

Perchta and Holda are often assumed to be ancient goddesses worshiped by early Germanic or Celtic tribes, but it should be kept in mind that Romanization of Celtic settlements in the Alps had already begun at the dawning of the Common Era, with Christian missionaries arriving and beginning conversion of the area by the 2nd century. Germanic tribes entering the areas had already converted by the 5th century. With the first mention of Holda-Perchta in the written record not occurring till around the year 1200, we're left with approximately seven centuries of Christianizing influence and intermingling of beliefs, making any precise equations with older, more pristine forms of Celtic or Germanic paganism questionable. Grimm's efforts to connect the medieval Holda (and consequently Perchta) to the ancient Germanic goddess Frigg/Freya are today viewed with skepticism.

Even the term "goddess" Grimm and countless others have used to describe the figures might be questioned. Particularly in the case of Perchta, it seems a little misleading. Depending on context, both Perchta and Holda might just as well be regarded as beings from the fairy realm, guardian spirits associated with a particular place (a mountain or spring) or with protected persons (children, women). In malevolent guise, they may be no more than bugaboos invoked by parents to frighten misbehaving children. This is especially the case with Perchta. These figures were indeed objects of cult veneration and ritual practices ultimately persecuted by the Church as witchcraft, but identifying cults like this only first described in the Early Modern Era with a paganism in its pre-Christian heyday remains a dubious affair.

This notion of Holda as a goddess of primordial provenance has its counterpart in romantic mythologies created by those involved with contemporary *Perchten* events. The webpage of the Steyrtaler *Perchten* from Steinbach, Austria, for instance, implausibly describes the *Perchtenlauf* as a "monument to a long-vanished nature religion, whose roots date back to the Stone Age." Perchta or Holda also show up in New Age circles as names for an impossibly old and multicultural "Divine Mother." As such, they are also celebrated in the relatively recent phenomenon of "Alpine Shamanism" in which drumming and crystal workshops (even Reiki) are jumbled up with hikes to various mountain destinations inevitably revered by local Celtic or Germanic tribes as "sacred sites." To compensate for the grandiosity of claims like this, I avoid the term "goddess" in discussing these figures when possible.

From Perchta to *Perchten*

The first mention of Perchta appears around 1200, but the word "*Perchten*" is not employed until centuries later. In 1468, there appears a reference to her retinue, but its members are not called *Perchten,* nor do they explicitly resemble *Perchten* as we think of them today. At this stage in Perchta's mythology, the company she leads is most often understood as spirits of the departed. With time, and frequent attacks from the pulpit, Perchta's pagan company came to be commonly feared not as ghosts but as demons, something presumably closer to the horned figures we now know. It's here, via Frau Perchta's horde, that we find a connection between the Krampus and the souls of the dead. This is the connection hinted etymologically by the Bavarian "*Krampn*" ("lifeless" or "shriveled") some believe to be the source of the devil's name.

In the same era we see the myth of Perchta's eerie night-traveling horde spreading, we also begin hearing of masqueraders impersonating this frightful host. Here the proper name "Perchta" seems to transform into the collective species, "*Perchten*." We have already seen how the name of a singular individual like "St. Nicholas" could unexpectedly pluralize in reports of rough "Nicholases" troubling towns. Likely the process with Perchta was analogous. Quite possibly, the early masker in a *Perchten* processions saw himself not as representing a demonic male follower of Perchta, but as Perchta herself, or more accurately, as one of a multiplicity of female Perchtas. The tradition of men costuming as female characters was, after all, part of folk-theater and Carnival traditions.

The very first illustration we have of Perchta seems to show not the figure herself, but in fact a masker. In South Tyrolean poet Hans Vintler's 1411 *Die Pluemen der Tugent* ("The Flowers of Virtue"), various superstitions are derided, including a belief in women like "Percht with the iron nose." Perchta's long or beaklike nose is a characteristic feature, and is often described as being of iron (as are, sometimes, her hands, teeth, and warts.) The illustration shows a figure with a face not only grotesque but seemingly artificial, with eyes peering out of what appear to be holes in a mask, and hands notably bulky and claw-like, as if gloved. Also occurring very early is the previously mentioned image of a Holda-Perchta

Frau Perchta (right) from Hans Vintler's
***Die Pluemen der Tugent* ("The Flowers of Virtue") (1411).**
Redrawn from manuscript by Lauren Church.

costume from a 1522 sermon by Martin Luther, that of "fraw Hulda" wearing "straw armor," something we can imagine, perhaps, as being similar to the *Schabmann* of the Bad Mitterndorf Nicholas play.

In the 17th century, we have the first reports of *Perchten* runs from the Pongau (the area around Gastein), and by the 18th similar accounts are appearing elsewhere. *Perchten* events in these days would begin around St. Nicholas Day and peak around Epiphany. This range of dates once more reminds us how the Krampus and *Perchten* traditions were earlier undifferentiated. The dates also tend to reinforce Grimm's notion that Holda-Perchta's connection with Epiphany is not intrinsic to the tradition, rather a matter of later ecclesiastical syncretization.

A creature we would today recognize as a *Percht* (or Krampus for that matter) has took shape by the 18th century. From the Tyrolean town of Kitzbühel, we have a 1736 report complaining of a late night disturbance by "most repulsive spirits, in devil masks" running about the town with noisy bells." By the early 19th century, documentation of *Perchten* events is not uncommon. Many of these clearly demonstrate an overlap with Nicholas-Krampus customs as well as deviation from the fixed date of Epiphany. In 1857, a J.V. von Zingerle reports on a Tyrolean *Perchtenlauf* held not on January 5 but weeks later on the last day of Carnival, and mentions not only frightening maskers, but also *Perchten* figures who distribute gifts in the manner of Nicholas.

The 1848 book *Bavarian Legends and Customs* describes the custom of youths impersonating "Iron Bertha" (Bertha being another derivation of Berchta or Perchta). Disguised in cowhides and horns, she goes about frightening some children and rewarding others with apples, pears, and nuts. In the same volume, we hear from Oberhausen, Germany, where a Nicholas ("Kläs") and a *Percht* were paired. The *Per-*

cht here appears with wild hair, soot-blackened face, and black rags. She is known as "*Buzabercht*," combining the name Bercht (or Berchta) with "*Buz*" ("bugaboo"), as we've seen in the 1750 woodcut, *Die Butzen-Bercht,* featuring the crone and her basket of children. While Nicholas performed his usual duties, the *Buzabercht* attacked the ill-behaved, not only with switches but also by smearing them with starch from a pot she carried for the purpose. In another account from Göttingen, Perchta arrives on New Year's Eve rewarding good children with undershirts, of all things.

Domestic Oversight and Female *Perchten*

Perchta's visits were primarily oriented toward ensuring compliance in certain household duties. Of particular interest was the spinning of flax, which was to be completed by Epiphany Eve. Should she find any unspun flax still on the distaff or about the house, it would be cut, tangled, or otherwise ruined by Perchta. Grimm mentions her burning the hands of lazy spinners. Austrian mythologist Lotte Motz goes further, stating that Perchta was said to wipe unspun flax with her excrement.

She was also interested generally in tidy housekeeping, and homes were to be thoroughly swept and scrubbed by the time she made her rounds. According to some scholars, this broader attention to tasks beyond spinning was a later development, appearing once the centrality of spinning as a cottage industry waned. Menial housekeeping in those days would naturally fall to young girls and unmarried women working as servants, making Perchta a creature of the female sphere.

While this may seem a long way away from the male dominated world of the modern *Perchtenlauf*, certain masked *Perchten* activities do directly reference Frau Perchta's role as enforcer of household order. In the small town of Rauris, about 30 miles west of Gastein, you'll find birdlike *Schnabelperchten* ("beaked *Perchten*"), who visit homes to inspect room for tidiness, while quietly and mischievously causing "accidental" messes in the process. Although played by males, performers cross-dress as old women, preferring grandmotherly kerchiefs, patched skirts, sweaters, and archaic straw slippers sometimes called "witches' slippers." Unlike the raucous bell-ringing *Perchten*, they move about with eerie stealth, slipping into homes in groups of four or five, softly clucking "Ga, Ga, Ga," in droning chorus. Their elongated beaks, probably inspired by Perchta's prominent nose mentioned by Vintler and others, are made of old linen and sticks, and are intricately rigged to clap with each chirped syllable. The *Schnabelperchten* bring brooms with which to sweep and large wooden scissors hinting at Perchta's tendency to cut open bellies. On their backs, they wear wicker baskets, sometimes fixed with large protruding doll legs, lest children forget that *Schnabelperchten*, like the Krampus, may abduct any who fail their obligations. *Schnabelperchten* of this sort are also found in the large, traditionalist *Perchtenlauf* held in Altenmarkt, Austria.

The Belly Slitter and Her Dreadful Ways

Rhymed text accompanying the previously mentioned woodcut depicting the "Butzen-Bercht," with her dripping, warty nose and basket of screaming children, clearly demonstrates that by 1750, when the depiction was created, Perchta's appetite for punishing wayward children was neatly suited to evolve into the figure of Krampus.

Here is my unrhymed translation of a portion of the Butzen-Bercht boast:

… So you shall not escape
My old broomstick, the whips, and the rod
With which I'll beat you till you're red with blood.
You hands and feet I'll bind
And throw you into the mire,
Set fire to your braids and hair,
Scratch your face, and cut your nose,
And rough you up quite well.
All your dolls I'll toss and burn,
And shred your finest Sunday dress.
The distaff I will fill so full of snot
That it drips and runs.
When I find you snoring late in bed,
I'll reel your intestines out from your belly
And fill the hole with wood shavings and tow …

("tow" = waste fibers combed from flax before spinning)

Perchta was particularly notorious for slitting open and gutting her victims. She might carry a sickle, knife, or scissors for this frequently required job. Sometimes, she would even perform this operation in order to remove foods consumed

Frau Perchta with butcher assistant. Drawing by Karel Rozum for *Den se krátí, noc se dlouží* ("The Day is Short, the Night Lengthens") (1910).

on her holy day not matching her dietary prescriptions. Straw, snow, dirt, pebbles, and assorted garbage as well as the above mentioned tow and shavings were then used to fill the cavity. She then finished up this bit of makeshift taxidermy by sewing the victim shut with a needle made of iron. Or in more hyperbolic stories, a ploughshare.

Another punishment associated with Perchta was her tendency to stamp on those who offend her. In certain regions, it is the *Stempe*, or the *Trempe* (from the German words for "stamp" or "trample") who appears to frighten the disobedient on Twelfth Night.

In a medieval poem, quoted in Grimm's *Deutsche Mythologie*, a child is threatened with the *Stempe* should he fail to eat the dinner served him. The manuscript from which Grimm worked featured an addendum re-titling the poem "Of Perchta with the Long Nose" confirming the identity of the two characters. Although undated, the poem was composed in Middle High German, spoken from approximately 1050 to 1350, making this one of our earliest references to a Perchta-like figure.

The unrhymed verse here is a translation from the English version of *Deutsche Mythologie*.

> *Now mark aright what I you tell:*
> *After Christmas the twelfth day,*
> *After the holy New-year's day*
> *(God grant we prosper in it),*
> *When they had to table brought*
> *All that they should eat,*
> *Whatso the master would give,*
> *Then spake he to his men*
> *And to his own child:*
> *'Eat fast (hard) to night, I pray,*
> *That the Stempe tread you not.'*
> *The child then ate from fear,*
> *He said: 'Father, what is this*
> *That thou the Stempe callest?*
> *Tell me, if thou it knowest.'*
> *The father said: 'this tell I thee,*
> *Thou mayest well believe me,*
> *There is a thing so gruesome done,*
> *That I cannot tell it thee:*
> *For whoso forgets this,*
> *So that he eats not*
> *On him it comes, and treads him.*

A Mother Goose Tale

Perchta's vengeful foot has also led to her being described as having large feet, or more often, a single large foot, i.e., *Berhte mit dem fuoze* ("Perchta with the foot") or *Berhta cum magno pede* ("with the big foot"). Grimm suggests this may recall Perchta's relationship to spinning and the heavy foot of a spinner constantly upon the treadle. He also explains the mismatched foot as an archetypal signifier of a supernatural being, as with the Devil's cloven hooves, or hoof. This physical marker seems to have been transferred to the Krampus as well, and is particularly prevalent in *Krampuskarten* showing the creature with one human foot and one hoof. Grimm also points to a conflation with the 8th century Frankish queen Bertrada of Laon, the mother of Charlemagne, known as Bertha Broadfoot thanks to Adenes Le Roi's 13th-century poem *Berte aus grands pies*. Le Roi does not make clear the significance of the large foot, which he also refers to as a "goose foot." From this evolved a French fairy figure Queen Pèdauca (from *pied d'oie* or "goosefoot"), who like Perchta is associated with spinning. Pèdauca is often presented as telling stories while she spins, thereby also relating her to the English Mother Goose.

Foods for Perchta

As mentioned, Frau Perchta can be quite particular about food. On the nights she appeared, there were specific foods to be eaten by those she visited as well as foods to be left as offerings to her. Omissions again resulted in gutting, but compliance at least ensured blessings in the coming year. From place to place, her requirements varied, but included fried dumpling dishes (*Semmede*), herring, eggs, and especially a milk porridge called *Perchtenmilch*, alternatively *Sampermilch* (boiled milk with bread slices) or *Bachlkoch*, a porridge drizzled with honey.

Families would be expected to eat their fill of these designated foods and reserve some uneaten for Perchta and company. Saved portions of this ritual meal would either be left on a specially prepared *Perchtentisch* (*Perchten* table) or fed to the farm animals to bless them with good health and fertility. For the convenience of her retinue, the offering might be left outside under a tree, or in the branches, or on a rooftop where night-flying spirits might most easily receive it.

Costumed *Perchten* visiting homes would also expect food in exchange for "bringing good luck." Their requests could mix threats and begging, as did trick-or-treaters in Halloween's wilder past. Perchta was, like the Krampus, sometimes said to abduct and/or eat children, and one rhyme used to shake down householders playfully threatened:

Kinder oder Speck,
Derweil gehe ich nicht weg.
("Children or bacon,
Or I won't go away!)

Feeding Perchta greasy foods could also save you from her iron grip, as it was said she must remove her iron gloves in order to eat such things. Alternatively, eating fried dumplings could save you from her knife, as greasy foods made the belly "too slippery" for her to slash. Milk porridge left overnight for Perchta and her entourage, even if apparently untouched, was said to be drained and mysteriously restored. How the bowl was found the next day could also serve as oracle for the coming year, as in this account from Hofstetten-Grünau, Austria, published in 1900:

> One should leave half of {the milk porridge} and leave the spoon stuck in it or lying on the edge of the bowl so that both ends hang free. Then around midnight, Perchta, with her host of children who have died unbaptized, will come to eat the porridge, and if you hear their slurping, you know the house is blessed for the entire year. The following morning … if the spoon you left is moved, you have misfortunes to fear in the coming year. If your spoon has fallen into the bowl, the next year will bring your death. If your spoon has fallen out, you will depart from your house. Unmarried people whose spoon has much milk skim on it, will soon be married.

Perchta and the *Heimchen*

Those invisible infants slurping *Perchtenmilch* in the night are called the *Heimchen*. This word also can translate as "cricket" and is used to describe a shy or retiring individual, especially a young female. Whether the evocation of diminutive, nocturnal, or evasive beings is etymologically related or intended is uncertain. The relationship of the unbaptized babies to the old lady Perchta Grimm describes rather neatly: "As the Christian god has not made them His, they fall to the old heathen one."

The *Heimchen* figure into many stories told about Frau Perchta, some identical to those told of Holda, also given charge over the unbaptized dead. In one of the best known, a peasant out late one Epiphany Eve encounters Perchta's entourage and notices a particularly small child repeatedly tripping on the tails of an overlarge shirt. The kind peasant cries out, "Oh, you poor ragamuffin!" and binds up the troublesome shirt. The *Heimchen* thanks the peasant for addressing him by name. In calling the child "ragamuffin," the stranger has christened the child with a sort of name, a de facto baptism that frees his soul from nocturnal wandering.

A final example has Perchta and the *Heimchen* blessing the farmers of a certain region with nocturnal attention to their crops. The story begins with Perchta wishing to leave the locality, arriving with her host of ghost children at the edge of a river, where she bids a ferryman take them across. The ferryman hesitates, seeing the massive throng she intends to board as well as the plough she wishes to transport. Nonetheless, he agrees to carry Perchta, her plough, and a portion of the children. As they drift over the water, Perchta tends to the plough, which needs mending, chipping away at the instrument, and leaving a pile of debris. When the ferryman hesitates to make additional trips for the rest of the *Heimchen*, Perchta offers a reward—the wood chips that lay around the mended plow. Angered by the gesture, the ferryman nonetheless returns to transport the rest of the *Heimchen*, grabbing three of the chips in disgust. After finishing his work, he returns home from the river. On waking the next morning, he finds the chips magically transformed into three gold coins.

Other folklore of the Heimchen has them visibly manifested as will-o'-the-wisps, the ghost lights, or ignis fatuus appearing particularly over swamps and said to lure from known footpaths unwary travelers mistaking them for village lights or helpful beings.

Usually consisting of unbaptized innocents, the company of Perchta (and perhaps even more Holda) may include others somehow misplaced by fate, in particular, those who have died before their time. Destined to wander until their appointed hour, these wards of Perchta, who failed to attain their allotted days, were later joined by others the Church found somehow worthy of neither heaven nor hell. These lost souls included suicides, those slain by arms, and later, witches and wizards. The ghostly followers of Perchta over time thereby came to be regarded as no longer merely eerie, but increasingly malevolent.

Holda-Holle

As mentioned, Holda's (or Holle's) domain is mostly identical to Perchta's. She is particularly associated with the twelve days between Christmas and Epiphany. During that period, she is said to travel about, sometimes riding a wagon or on horseback. While she's also given charge over spirits of the unbaptized or those not ready to enter heaven, her entourage may at times also resemble a ghostly hunting party, and as such merges with the mythologem of the Wild Hunt, a theme explored in greater detail later. Like the classical Goddess Diana, with whom Latin-trained clerics often compared her, Holda might appear as a huntress, blowing a hunting horn, or be followed by a train of dogs. Perchta too, as in Tyrol's Eisack Valley and elsewhere, was sometimes accompanied by the souls of children taking the shape of dogs.

Holda-Holle also oversees spinning and domestic order, and rewards and punishes those who fulfill these responsibilities. In Hesse, where her tradition remained strong, children until recently would set out bowls on New Year's Eve, which would be filled by morning with sweets if merited. For the poorly behaved, she would leave switches.

Frau Holle Tales

Domestic duties figure prominently in the best-known tale associated with Holda, one published in 1812 in Grimm's *Children's and Household Tales*. Rendered in English as "Mother Hulda," in German it's known as "Frau Holle," using the more common name for the figure in Grimm's native Hesse, where the story was collected.

In the tale, the stepdaughter of a rich widow is treated cruelly by her step-mother and lazy stepsister. One day while spinning by the family well, the step-daughter pricks her finger on her spindle. As she washes the blood at the well's edge, she accidentally drops the spindle into its depths. Fearing her stepmother's wrath, she leaps in to retrieve the item, falling into darkness and awakening in a magical landscape. There she encounters an apple tree begging her to pluck the heavy fruit from its limbs and baking bread asking to be removed from the oven. After successfully performing these tasks, she meets old Mother Hulda, whom she dutifully helps with household chores. One of these is to help Hulda shake out her feather bed, which scatters down that falls as feathery snowflakes into the mortal world. As the stepdaughter grows homesick, Mother Hulda sends her back to her world, but not before rewarding her with a shower of gold, that transforms her into the glittering "Gold-Marie." Her envious stepsister plunges into the well in hopes of obtaining the same, but is too lazy to complete her tasks, and returns from Hulda's magic realm showered with pitch and known as "Pitch Marie."

Along with her association with spinning, the story reflects the figure's con-nection to winter, incorporating an old superstition about Holle bringing snow. Additional stories depict Holle doling out rewards and punishments according to behavior. Incognito as an elderly "Aunt Mählen" she begs for food and shelter, magically rewarding those who show generosity. Asking such charity of a bee-

Frau Holle and the *Heimchen*, from *Das festliche Jahr: in sitten, gebräuchen und festen der germanischen Völker* by O. Spamer (1863).

keeper, Holle/Mählen is fed by his daughter, provoking an angry blow from the girl's stingy father. In retribution, Holle sets the apiary and estate ablaze, killing the father, but miraculously preserving the daughter even within the flames.

Just as Perchta's association with agriculture is represented by her plough in the tale of the ferryman, even more stories emphasize Holda's connection to nature and the fertility of crops, animals, and humans. Her passage over a farmer's land was said to ensure a bountiful harvest. She is also strongly associated with the life-giving waters of springs, ponds, and streams, and is sometimes spotted in the noonday sun near bodies of water, dressed in shining white and only visible for an instant before vanishing.

Frau Holle Country

Particularly powerful is her connection to the Frau Holle Pond on the Hohen Meißner mountain complex in Hesse. Since at least 1641, the landmark has been identified with her name, but the association may have begun much earlier, possibly even as a site of sacrifices as suggested by the discovery of medieval potsherds and 1st-century Roman coins in its depths. Legend describes the pond as deep beyond measure, and somewhere within is Holda's silver palace amid a luxuriant world of fruit and flowers.

The waters have long been sought out by female bathers seeking health and fertility. Up into the 1930s, women gazing into the pond were said to be able to discern their unborn children sleeping below, and would see the tips of the hairs on these children's heads in the reeds protruding from the surface.

Since 2004, a sculpture of Holle has stood on the banks of the pond, which has been incorporated into a 115-mile Frau Holle Path, a route connecting various sites associated with the figure and marked by informational displays. Among the local sites where Holle's blessings are sought and flowers may be left are a rock formation on the south side of the Meißner, known as the "Frau Holle Chair," two dolomite crags (known as the Holle Stones). The subterranean waters of the Holle Cave and the Witches' Pond, are said to be particularly salubrious, particularly for bathers who visit on Christmas or May Eve. Nearby, the town of Hessisch Lichtenau bills itself as "The Gateway to Holle-Land." In 2011 the municipality reopened its old cross-timbered courthouse as the Frau Holle Museum or "Holleum."

Enchantress in the Mountain

While the ugly, large-toothed character Grimm describes as "Mother Hulda" is now mostly remembered as a charming grandmotherly type, the Holda of folk tales and legends also possessed a darker side more reminiscent of Perchta. Like Perchta, who is said to reside in certain Tyrolean caves with the spirits of the unbaptized and unborn, Holda sometimes eerily merges cradle and grave and makes clear her identity as matron of both death and regeneration.

A geographical focus of this darker aspect is the Hörselberg, a mountain near Eisenach, Germany, where Holda and her host are said to reside in underground caverns. The mountain has a long history associating it with the otherworldly. Legend credits medieval monks for naming the mountain "Hear-Souls Mountain" ("Hör-Seel Berg") after perceiving the wailing of lost souls from within. Local tradition, for centuries, has described Holda emerging from the mountain with her horde either on Christmas Eve, New Year's Eve, or the Winter Ember Days. Though not as common,

"Frau Hulla and the Wild Host" by Joseph Sattler for *Hörselberg Monthly*, vol. 1. (1927).

a similar legend attached itself to Kyffhäuser, a mountain in Central Germany where a 12th-century Holy Roman Emperor Friedrich Barbarossa and his armies are said to repose, waiting to be called forth in Germany's hour of greatest need.

First mentioned in the late 1400s, the notion of the Hörselberg as home to Holda and her phantoms may have been influenced by earlier Italian tales of a witch queen, Siballa. Named after the oracular Sibyl of Cumae, Siballa was said to reside under the mountains near the Umbrian town of Norcia, an area for centuries associated with witchcraft. Roughly a century before Holda's residence in the Hörselberg is mentioned, tales of the Italian Siballa's subterranean existence around Norcia began to circulate. In 1442 French courtier Antoine de la Sale visited the areas, claiming to discover the entrance to the witches' caverns. Finding inscribed on the portal names of knights and sorcerers who had entered but never returned, La Sale turned away, content with his discovery and the local legends he had collected telling of bacchanalian orgies enjoyed within the mountain.

By the early 1400s, German balladeers were telling a similar tale of Tannhauser, a 13th-century Minnesinger, recast as poet and knight who enters the Venusberg, a magical realm where he devotes himself to Venus, endless revels, and erotic adventures. Goaded by Christian conscience, Tannhauser attempts to revisit the mortal world, but is condemned to return to the Venusberg. Tannhauser's tale, with characteristic reworking and the addition of an umlaut, was recast as Wagner's 1845 opera *Tannhäuser*, one notorious in its day for its lurid opening scene depicting the erotic indulgences of Venus' court.

In 1501, Wolfgang Heider, a professor at the University of Jena, placed the Venusberg in the forests of Thuringia, where both the Hörselberg and Kyffhäuser are found. He also marked Christmas as the time at which the supernatural horde emerges, describing ghostly troops of men on horse and on foot, as well as "lemurs, larvae, and empusae," the first two being malignant ghosts that haunted the Romans, and the latter monstrous servants of the goddess Hecate.

Holda Becomes a Witch

Heider's use of classical terms to describe the superstitions of German peasants is typical of clerics trained in Latin. The writings of the 15th-century Bavarian Dominican Johannes Herholt are illustrative here. In this *Sermones*, Herholt expands upon Burchard's comments about a "Diana" called "Holda" by the peasants. To Burchard's equation of Diana with Holda, Herholt adds "Fraw Berthe" (Frau Perchta) as yet another equivalent name. He also changes Burchard's "Holda," to "Unholde." We already understand the identity of Holda with Perchta, but where does this "Unholde" come from?

In modern German, "*unhold(e)*" means unholy or monstrous, while the word "*hold(e)*," if not the exact opposite, means graceful, charming, or dear. In providing an etymology for Holda's name, Grimm has pointed out that in the Middle

High German current when these documents appeared, "*unhold(e)*" was used to describe a "dark, malign, yet mighty being." The "mightiness" attached to the word is not shared in modern German, but Grimm seems to associate it with dread or a sense of the supernatural. He suggests that by extension, the then-less-common "*hold(e)*" might also be "commonly used for ghostly beings." Both words, then, would have a supernatural aura to them and differ primarily in moral valences.

Philologist and folklorist Claude Lecouteux, from his studies of the word in Early and Middle High German contexts, concludes similarly that the word "*hold(e)*" is related to the realm of the fairies, a world where both benevolent and malevolent beings can be found. Perhaps this reflects the dual aspect Holda shares with Perchta. Or it may reflect the opposing perspective of those revering and opposing her.

In various rewordings of the original *Canon Episcopi*, we find not only Holda and Unholde, but also "*striga holda*" and "*striga unholda*," with the Latin "*striga*" used of witches and other evil spirits. These changes seem to document a gradual process of demonization of a Lady Holda whom followers saw as graceful and benevolent. The records of Early Modern Alpine witch-trials, which we'll examine shortly, not only give us a clearer picture of beliefs common to the cult of Holda, but also have influenced centuries of *Perchten* tradition as well as contemporary customs associated with Krampus and St. Nicholas.

Herodias, Perchta, and a Hissing Head

Herodias is another ancient figure equated to Diana and Holda by Burchard of Worms and many other medieval clerics. From the 11th century onward she is frequently portrayed as a queen of witches. This biblical villain was the mother of Salome and wife of King Herod Antipas (son of the Herod responsible for the Massacre of the Innocents). She is known primarily for encouraging Salome to demand the head of John the Baptist after performing an erotic dance, a performance Herod had offered to reward with any price she asked. Not only the wickedness of this deed, but also a legend that represents Herodias doomed to forever fly in the nocturnal winds, associated her with witchcraft.

The latter is most prominently articulated in *Ysengrimus*, a Latin collection of fantastic tales (including fables of Reynard the Fox) probably written by the poet Nivardus around 1148. In an English version of the work, translator Jill Mann relates Nivardus' story of Herodias, who during the Middle Ages was often conflated with Salome. Here understood as the one who had performed the dance, and smitten with John the Baptist even after his decapitation, Herodias attempts to kiss the head with unforeseen results: "The head miraculously moved away, and hissed at her with such force that she was blown up into the air and out through the sky-light. Ever since then, the story concludes, she has been driven through the skies by John's implacable anger; at night she perches on oaks and hazel-trees, and a third part of mankind is subjected to her sway."

The legend gained lasting traction in German-speaking lands. Commenting on the medieval equation of Herodias, Diana, Holda, and Perchta, Grimm presents the myth as very much alive in his 1835 *Deutsche Mythologie*, remarking that winds in Lower Saxony were still said to be stirred by the whirling of Herodias' tormented dance. In the region around the towns of Virgen and Prägraten in Tyrol, Herod's daughter is traditionally feared as a child-stealing demon. In the Austrian state of Carinthia, she was especially dreaded, and in the town of Mölltaler, legend has it that Herodias continued her erotic dance teasingly on the ice-covered Lake Ei-sten. Breaking through the ice, she died and was condemned to return every year as the night-flying Perchta.

Loyal Eckhart, Ghosts, a Jug of Beer

By the mid 17th century, most of the elements of the Holda myth were in place. She was firmly connected to Diana, Herodias, and (in legends of the Venusberg) Venus. In 1663, Leipzig historian and polymath Johannes Praetorius-related a story that adds one further element. He writes of "the Loyal Eckhart" who "goes before her troop to warn any folk they encounter, asking them to remove themselves from its path so that no misfortune befalls them."

Eckhart is a figure from earlier Germanic knightly legends grafted into the Venusberg story. In the appendix to the *Heldenbuch* (a 15th–16th century collection of epic poems), he is stationed eternally before the opening to Holda's underground realm to warn away those who would enter. In the folklore of Holda's Christmas entourage, he functions as a sort of chamberlain to the queen, a stern but helpful intercessor between mortal and immortal realms, whom Grimm compares to a psychopomp, a leader of souls. When described, he is usually a hoary figure with long beard and white staff.

Praetorius' story of the encounter with Holda's train continues: "Several lads of this village claimed to have seen it when they were on the way to the tavern in search of beer to bring back home. Because the ghosts were taking up almost the entire width of the road, they were pushed a little to the side with their jugs. Some of the women of this troop supposedly took the jugs and drank their contents.

Faithful Eckart, from *Das festliche jahr: in sitten, gebräuchen und festen der germanischen Völker* by O. Spamer (1863).

Struck with fear, the lads kept their peace about this, overlooking how they would be greeted back home with their empty jugs. Finally, Loyal Eckhart allegedly told them, 'God inspired you to say nothing—otherwise they would have wrung your necks. Quick, return home and say nothing to anyone about what happened. Do this and your jugs will ever be full and you shall never want for beer.'"

As promised, the beer remains inexhaustible until the lads give up their secret. After this, the jugs run dry.

The Inexhaustible Sacrifice

An interesting element in Praetorius' narrative is the motif of the jugs as cornucopia. Here the beer drunk and replenished by the phantoms should remind us of the *Perchtenmilch* set out on Twelfth Night. In the mythic view, the notion that the porridge was simply never touched does not enter the picture. Instead, it is a sacrifice offered the spirits, which like the beer offered Holda's troupe, is magically replenished. Such instances may seem like minor details easily dismissed as a beer-drinker's fantasy or an entertaining tale for children, but these are not isolated cases. In fact, they are part of a golden thread that connects Holda and Perchta to a widespread complex of myths and rituals central to the earliest trials of the witch persecutions.

Already in the 1200s, Bertold of Regensburg warns his flock against an array of pagan superstitions, referencing a number of beings resembling Holda and her horde as well as food offerings left for them. He writes: "You should not believe at all in the people who wander at night (*Nahtwaren*) and their fellows, no more than the Benevolent Ones (*Holden*) and the Malevolent Ones (*Unholden*), in fairies (*Pilwitzen*), in nightmares (*Maren, Truten*) of both sexes, in the Night Ladies (*Nahtvrouwen*), in nocturnal spirits, or those who travel by riding this or that: they are all demons. Nor should you prepare the table anymore for the Blessed Ladies (*felices dominae*)." The table here, of course, refers to food offerings.

The very earliest explicit mention of Perchta occurs in a 1350 tract entitled *Mirror of Conscience*, mentioning such a table and condemning those "who, on the night of Epiphany, leave food and drink upon their table so that all shall smile upon them over the coming year and good luck will grace them in all things … Therefore also sinning are they who offer food to Percht …" And again in 1468, in the Bavarian *Thesaurus Pauperum*, we find a condemnation of the "idolatrous superstition of those who left food and drink at night in open view for Abundia and Satia, or, as the people said, Fraw Percht and her retinue, hoping thereby to gain abundance and riches."

The idea of ghostly beings at once consuming and replenishing food during nocturnal visits is also found further west in Switzerland. There the folkloric cousins to Perchta's train were known as the "Blessed Ones" (*säligen Lütt*). In an account written around 1600 by Renward Cysat, a city clerk of Lucerne, they are described as the "souls of people who died violent or premature deaths, who must wander the earth until the day that fate has fixed for their passing; these folk are friendly and kind, and enter the homes of those who speak well of them at night, cook, eat, and then leave again, but the amount of food does not diminish." Elsewhere Cysat quotes a peasant woman speaking of the Blessed Ones who makes clear that these spirits share Perchta's concern with domestic order. "Among other idiocies," Cysat writes, "she said that these folk that roam the night become irritated when the kitchen has been left untidy. "

Witch from Gruabtoifi Saalfelden, Austria. *Photo © Günther Golliner.*

Magic in the Venusberg

Another element worth examining in Praetorius' story has to do with the secrecy surrounding the magical filling of the jugs. Sharing the secret of this boundless source, of course, could lead the greedy to seek out encounters with Holda and her host. Preventing this danger is precisely why Eckhart had been added to the myth, why he goes before the horde to warn away onlookers, and why he guards the gate to the Venusberg.

Even to look upon the phantoms was regarded as a great danger, and in some regions, those caught unawares by Holda's passing were advised to throw themselves face to the ground with arms outstretched in the shape of the cross. Even where Eckhart is not named, there is often an anonymous forerunner posted before the horde to offer similar warnings. Likewise Perchta, according to one tale, blinded for a year an overly curious peasant who dared to peek at her through a keyhole. Already imperiled for having glimpsed the specters, the boys in Praetorius's story, as Eckhart tells them, would have surely lost their lives had they dared to speak to the ghosts. The jugs' magic can only work if hidden, not if made manifest.

The terror of contact with the dead, and the notion that interaction might somehow be mortally contagious seems intuitive. Yet there is also something confusing in these Holda narratives—namely the restyling of the Hörselberg, a grim abode of lost souls, as the Venusberg, with its endless feasting and erotic pleasures.

Some of this may be due to the early modern era's idealized fascination with classical paganism as a playground outside purview of the Church. As an already ambivalent figure both *hold* and *unhold*, as a mother of both cradle and grave, perhaps Holda's identification with such diverse and contradictory figures as Venus, Sibyl, Herodias, and Diana becomes more understandable. Also entering into the Venusberg legends may be a bit of Christian myopia and envy, blurring diverse and contradictory pagan figures into a single enticingly unchristian fantasy figure associated with erotic indulgence.

As a realm of pleasure from which there is no return or escape, the Venusberg has many parallels in folk tales and legends. Whether the gold-filled subterranean halls of dwarves, enchanted fairylands, or a kingdom under sea, these lands of no return have been understood by many folklorists as representative of death and eternal reward. Entering this realm, the soul may never again participate in mortal life, but instead partakes of immortality and the immortals' power to know and control man's fate.

This is the sort of contact sought by the necromancer, who by calling on the dead obtains hidden knowledge, boons, or control over destiny. The food offering left for Perchta's company, like the necromancer's invocation, is a magical summons. It draws in and feeds the dead so that the dead may feed the living. The impoverished mortal, through this small offering, can connect with immortal abundance. The magically replenished beer and *Perchtenmilch*, in their small way, illustrate this ritual transaction with the dead.

Despite the danger implicit in mortal contact with the immortals, there have been many who hoped to gain magical powers by seeking out Holda in her realm. One account of this is provided in records from a 1497 trial of the witch Zuanne (Giovanni) delle Piatte in the Italian town of Val di Fie Fiemme in German-settled South Tyrol. Previously accused of possessing magical crystals and "many signs and diabolical formulas in the German language," delle Piatte claimed to have been allowed to visit Herodias's home in the Venusberg ("*el monte de Venus ubi habitat la donna Herodiades*") where he encountered "a whitebearded old man called 'loyal Eckhart.'" Adopted into the supernatural society within the mountain, delle Piatte, along with select mortals, feasted and drank, and enjoyed the ability to undertake magical flights around the world during the Christmas Ember Days.

Similarly, in a trial held in Hesse in 1630, the accused, Diel Breull, claimed to have woken from sleep within the Venusberg where he encountered "Fraw Holt," enjoyed feasting and drinking, and was granted visions of the dead seated in purgatorial fire. Like delle Piatte, he was adopted into Holda's troupe and subsequently transported to the Venusberg four times each year during the Ember Days.

Renward Cysat's informants from 17th-century Lucerne offered similar stories of adoption by and travels with the "Blessed Ones." The wife of an acquaintance of Cysat's claimed these trips into immortal realms granted her visions of things "that no one in our fatherland knows of yet." When asked if her husband knew of these fantastic flights, "she answered no, because her body remained lying in bed." As these visionary trips repeated on set calendric dates, they were understood to be more than randomly occurring dreams, rather they were purposeful excursions of the soul, which, according to medieval belief, travels out from the body in sleep.

Witchcraft Born in the Alps

At the beginning of Chapter One, I mentioned traveling on my way to Gastein through Italy's Friuli region, where important 16th and 17th-century witchcraft trials related to our story had taken place. The accused, in this case, were members of the *benandanti* ("good walkers"), a visionary cult whose members saw themselves as the benevolent opponents of malevolent witches (*malandanti*) and claimed to do battle with these witches in spirit form. At stake in these battles was said to be the fertility of the fields and welfare of their community. Like Diel Breull arriving at the Venusberg in sleep or Cysat's acquaintance traveling with the Blessed Ones in dreams, the *benandanti* claimed to conduct their excursions against the witches on the Ember Nights while their bodies lay in a state of trance.

The female *benandanti* also claimed that in their nocturnal travels they celebrated feasts and dances like those within the Venusberg. In trial records one of the *benandanti* reported "bowing her head to a certain woman called the Abbess, seated in majesty on the edge of a well." Given that the Friuli region had been settled by Germanic tribes, the Abbess and her well might remind us of Holda and her sacred pond. Those who followed that Abbess did so in spirit, like certain travelers to the Venusberg.

Historian Carlo Ginzburg, in *The Night Battles: Witchcraft and Agrarian Cults in the Sixteenth and Seventeenth Centuries*, regards the *benandanti*'s Abbess, like Holda, as belonging to a family of nearly identical cult figures found throughout the Alps, northern Italy, and beyond. Typical of spirit travelers following these figures, the *benandanti* visited homes by night, slipping in to drink wine from casks in the wine-cellars, leaving these, like the jugs of beer, magically replenished. Even more significantly, Ginzburg regards the spiritual opposition of the *benandanti* vs. *malandanti* as a likely reflection of the *Schönperchten-Schiachperchten* duality, a notion I'll later discuss.

The case of *benandanti* and many similar trials in the Alps make the region particularly significant in the history of witchcraft. The early dates of these prosecutions, their number, and the tenaciousness of these beliefs and practices in remote mountain valleys have caused many scholars to regard the Alps as the birthplace of the modern European notion of witchcraft. As it was clerics from this region and nearby German-speaking lands who defined this concept, the folklore of Holda-Perchta was naturally a central element.

Heinrich Kramer, who in 1486 authored the infamous *Malleus Maleficarum* ("The Hammer of Witches"), began his career prosecuting witches in Tyrol and also functioned as Church-appointed Inquisitor over the German-speaking Salzburg, Moravia, and Bohemia. Though he initially failed in his Tyrolean persecutions and was expelled by the bishop of Innsbruck for behaving as a "senile old man," Kramer responded by soliciting, and receiving in 1484, a bull from Innocent VIII allowing him free hand in these efforts.

Not long before this, in Switzerland, where the *säligen Lütt* roamed by night, battle lines were already being drawn at the ecclesiastic Council of Basel. Convening in 1435, in part to discuss the witch cults coming to attention in the Alps and beyond, clerics gathering there, according to historian Wolfgang Behringer, "could exchange opinions as if at a European trade fair; they heard not only reports of the trial of Joan of Arc, but also got the first public view of the new image of the witches' sabbath, an idea that had been invented in the region around Lake Geneva." German theologian Johannes Nider was largely responsible for shaping this view, and his witch-hunting guide *Formicarius*, Behringer says, characterized these pagan beliefs "as a specifically Alpine vice."

The paradigm shift Nider and Kramer created conceived of witchcraft as a more immediate and present danger than ever before. Older canon law as interpreted by Burchard of Worms in his comments on Holda regarded the matter as one of misguided peasant superstition. Tales of spirit travels were viewed as mere dreams or foolishness encouraged by Satan, and relatively lenient penances were proscribed. But with Nider's and Kramer's work, these travels became literally real and dangerously demonic. Inquisitors were to press defendants for information on a previously unseen male figure appearing at real-world gatherings, one who could easily be identified with Satan. Also aggressively sought was evidence of abjurations of Christ, the trampling of the host or crucifix, and the like. The feasting of the Venusberg and drinking in wine cellars was thereby slowly transformed to the more Satanic revels of the modern witches' sabbath.

Witch mask. Barmstoana Perchten, Hallein, Austria. *Photo © Roland Käfer.*

Witch Hunting and Hauntings in Tyrol

South Tyrol, which has already been discussed in terms of its significant influence on Nicholas and *Perchten* traditions, also seems to have been the site of particularly important witchcraft activity associated with figures like Holda. Traces of this still survive in certain landmarks, local legends, traditions, and even regional tourism, and the same might be said of the adjacent Italian state of Trentino, once part of the Habsburg state of Tyrol.

The nearby valleys of Fassa and Fiemme, nestling between the uniquely eerie crags of the Dolomites, were both sites of early trials. The investigation of two women in Val di Fassa, conducted in 1457 by the German theologian, Nicholas of Cusa produced testimonies of participants traveling by night "to a place full of dancing and festive folk." Like the activities of Holda-Perchta, these gatherings took place on the Ember Nights and were presided over by a mistress identified by the defendants in Italian as "bona domina Richella," or "the good mistress of fortune," which Cusa translated with the Latinized "Fortuna" and also the German "Hulda" (Holda).

Trials in Val di Fiemme, during which 14 people were executed from 1501-1505, were partially instigated by the magician Giovanni delle Piatte mentioned above for having allegedly encountered Herodias and Loyal Eckhart in the Venusberg. Instead of facing execution, Della Piatte was merely banned from Fiemme after naming others prosecutors might pursue for witchcraft. The most famous of these was Margherita Tesero (called Vanzina) who also referred to a mysterious mistress presiding over activities. Vanzina mentioned two troupes, or spiritual societies, perhaps akin to those of the benandanti and malandanti. One was said to be devoted to the "game of the devil" and composed of incubi and nightmare-spirits, while the other was led by the "Mistress of the Good Game."

Not far away is the Schlern (Sciliar) mountain where witches have for centuries been said to hold their Sabbaths, congregating on ancient stone slabs known as "witch benches." The notorious *Schlernhexen* (Schlern witches) are reimagined today as tourism icons, adorning signs of local businesses and showing up as rather grandmotherly dolls and figurines. Mountain legends here are rich with stories of herb-women, "wild folk," wood and water spirits, giants, and a magical garden of roses blasted to a naked crag by dwarf King Laurin. Also cursed by Laurin were protective mountain spirits who tended his roses, the *Säligen*, who were thereby transformed into witches, either flying off to their sabbaths or left clinging to the mountain slopes in the form of wildflowers, the *Aquilegia einseleana*, commonly called "*Schlernhexen*."

Court records of witchcraft in the area present a decidedly grimmer picture. Nine women accused of witchcraft between 1506 and 1510 met their death, either by fire or, more gruesomely, were drawn and quartered (i.e., torn asunder by charging horses to which they were tied). During trials Juliane Winklerin, Anna Miolerin, and the Austrian Anna Jobstin used the term "the Game of the Good Society," to describe their nocturnal dancing and feasting on the Schlern as well as night flights (on broomsticks, benches, chairs, and a cow).

Prompted by the newer, diabolical image of witchcraft promoted by Nider and Kramer, as well as the torture to which Inquisitors here resorted, the Schlern witches confessed not only to initial allegations of having manipulated the weather and cursed neighbors, but also to fornicating with the Devil and killing, cooking, and eating a baby. After the child was eaten, defendants related that the baby's bones were collected, and from these it was possible to magically restore the child to life.

Apart from the regrettable part torture may have played in the confession, this miraculous control over life and death, found in many other accounts of witches feasting on cattle or game, may have been a genuine element of the cult's beliefs as it symbolically reinforces the Good Lady's ability to miraculously replenish food, restore life, and grant abundance—elements we have already learned to associate with Holda.

From the 1540 trial of Barbara Pachler, not far away in Sarnhein, come more stories of babies being cooked and eaten. Originally accused also of manipulating the weather, Pachler confessed to having met the Devil and a company of witches at a site dotted with weird stone monuments known as the *Stoanerne Mandln* or "stone men." Roughly 100 in number, these towering spires of stacked stones remain mysterious in terms of origin or purpose. While some may have merely been constructed by bored shepherds in recent years, carvings on the rocks, and flint tools found nearby, have suggested much earlier, possibly Celtic, some say even Neolithic, origins. The uncanny presence of these monuments, along with the preternatural activities associated with them, have done much to fuel ongoing local legends of the witch Pachler, or Pachlerzottl ("ragged Pachler"), as she is called, flitting amid the stones on moonlit nights.

Witch Fires   The fear of witchcraft that exploded in the Alps of the 15th and 16th century has left vestiges in folk rituals and traditions involving fires and witches, many of which take place around Carnival, particularly Epiphany, Perchta's day.

During Epiphany week in the South-Tyrolean-Trentino town of Cavalese, the witch trials of Val di Fiemme are commemorated with a re-enactment. Accompanied by drums and torches, the accused are marched to a park outside the pal-

Witch torments horses in the Egga-Spiel (Egga Play), Sonthofen, Bavarian Alps.
Photo by Flodur63 (2010) (CC BY-SA 4.0).

Twelfth Night reenactment of Val di Fiemme witch trials in Cavalese, South Tyrol/Trentino.
Photo © Massimo Piazzi (2011).

ace, seated around an ancient stone table, and dialogue from court transcripts is read. After the inescapable verdict, four effigies are staked and set ablaze. Similarly, in the Bavarian Alps, the town of Burgberg performs the Eggaspiel, a folk play inspired by a rash of witchcraft trials that took place in the region between 1586–1592. The masked performance portrays scenes of a farming couple and their livestock (portrayed by animal-masked locals) tormented by a witch who is eventually chased through the town, captured, tried, and burned in effigy. The play takes place every three years during Carnival.

Throughout northern areas of Italy bordering or within the Alps, the burning of a witch effigy traditionally takes place on Epiphany, or on the last Thursday of January in Lombardy (Thursdays being favored for witches' Sabbaths). In the Veneto and Friuli regions bordering Austria, the burning of the effigy is called *panevin*, while in Piedmont and Lombardy, the puppet burned, and by extension the tradition itself, is known as the *Giubiana*. The custom is particularly elaborate in the Lombard town of Canzo with a theatrical masked procession accompanied by drum and bagpipe to the bonfire. Dispatching the witch drives out the winter and ensures annual protection from the baleful influence of witchcraft. The direction and motion of the flames and smoke are carefully observed for omens regarding the weather and harvests of the coming year. Sometimes prognostications of this type are also offered by a costumed witch presiding over the proceedings.

La Befana

In Veneto and Friuli, the costumed witch present at these fires, as well as the rag or straw effigy burned, is known as La Befana, a name understood to be a corruption of the Italian word for Epiphany (*Epifania*). Far beyond the northern bonfire customs, throughout Italy, and even Sicily, La Befana is known to most every Italian. Now conceived as a mostly benevolent grandmotherly character, and often represented by small broom-riding dolls displayed in windows or on chimneys, La Befana is said on Twelfth Night to stuff stockings of good children with small gifts of fruit and candy while leaving "coal" made of sugar for the less well behaved. The custom of burning her in effigy, however, suggests that La Befana was in former centuries a more fearsome character. While noting her benevolence to good children, Jacob Grimm in 1835 refers to La Befana as a "misshapen fairy" whom he characterizes as "black and ugly." Quite understandably, he regards this Epiphany witch as the Italian version of Frau Perchta. According to folk songs and stories, she comes, like Holda or Perchta, "from the mountains," and is occasionally said to reside in a cave.

La Befana

Opposite: **La Befana figure.** *Photo by soniadal82 (2009) (CC BY 2.0).*
Above: *La Befana*, **by Achille Pinelli, after 1820.** *Courtesy of Harvard Art Museums/Fogg Museum.*

While a pagan origin is presumed for La Befana, various legends have arisen to place her in a Christian context. Usually she figures into a story of the Three Magi en route to find the newborn Messiah. In one version, she provides the Magi overnight lodgings, is asked to join them on their travels to Bethlehem and refuses. In another, they find her too busy with chores to provide hospitality and depart. In both cases, she later regrets her decision, and sets out in search of the infant Jesus, an act she's fated to endlessly repeat each Twelfth Night. In another darker version, she has recently lost her newborn child and is delusional with grief. Encountering Christ in the stable, she mistakes Him as her own and presents Him with gifts. Pleased by her charity, Jesus blesses her, declaring her the spiritual mother of every child in Italy.

Though La Befana is traditionally said to cloak herself in invisibility or administers a sharp blow with her broomstick to children she catches spying on her, people costumed as the witch (both men and women) nonetheless make appearances throughout Italy at public holiday events or as gift-givers in homes.

In Rome, La Befana's tradition is particularly associated with the Piazza Navona, which for centuries has been the site of an annual holiday fair and market specializing in La Befana dolls, puppets, and figurines, as well as toys, sweets, and sugar coal of the type she distributes. On Twelfth Night, Romans from all quarters make their way to the square, welcoming the old lady with as much noise as possible from trumpets, whistles, and other noisemakers sold in the piazza and across the city.

The Tuscan town of Barga, in the foothills of the Apuan Alps, bills itself as the "*Citta della Befana*" and its particularly well preserved traditions offer another hint at La Befana's origins. Here, and in several towns of southwestern Tuscany's Maremma region, the costumed Befana is accompanied as she makes her rounds from house to house by carolers known as *befanotti*. Like the witch, the singers dress in ragged, old-fashioned peasant clothes, and as they are said to represent departed ancestors, they may also blacken their faces with soot to give themselves a more otherworldly appearance. Among many theories attempting to account for La Befana's origins, is the suggestion that she originally was part of just such a troupe of ghostly beings. Whatever the case, the witch's connection with the dead as represented by the *befanotti* could only bolster Grimm's assertion that La Befana and Holda-Perchta are equivalent.

Like Perchta, Befana goes by a myriad of regionalized names. In the Veneto and Friuli regions, she is sometimes known as Redosa, Redodesa, or Aredodese, the latter, according to some scholars, a corruption of Herodias. Sometimes she is accompanied by twelve children, recalling Perchta's *Heimchen*. In the province of Belluno, along the Austrian border, Redosola emerges from her cave once a year to be burned in effigy. In Tuscany, Befana is said to emerge from a cave alongside

Redodesa and Marantega, the folkloric names given the Three Fates in that region. The connection with caves in these stories further links the figure with Holda and her underground dwelling in the Venusberg, or perhaps more directly Siballa and the cave in Norcia.

Perchta by Any Other Name

The Italian *strega* (witch) is Germanicized in the name of the Sträggele, the frightful crone said to arise in Switzerland on the Ember Night before Christmas. She also concerns herself particularly with spinners and the proper conduct of their work. She is regarded as the wife of the ghost hunter Türst, and is often seen in his company with a pack of phantom hunting dogs.

Posterli was the name of another witch associated with the holiday in Switzerland. Envisioned as an old hag, she-goat, or sometimes as a donkey, she was either represented by a costumed youth or by an effigy fixed to a sled. On the Thursday Ember Night before Christmas in Lucerne's Entlebuch district, village youths gathered for "Posterli Hunts" to symbolically rid their community of the witch's evil. Amid the sound of clanging cowbells, horns, and cracking whips, the Posterli was captured and paraded out of town and transported to the perimeter of a nearby village. This rather un-neighborly tradition was eventually abandoned around the end of the 18th century.

In the sub-alpine Jura Mountains between Switzerland and France, another witch known as Tante ("Aunt") Arie appears on Christmas Eve or the 15th day of Advent. Like Perchta, she brings sweets for good children, and for the bad she leaves birch switches or dunce caps. She likewise appears with the mismatched feet of a goose and has iron teeth recalling Perchta's iron nose. She wears a bell on her nocturnal rounds, which rather than awaken children is said to magically lull them to sleep, as she prefers not to be seen. Like Holda, she would sometimes appear incognito asking for charity to test and reward the kindness of strangers, and was similarly the protector of pregnant mothers, or women hoping to marry and conceive.

Tante Arie also resides underground, sometimes in a cavern filled with treasures, and rides out from her mountain home on a donkey named Marion. Like Holda, she was said to enjoy bathing and would swim in underground lakes within her caverns, sometimes changing into a serpent-like creature, known as a *vouivre*, to do so. There are a number of locations on the French side of the border purported to be her caves—la Roche de Faira (fairy rock) in Franche-Comté, and the grotte de la Combe Noire (or la grotte de la tante Arie) near Villars-Lès-Blamont.

At the latter, one can still find offerings of bread, milk, flowers, and mistletoe left by women desiring her aid.

In Germany, north of the states of Thuringia and Hesse, outside regions where Holda or Holle is found, there are other figures comparable to Perchta. Frau Gaude (also Gaue, Gode, or Wode) appears at Christmastime with a ghostly entourage, but these most often are described as phantom dogs, and though she may occasionally concern herself with spinning, by and far the real object of her passion, is the hunt. Some tales present her as cursed to wander eternally with her dogs after imprudently making a wish that she could hunt forever. Other stories have her sending her dogs into homes where they are impossible to expel, and if killed turn to stone that if moved, is the cause of still greater torment.

Gaude has also been described as riding a cart about during the Christmas nights accompanied by her pack. A legend paralleling Perchta's encounter with the ferryman has Gaude requesting repairs of a passing stranger when her wagon breaks down at a crossroads. Gaude similarly offers an apparently worthless reward that later transforms into gold. In one case, the magically transforming material is the wood shavings spilled from the repairman's tools, and in another, the excrement dropped by Gaude's waiting dogs.

In the historical region of Mecklenburg (now the German state of Mecklenburg-Vorpommern), Frau Harke (also Herke, Hacke) seems to be little more than a regional name for Frau Gaude, as she is likewise associated with dogs, the nights around Christmas, and the punishment of spinners not mindful of their work. Farmers also may offer tribute to both Gaude and Herke at the time of the harvest, when a sheaf of grain is left standing as an offering to her, thereby ensuring the success of the next year's crops.

Gaude is sometimes said to be the wife of Odin, the commonly cited leader of the *Wütende Heer* ("furious" or "raging" army), a ghostly nocturnal horde traversing skies especially around Christmas. Sometimes she rides alongside Odin, or at other times, she is said herself to lead the host of phantoms. Some folklorists even see in her name a regional corruption of the name "Wodan" (Odin/Wotan), and regard her as little more than a female aspect of the Norse god. In this sense, she is also often identified with the better-known consorts to the god, Freya or Frigg.

Even in Iceland, there is a menacing female figure associated with Christmas by the name of Grýla. This giant ogress also lives in a cave, emerging from her lair as the holiday approaches to capture children who have been badly behaved, carrying them off in her sack to later eat.

Ghostly Company

The motif of the Furious Army strongly overlaps with myths of the Wild Hunt (*Wilde Jagd*). The latter, as previously mentioned, can be led by Holda and differs primarily in the absences of slain soldiers among the specters. The seasonal apparition of Perchta's company of wandering souls, usually portrayed as unbaptized infants or other lost souls, is also often compared with these, though unlike the raging spirit of the Wild Hunt or Furious Army, Perchta's train is usually imagined as quiet and somber, closer to the *Canon Episcopi's* description of witches who, "traverse great spaces of earth in the silence of the dead of night … to be subject to her laws as of a Lady, and on fixed nights be called to her service." Such supernatural flights on the Christmas Ember Nights too are part of this family of folkloric phenomena.

All these species of ghostly perambulations through winter skies, just like the seasonal burning of effigies to drive off maleficent influence, should again remind us how the Christmas season was formerly a time of menacing supernatural activity. Exploration of this annual climate of superstition in the following chapter, like our previous discussion of the Alps as an incubator of witchcraft, should help make sense of the Krampus as much more than a bogey useful in Christian parenting. Recognizing the old *Percht* behind the Krampus mask, reframes the character not as a domesticated servant of the Church, but as a member of Perchta's supernatural train, and as such, more dreadful and capricious. Understanding these deeper roots extending into the fairy caverns of Holda's mountain or Perchta's realm of the dead, may help us grasp that sense of fearful wonder that once saw offerings of porridge placed on snowy Alpine rooftops, and lingers perhaps today with cookies, milk, and notes for Santa left in dark suburban kitchens.

Chapter Six

THE HAUNTED SEASON

Unholy Nights

Though it's hardly a feature of the modern horror film, up until at least 1860, according to *German Folk Superstitions of the Present*, Christmas and werewolves went hand in hand. The seasonal fear of these beasts was so great that simply to utter the word "wolf" between Christmas and Epiphany (or even during the entire month of December) was to put oneself at risk. To avoid being "torn apart by werewolves," so goes the superstition, one should replace the word "wolf" with "enemy," "pest," or some other circumlocution less likely to summon the beast. Not only was this (along with the summer solstice) one of the primary times for werewolf transformations, but in German-speaking lands (as well as in Italy, Romania, and Russia), to be born on Christmas Day could be considered an affront to Christ and thereby result in one being cursed to life as a werewolf.

It was not just the werewolf that haunted the snowy forests and mountains this time of year. Along with witches and spirits of the dead led by Perchta or Holda, the season brought encounters with the *Drud*, a sort of night hag that smothered and sickened sleepers and could only be repelled by the *Drudenfuß*, or pentagram. In Alpine regions, families listened for the eerie cry of the demonic goat-like *Habergeiß*. In marshes, travelers feared the *Nebelfrau* ("mist woman") who seduced travelers from the safety of their paths. Impending death might be announced by the arrival of the *Seelvogel* ("soul bird"), whose claws transported the doomed to the other side. The nocturnal forests and moors swarmed with spirits: the *Moosweiberl* ("moss woman"), *Holzleute* ("Wood Folk"), and the *Schratzln* (forest goblins).

Rindbacher Glöckler, Ebensee, Austria. *Photo © Ferienregion Traunsee, Ruber.*

Even places of industry were endangered by malevolent beings this time of year. The *Melhweibl* ("flour woman") could drag the miller into the grinding gears of his mill, and the *Durandl*, a sort of goblin haunting the glowing depths of the glass furnace, could emerge to destroy the day's work or even set the foundry ablaze.

Historical and semi-historical figures too joined the season's ranks of threatening ghosts. Frightening travelers in the Lower Bavarian Forest was Woidhaus-Mich, a monstrously large and powerful cowherd said to occasionally devour the raw flesh of his own animals, dispatching them with a club made of a dried bear claw. And in the same region, chatelaine Maria Freiin of Castle Rammelsberg lived on as the witch Wecklin, condemned to dance in burning slippers during the Twelve Nights of Christmas because she once used her own slipper to beat to death a child who'd spilled some milk. Even the "Forest Prophet" Mühlhiasl of Apoig, after his death in 1805, became a sort of seasonal phantom, thanks to his eerie prophecies of human extermination that caused him to be refused burial on consecrated ground.

Even the saints themselves twisted into sinister forms during the month of December. On St. Lucy's Day, the shrouded *Lutz* or *Lutzelfrau* once threatened children with evisceration or drowning, and on St. Thomas Day, "Bloody Thomas" stalked the forest with a gore-drenched hammer. We'll examine these characters further in a bit as they represent the same sort of monstrous inversions of a Catholic saint we find on St. Nicholas Day with the Krampus.

Companies of Ghosts   Of all the terrors unleashed during the nights around Christmas, the most widespread in German-speaking lands were those ghostly processions previously mentioned—both the solemn train of souls led by Holda or Perchta as well as the stormier apparition of the Wild Hunt or Furious Army.

Broadly amalgamating and sometimes blurring together elements of hunting and diabolic hunters, lost souls, and slain warriors, stories of ghost hordes are widely dispersed across Central Europe, Scandinavia, the British Isles, and even North America, where the spirits appear in cowboy legends, and made their way into the 1940s country-western ballad "Ghost Riders in the Sky."

The terms "hunt" and "army" can sometimes be misleading. The prey hunted by the Wild Hunt, if one is actually hunted, is rarely seen or specified. "Hunt" may be understood as merely describing the quality of the apparition's movement—a racing stampede of figures chasing one after the other. Likewise, the word "*Heer*" (army) can also simply mean "a great number," as in "horde," and needn't always designate a specifically military assembly. This usage is evident in a 1508 sermon by the German preacher Johann Geiler von Kaiserberg in which he characterizes this army or horde not as fallen soldiers, but otherwise:

> You ask, what shall you tell us about the Wild Army? But I cannot tell you very much, for you know much more of it than I. This is what the common man says: those who die before the time God has fixed for them, those who leave on a journey and are stabbed, hanged, or drowned, must wander after death until there arrives the date that God has set for them … Those who wander are especially active during the Lenten days, and first and foremost during the lean times before Christmas, which is a sacred time.

Those who have died before their time could also describe the spirits led by Holda, and in a more limited way Perchta's *Heimchen* who did not live to be baptized. Slightly more martial, and specifically mentioning dead soldiers, is this account from 1516 by Strasbourg historian Jacques Trausch:

> At night, the Army hastens through the fields, playing drums and fifes, and also it travels through the towns, its members carrying lights and making loud cries. Such ghosts number sometimes fifty or eighty and even one hundred or two hundred. One carries his head in his hands, another carries a cross or sometimes an arm or a leg, depending on the manner in which each found his death in battle. They carry candles that cast enough light so that it is possible to recognize who they are and if they died in war or elsewhere. A man always preceded them, ceaselessly shouting, "Make way, make way, lest you suffer!"

The unnamed forerunner is clearly comparable to Loyal Eckhart, and it should be noted that the ghostly horde here is not exclusively made of soldiers, but those who "died in war or elsewhere." The warriors among them are not in the throes of that battle fury evoked by the term "Furious Army." All of this points to the difficulty of conceptually sorting such apparitions. Names like "Wild Hunt" or "Furious Army" rarely represent clear-cut categories, so for the sake of simplicity, I will occasionally refer to the collective spectrum of ghostly processions as "The Wild Hunt."

To understand these apparitions, we must examine sets of intermittently overlapping traits. One of these is the perceived function or mission of the phantoms. This might include hunting or making war, heralding a dire event, bestowing blessings, or participating in ghostly revels. Christianity often reshaped this essentially pagan phenomenon, and displaced and departed souls began to be portrayed either as damned souls condemned to wander, or as demons. Or demons might be mingled with the damned as their torturers driving them onward.

The location of the sightings may also be a differentiating factor. Perchta's company, or the Swiss *säligen Lüt*, for instance, are said to move through towns and visit homes, while the Wild Hunters naturally appear in wilderness areas. The Furious Army may appear either in areas populated or wild. Most apparitions appear at night, but there are occasional daytime exceptions to the rule.

Where there is no direct interaction with mortals, the company passes through at some elevation, either high above in the clouds, or quite typically, floating several feet above the ground. As these ghosts frequently remain invisible, eerie sounds may be all that characterizes the experience. Witnesses may find themselves enveloped by the sound of sweet otherworldly music, the clamor of a passing army, or the barking of invisible hunting dogs. Unsurprisingly, the sound of wind howling through Alpine peaks and ravines is often mentioned and said to assume a supernatural quality betraying the passage of spirits.

Lo Stregozzo (the Witches) by Marcantonio Raimondi and Agostino Veneziano (ca. 1520). Some historians have seen this engraving as a depiction of the Wild Hunt.

Wuotan and the Wild Hunt

The Norse Wuotan (Wotan/Odin) is particularly associated with these winter apparitions. As a deity concerning himself with death and warfare, he is naturally connected with the Furious Army, and serves as its most frequently named leader. His traditional wolf companions, Geri and Freki, might be associated with the ghostly hunting dogs found elsewhere. As the phantoms usually appear amid the clouds, Odin's role as god of the storms and winds further associates him with these apparitions.

Throughout that region, particularly in the German state of Mecklenburg-Vorpommern, east of Hamburg, the apparitions were reported with particular frequency. Around the town of Rostock, it was called the "Wohl," a name equated

Detail of *Åsgårdsreien* (Asgard riders) by Peter Nicolai Arbo (1872).
A Scandinavian depiction of the Wild Hunt.

with "the Wild Hunt, *also called the Furious Army*" (italics mine) in an article by one Professor Flörke, writing for his local paper in 1832. He writes:

> Our agrarian laborers, who seek to profit from the cool of the evening air to bind the rye, were so terrified by the Wild Hunt they would barely dare go into the fields, shivering all the while. First, they heard the baying of hounds, which then mingled with the fairly harsh voices of men and others that were fairly sweet. They saw fires that passed rapidly through the air, then, if they did not flee, the entire army paraded before them in a terrifying din made up of barking, instruments that sounded like hunting horns, and panting.

Professor Flörke equates the *Wohl* with Wuotan, he says, thanks to the example of "a pious preacher," who'd convinced him, "that this was nothing other than the devil himself accompanied by several fallen angels, who took pleasure in frightening people. The devil, he said, took the form of Wuotan, the old pagan idol." Though most common in the north, Wuotan also plays the role of Wild Hunter in Germany's Alemannic regions further south, in Swabia, and in Switzerland, where the apparition is know as *Wuotis Heer* ("Wuotan's Army").

While Wuotan's association with the Furious Army or Wild Hunt is undeniable in the areas mentioned, there has been a historical tendency among German writers to universalize his importance and interpret any folkloric motifs in terms of the Nordic pantheon. In the case of those Alpine regions where the *Perchten* and Krampus mythology evolved, though, connections with Odin are not explicitly present, and historians seeking these may overlook the obvious possibility of influence from non-German-speaking but geographically closer regions. The myth of nocturnal sightings of phantom hosts, are, after all, present not only in countries surrounding the Alps but also extend geographically and chronologically to the classical world, where stories of ghost armies are mentioned by Greek and Roman writers such as Herodotus, Tacitus, or Ovid, who writes of an omen heralding Caesar's death, describing "the rattling of weapons in the black clouds, the sound of terrifying trumpets and horns in the sky."

This emphasis on the Nordic stems, in part, from Jacob Grimm, German Romanticism, and the desire to forge a language-based cultural identity prior to the 1871 formation of the German state, a tendency further cultivated by late 19th-century *völkisch* (from the German word for "folk") movement searching for ancient pagan roots of a pan-Germanic culture. All of this reached fever pitch in the Third Reich, with Wuotan's association with war providing a mythic grounding for Himmler's fantastical worldview. His occult initiatory order, the SS, drew inspiration from an ancient Germanic tribal model, namely blood bonds between warriors and a leader embodying Wuotan. The fury (*Wut*) of the Furious Army (*Wütende Heer*) was etymologically linked to Wuotan and celebrated as the ecstatic state in which Viking Berserkers went to war. While not consciously referencing Third Reich ideology, this tendency occasionally surfaces today on websites and in articles proposing specious connections between the costumes of the *Perchten* and the wolf and bear pelts or animal masks worn by the Berserker.

In Scandinavian countries, Wuotan is even more prominent. The Wild Hunt in Norway, for instance, is called "*Oskoreia*," a corruption of "Åsgårdsreia" ("riders of Åsgård"). Witches and trolls might join these *Julereia* ("Christmas riders") as well as the spirits of the dead. Departed ancestors might be envisioned as part of this company, and to insure their comfortable passage during these nights, a meal and ale might be set out, a fire might be left burning for their warmth, candles to light their way, or even sometimes a warm bath might be drawn.

The figure of Wuotan in the Scandinavian Wild Hunt does not inevitably represent some sort of archaic survival of pagan belief. In an explicitly Christian tale from Swedish, for instance, the Wild Hunter Wuotan is identified as a nobleman who defied Church law by hunting on the Sabbath and is therefore doomed to hunt throughout eternity. An even later incorporation into the myth occurs in Denmark, where Odin does not show up as the wild huntsman until the 18th century.

The Night Folk

Less aggressive than the hunters or warriors associated with Wuotan are the Night Folk (*Nachtvolk*) and Night Throng (*Nachtschar*) who appear especially around Christmas in the Alpine area where southern Germany, western Austria, and northern Switzerland meet. These two names designate similar groups, and some regional sources do not differentiate, also using the terms "Death Folk" (*Totenvolk*) or "Death Throng" (*Totenschar*) interchangeably. As these specters are not hunters or warriors, they distinguish themselves by moving in a slower procession, and on foot. Despite this, they are inescapable, and they may inexorably follow given paths. Obstructing their progress over these routes is dangerous. Doors on opposite sides of a house must sometimes be left open to create a ghostly throughway, and tales are told of havoc wrecked if houses are not thus readied, or of houses blown down if constructed on a route the spirits follow. The same is also often said of obstructing the Wild Hunt.

A few tales of the Night Folk from a volume of Austrian legends collected in 1911 illustrate more of their characteristics. The first is told of a wanderer in Eastern Austria's Vorarlberg region:

> On a moonlit night, a farmer from Montafon arrived in a nearby ravine and sat down upon a stone to rest, and drawing out his mouth harp, he played to pass the time.
>
> Then all at once, the Night Folk appeared in a long procession moving through the ravine. A shadowy figure stepped up to the farmer and said, "Hear now, if you choose, I can instruct you to play so beautifully, the pine cones will rise and dance round about us."
>
> "That would please me," replied the musician.
>
> Scarcely had the lessons begun, when from the throng emerged a woman who drew the shadowy figure back into the crowd, whispering to him: "Come, this one is not worth your time. Only this morning, he has taken holy water."
>
> The lonely wanderer crossed himself, realizing with horror the danger he had so narrowly escaped.

Bestowing supernatural musical ability is a particularly distinctive trait of the Night Folk. As with the shadowy figure in our tale, they are usually described as black silhouettes, or may be dressed in black like priests or monks. They produce striking music, sometimes described as "heavenly," or "as if the angels were playing," but often as a tool of seduction for those they would abduct from among the living. They may hold nocturnal revels similar to those of the witches, usually in isolated wilderness areas, but occasionally closer to areas of human habitation, or even during the day, as in this tale from the above-mentioned volume:

Once, however, the Night Folk appeared in the tiny hamlet of Walsertale during daylight hours to hold a merry feast. While mass was being said in a nearby church, they snatched a farmer's finest cow from the stable and hurriedly slaughtered and consumed it amid dancing, shouting, and the sweet sounds of stringed instruments. To the children who had remained in the house, the Night Folk kindly gave some of their meal, but warned them not to break or discard the leg bones. After the meal, all the bones were collected but one, which despite all the searching could not be found. Then they wrapped the remains in the skin of the slaughtered animal and declared that because of this, the cow will limp home. When the Night Folk had withdrawn, the living cow again stood in its stall as before, but thereafter dragged one of its feet.

This sort of slaughter, consumption, and restoration of a living creature, dubbed the "Miracle of the Bones" by historian Wolfgang Behringer, is a common feature in accounts of the Night Folk. As we've seen, it is also figured into tales of witchcraft revels in Tyrol, usually in reference to butchered livestock but also to human children who are eaten. Behringer regards this re-animating "Miracle of the Bones" as symbolizing "the most extreme form of benevolence," providing "the best thing in the world: life itself."

The benevolence of the Night Folk, however, was not so evident in the Swiss cantons of Glarus, St. Gallen, and Graubünden, where the ghosts behaved in a less civilized manner, did not play music, tended to blind or abduct witnesses, and often through their appearances heralded death or epidemics. Seeing those still alive amid the throng of departed souls never bade well, as in this tale collected by the folklorist Theodor Vernaleken in the canton of Graubünden in 1858:

Midnight is the hour when the Death Folk move about, at their front, the bony figure of Death leading with his violin all who will die within the year. At the time of the plague known as the Black Death, a man in the Churwalder Valley heard by night a soft music passing close. He leapt up, and throwing one leg into his pants, rushed to the window, flung back the curtains, and saw the Death Folk. Among them were many of his acquaintances, and there at the end of their train, with pants pulled over one leg only—he himself! Pale and rigid with terror, he sank back, knowing that he would be the last of all to die of the plague. And that was how it happened.

Because it was advisable not to look upon any class of these wandering specters, and because—from an empirical perspective—sound divorced from vision left more room for the play of imagination, what was *heard* of these apparitions was often featured more prominently than what was *seen*. A peculiar sound almost always anticipated the troupe, which itself might remain invisible. It is often described as musical. At times it was the martial sounds of drums and pipes, at others, more ethereal. Or it may have come as "a droning murmur," "a strange hum like the buzzing of bees," a "song sounding like a Psalm," or "the rattling of bones and many voices in prayer." It could build to a crescendo described by one storyteller as "the music of a thousand instruments, followed by the crash of a storm breaking through the oaks of the forest," building finally to the noise of "a great rolling black coach, in which hundreds of spirits sit joined in wondrous song." The sounds accompanying the host could also predict the future. Should the ghosts' "appearance signify a good year, it brings music," and "if war or sickness await, a discordant noise accompanies it."

Wild Hunters

In the case of ghosts recognizable as soldiers, the leader can be Wuotan or also a historical warrior, as is the case with Charlemagne, who rises from within Austria's Untersberg mountain to lead his ghostly army at the time around Christmas. In the case of a phantom hunting party, particularly in Thuringia, the leader can be Holda, as we've seen, thanks to her association with the huntress Diana. Further north toward Scandinavia, the rider can be the tragic and vengeful Gudrun (Kriemhild) of the Germanic Nibelungen legends.

Local legends may also position a cursed nobleman as the Hunter. In the former northeastern German province of Pomerania, it was Count von Ebernburg who was doomed to hunt forever. Riding out one Sunday morning rather than attending church, legend says the count found two strangers in his hunting party, one angelic and the other devilish. While the angelic rider counseled Ebernburg to return to church services, the wicked one mocked this and was soon joined by Ebebernburg in his ridicule. Eventually the strangers vanished, and soon enough, the riders found their horses running not on the ground but with hooves in midair as the whole party was swept into the sky where they still ride today.

More commonly, particularly in Westphalia and Lower Saxony, the hunter named is Hackelberg (sometimes Hackelbärend, Hackelblock, etc.). Like Count Ebernburg, he is often cursed to wander thanks to his disregard for the Church. During the Twelve Nights of Christmas, or during thunderstorms, the sound of his hunting horn may be heard, and amid a pack of hellhounds, the figure may be seen upon a black steed with smoke trailing from glowing nostrils. Sometimes the party is preceded by Tutosel, an owl, inhabited by soul of a nun, whose dreadful singing in life approximated the hooting of that bird.

Legends often mention female forest spirits as the prey of the Wild Hunter,

Odin as the Wild Hunter, from *Die Götterwelt der deutschen und nordischen Völker* (1860).

either the *Holzweibl* ("wood woman") or *Moosweibl* ("moss woman"), both of whom are said to be diminutive, dressed in moss, leaves, or other vegetation, and generally friendly to man. Some scholars have suggested that the image of this hunt is suggested by the wind (associated with the Wild Hunter) chasing leaves or woodland debris across the forest floor. Woodcutters, sympathetic to the plight of these kindly forest beings, would sometimes protect them from the Wild Hunter by marking trunks of felled trees with three crosses, thereby rendering the stumps safe havens from the phantom huntsmen.

Stories of these forest folk pursued by the Hunter are particularly prevalent in the Thuringian Forest. In Germany's Vogtland, a region straddling Thuringia, Bavaria, and Saxony, on the Czech Border, the *Moosweibl* and *Moosmännel* ("moss man"), are important in Christmas tradition. During the Twelve Nights, they are said to flee the inhospitable frozen forest and seek the warmth of human habitation. Handmade representations of the figures covered in moss and holding candles are still traditional in Vogtland homes during the holiday. These mossy figures, which have become popular beyond the Vogtland, originated in the second half of the 19th-century as an inexpensive handicraft item poorer rural folk could create and sell in bustling Christmas markets.

The suffering of those who fail to treat the Wild Hunter with due respect is another popular theme in the folklore. One tale tells of a woodsman who hears the Wild Hunter pass and impudently imitates him, crying "Ho, ho, ho." Another has the woodsman calling out after the Hunter asking to join his hunt. In both cases, their disrespect is rewarded the following morning as they find a grisly gift—a portion of a slain *Moosweibl* nailed to his stable door. In another tale related by Grimm, an overbold carpenter is startled when "a black mass came tumbling down the chimney on the fire, scattering sparks and brands about the people's ears: a huge horse's thigh lay on the hearth, and the said carpenter was dead." Another legend warns that the impertinent will be devoured by the Hunter's dogs.

The Wild Hunter Türst

Riding the winds during the nights around Christmas, the Wild Hunter in Switzerland goes by the name Türst. Legend most famously associates him with Mount Pilatus near Lucerne, but he also appears elsewhere and in regional variations. The specter is known by the sound of his hunting horn and the eerie barking of his three-legged hunting hounds led by a one-eyed canine. In some regions, this pack is a monstrous hybrid of dog and swine. In other regions, Türst himself transforms into a dog for the hunt, or turns those who impede his path into dogs compelled to join his ghostly party. Livestock whom the phantoms passed by would scramble, go mad in their stalls, or cease giving milk.

As a spirit of the mountains and wilderness, Türst functions as a sort of gamekeeper, and his hunting horn has the power to summon any wild creature. In some tales, Türst is also master of the goblins who reside on Santenberg mountain near Lucerne, and together they were said to protect a unicorn living amid the crags. As spirit of the wind, Türst, like other embodiments of the Wild Hunter, would blow down structures not left open to his passage. As spirit of the storm, however, his power was especially feared and gave rise to the erection of *Wetterkreuze* (weather crosses) to calm or repel his destructive force. One such cross once stood on the Santenberg with the inscription, "Here hunts Türst."

Sometimes the hideous witch Sträggele accompanies Türst as his wife. Said to abduct or eat children, she was used as a bogey to frighten misbehaving children. Like Perchta, she could also have a kindly side, and was likewise associated with spinning and the Twelve Nights. Sträggele and Türst were also sometimes joined by the *Pfaffengälern*, a mysterious wild phantom with flaming eyes.

The Twelve Nights, the *Rauhnächte*

Apparitions that have thus far been mentioned as occurring "around Christmas" specifically tend to fall within those twelve days between Christmas and Epiphany. For most Americans, these Twelve Days have little significance beyond partridges, pear trees, and a vague notion of extended merriment in picturesque old England. But in the folklore of German-speaking lands, when "the Twelves" (*die Zwölfte*") are counted, it's not a matter of *days* but uneasy *nights*. The period is regarded as a sort of calendric limbo in which one year dissolves into the other, and the otherworldly leaks into the mundane. In Germany's Vogtland, it's referred to as the "between-nights," the "inter-nights" or "under-nights." In other regions it's the *Losnächte* ("oracle nights") because fortunetelling is practiced then. *Glöckelnächte* ("knocking nights"), is yet another expression arising from the custom of groups of young people going out by night and mischievously thumping doors and windows and demanding treats.

The most common name, however, is the *Rauhnächte* (singular: *Rauhnacht*). The etymology of the term is much debated. Some scholars suggest it originates with the Middle High German word *rûch* for "hairy," referring presumably to fur-wearing performers, like the *Perchten*, who roamed these nights. Others believe the term related to the word for smoke, "*Rauch*," thanks to the practice of censing homes, stables, and barns during these nights to drive off evil influence. In some regions, the name *Rauchnacht* ("smoke night") rather than *Rauhnacht* is used, but this may be a more modern development. The most significant nights within the twelve are Christmas Eve, New Year's Eve, and Epiphany's Twelfth Night. In other regions, however, the twelve-day period is shifted to end on the New Year, and begins instead on the eve of St. Thomas Day (December 21) instead of Christmas. While not technically a *Rauhnacht* or within the twelve, St. Lucy's Day (December 13) is also often associated with similar beliefs and practices.

Exactly when these nights acquired their significance is unclear, but the notion of this as a time of supernatural possibility seems to consolidate at some point during the Early Modern Period. Some scholars have suggested that the 12-day difference between lunar and solar years point to much older origin in attempts to synchronize ancient Germanic or Celtic lunar calendars with the Roman solar year, but there is no clear evidence for this in the historical record.

While the *Rauhnacht* traditions are historically strongest in German-speaking lands, related beliefs and practices are scattered throughout Europe and Russia with Epiphany fortunetelling being the most common.

Rauhnacht Superstitions

A surprisingly large number of regionally diverse and sometimes contradictory superstitions cluster around the *Rauhnächte*. Along with the notion of opening doors or windows to facilitate passage of the Wild Hunt, clotheslines or hanging laundry were not to be left out at night for fear of entangling flying ghosts. On New Year's Eve, it was specifically the back door that was to be opened, because only through this door could good luck arrive; all others were to remain shut. Doors were to be closed quietly as slamming doors on New Year's Eve caused lightning strikes in the coming year. Washing, baking, and other chores were at least partially restricted during the period, but clean homes were to be maintained as dirt and disorder attracted malevolent spirits. Garments missing buttons needed to be mended before the *Rauhnächte*, lest financial hardships result. Neither hair nor nails were to be trimmed as doing so could cause headaches and inflammation in the fingers. Spinning wheels, wagon wheels, or geared machines were to be stopped as only the Wheel of Fortune was to turn on these portentous days.

Women and children would not to go unescorted after sunset for fear of the Wild Hunter, roving spirits, witches, and werewolves. But those who did venture out might be rewarded with wondrous sights. At midnight on Christmas Eve, running brooks turned to wine, bees buzzed and swarmed in the frigid air, and standing under an apple tree, one might look up and see the heavens open. At that same hour, animals spoke in their pens, stalls, and stables. Their utterances could reveal the future, but none could share these secrets, as death would quickly overtake any who witnessed the miracle. During the *Rauhnächte* dog barks heard in the distance acquired special meaning; those you heard following a private thought confirmed the truth of that thought; those heard after midnight presaged a coming death. Domestic animals might also use the gift of speech to speak to the *Hausgeist*, the protective spirit or fairy resident in each home. Should the animal complain of ill treatment by its master, the *Hausgeist* would ensure retribution. These domestic spirits were particularly active during this time, and families did well to placate them with small gifts set out overnight.

A number of Christmas Eve customs surviving into the 19th and 20th century recall seasonal food offerings left for Frau Perchta centuries before. On Christmas

Eve in Lower Bavaria, sausages would sometimes be prepared to break the fast after midnight mass, with a portion of these set aside for the departed. When on Christmas morning the food appeared untouched by specters, it was donated to a needy person promising to pray for the dead and thereby offer sustenance in another form. Elsewhere, the spirit visitors were said to be the Holy Family. In Tyrol, milk was set out for the Christ Child and his mother after midnight mass, and elsewhere in Austria, candles were set out to light their way. In Northern Germany too, lights were left burning and food was left on tables for the Virgin and the angels.

The period of the Twelve Nights lends itself to prognostication as events of each day can be correlated with each of the coming twelve months. One method of prognostication used an onion split into twelve bowl-shaped parts. Each was marked with the name of month and sprinkled with salt. In the morning, the amount of moisture found in the hollow of each slice showed how wet or dry each month would be. Generalized predictions for the entire year could also be inferred from weather observed on New Year's Day. High winds announced a troubled year; clear skies, pleasant times; frosted windowpanes or heavy snow, a year of healthy profits. Vintners hoped for clear skies, anticipating a robust harvest and superior grapes. Epiphany's sunny skies heralded a peaceful year for all.

For unmarried women, the identity of one's future lover or bridegroom was best discovered during the *Rauhnächte*. Swabian women drew sticks at random from a woodpile; long, short, straight, or crooked, they foretold similar qualities in future mates. Women in Baden-Württemberg sometimes formed a circle around a blindfolded gander, waiting to see who would be approached first by the animal and therefore next to marry. Tyrolean women put an ear against the side of a warming oven, straining to make out prophetic sounds; music foretold a coming wedding, while the sound of bells represented a death knell for the listener. A young woman who waited at the crossroads during a *Rauhnacht* might encounter an apparition of her future bridegroom, but she must resist the temptation to address him for this would mean her death. Death or exile in the coming year could be predicted by a curious ritual involving a slipper thrown against a door; however it landed, its toe pointed to the individual who would depart within the coming year.

While most all of these superstitions have long been forgotten or fallen into disuse, one method of fortune-telling long associated with the *Rauhnächte* is still practiced, though usually in a more skeptically playful spirit. This is *Bleigießen* (lead-pouring), divination from shapes formed by molten lead cooled in water. One of the many tools of prognostication employed by Roman augurs, this technique, known as Molybdomancy, spread via imperial expansion throughout Europe. While otherwise unused today, it has been retained as a New Year's Eve recreation in Germany, Austria, Switzerland, and Scandinavian countries. As originally practiced (on any of the *Rauhnächte* , not just New Year's Eve), leftover bits of lead used in farm repairs would be melted and dropped into water. Not only the shape of the solidified metal but the shadow it cast could be scrutinized for clues.

Of typical concern might be the trade practiced by a future bridegroom, so blobs would be scrutinized for resemblances to a tailor's shears, a miner's pick, or blacksmith's hammer. Later, Christmas tree tinsel, in the days it was still made of lead, was melted down. Today commercially produced kits are seasonally available, and include, along with spoon and lead pellets, a prepared guide to aid interpretation. Though still quite common, lately the substitution of wax for lead has been promoted due to certain degrees of toxicity associated with the use of lead.

Ausräuchern (Censing)

As mentioned, censing the property to provide protection from evil is one possible source of the name *Rauhnacht/Rauchnacht*. Though far more rare than the practice of *Bleigießen*, this custom has not completely died out in rural Alpine areas, though is now conducted more as a matter of family tradition than for spiritual safekeeping. This was not the case, however, in the 19th century, when even in urban areas such as Munich, censing of commercial sites and office buildings was regularly carried out. In its current survival, *Ausräuchern* only exists as a Twelfth Night custom, but formerly the practice was also associated with Christmas Eve, and or on Thursdays throughout Advent.

Even outside rural areas where *Ausräuchern* is practiced, the custom of burning incense at Christmas survives in the contemporary popularity of figurative wooden incense burners (*Räuchermännchen* or "smokers") sold at German Christmas markets alongside nutcrackers and other ornaments. Usually carved in the Erzgebirge Mountains, a region famous for its handcrafted wooden toys and Christmas decorations, the *Räuchermännchen* typically take the shape of rustic lederhosen-wearing peasants, night watchmen, hunters, or other traditionalist figures. To some small extent, the practice of *Ausräuchern* has also been rediscovered in certain New Age quarters, where it is naturally reframed in terms far removed from the folk Catholicism of its origins.

Traditional *Ausräuchern* is carried out with a small pan or pot filled with burning charcoal and frankincense. In earlier times, a mix of juniper berries and herbs selected for their magical properties might also be used. The head of the household carries this through the home, barn, and animal pens accompanied by the eldest child, wife, or servant who sprinkles holy water along the way. Ideally this would be *Dreikönigswasser* (Three Kings' water) blessed during the Epiphany mass of the previous year. As the party moves about the property, smoke is blown

The initials of the Three Kings (Kaspar, Melchior, Balthasar) chalked over a door on Epiphany, 2012

from the censer to the four directions, and prayers are offered. Each cow is individually censed and sprinkled with holy water, and specific prayers are offered for their protection from disease and epidemics. After their normal feeding, the cattle might also receive consecrated bread, cabbage, salt, and water. Before fumigations are complete, any headgear in the house is set over the pot to collect the smoke, thus making its wearer immune to headaches. Feet or shoes may be similarly smoked for safe travel. After all this has been done, the censer is left overnight in the herb garden to provide a final blessing there as it cools.

As well as fumigating all corners, above all doors, and even the pigsty, an inscription is traditionally chalked for further protection over all who enter. Usually, this took the form of the letters K, M, and B joined with crosses and sandwiched within numerals representing the years, so for 2016: "20 + K + M + B + 16." The letters are said to represent the Magi's traditional names: Melchior, Caspar (German: "Kaspar"), and Balthasar. Sometimes the letters may be altered as C + M + B, more recently said instead to represent the Latin *Christus mansionem benedicat* (Christ bless this house) or K + M + B, inserting the Greek *Kyrios* ("Lord") into the formula. The inscription is to remain over all doors until the following Twelfth Night. Sometimes, a pentagram may also be drawn over animal pens as additional insurance against the *Drude* and other evils.

Historically, the practice seems to have been borrowed by the laity from monasteries, as monks were the earliest settlers in many Alpine regions. Already in the 14th century, incense was a traditional feature of Nicholas plays and parades organized by the monasteries, and clerics were often called upon to cense non-ecclesiastic property in times of need. For example, in Bobingen, Bavaria, it's recorded that a sacristan was recruited during the plague of 1635 to cense and bless homes after Christmas, New Year, and Epiphany services. In the 16th and 17th century, church incense was often sought by the laity, not only for such protective purposes but also for use in love-spells and other magic. After unsuccessful attempts to ban this sort of private use, the Church eventually conceded informally to such use when associated with particular feast days such as Epiphany.

The *Rauhnächte* are an ideal time for the fabrication of charms and the casting of spells. Magical herbs collected during this period are said to be particularly potent, and a broom made during these nights is able to sweep away evil spirits and disease. On Twelfth Night, water dipped from a spring or well at midnight possesses the power to heal, and divining rods cut on this night are infallible. Those blessed in the name of Caspar find gold, Melchior locates silver, and Balthasar yields water. The names of the Three Kings, written on slips of parchment and attached to the traveler's leg, bless his journey and protect him from predators, robbers, and accidents. Water, salt, incense, and the chalk consecrated in a church on Epiphany have special power, and if windows are opened at midnight, the wind that passes through expels all evils. Midnight of the New Year offers similar potential. A glass from which all family members drink at this hour wards off ill fortune. Jumping from a table or chair at the stroke of midnight does likewise, and four stakes pounded into the earth at the cardinal points around a home safeguards the property from fire. Lentils, peas, and beans eaten on that night bring a fruitful year.

Knocking Nights

The "Knocking Nights" (*Klöpfelnächte*, *Anglöckelnächte*, or *Glöckelnächte*—all from the German for "knock") were celebrated in Austria, southern Germany, and Switzerland, usually on the three Thursdays preceding Christmas. One of the earliest mentions of knocking customs comes from German scholar and writer Thomas Naogeorgus, who in the mid-1500s describes the practice in this poem translated from the Latin:

> Three weeks before the day whereon was borne the Lord of Grace,
> And on the Thursday boys and girls do run in every place,
> And bounce and beat at every door, with blows and lusty smacks,
> And cry, the Advent of the Lord not borne as yet perhaps.
> And wishing to the neighbors all, that in the houses dwell,
> A happy year, and every thing to spring and prosper well:
> Here have they pears, and plums, and pence, each man gives willingly,
> For these three nights are always thought, unfortunate to be;
> Wherein they are afraid of sprites and cankered witches' spite,
> And dreadful devils black and grim, that then have chiefest might.

The Knocking Nights, like the Twelve Nights, were a time of ghosts and supernatural happenings, including the gift of speech endowed upon animals on these nights. The name comes from the custom of knocking on the walls of barns where livestock slept, thereby provoking the beasts to vocalize. In those sounds, one might discern the names of anyone in the village who would die within the coming year. Assuming Tyrolean kids of the 16th century were not so different from those today, it's easy to imagine this custom propagating as groups of young people ran from barn to barn in search of spooky thrills.

At some point the emphasis of the practice shifted, and the nocturnally roaming youths themselves came to represent wandering ghosts, and their mischievous knocking would resemble the "*poltern*" ("noisemaking") of the poltergeist. Some accounts make this clear, mentioning visiting youths knocking on doors and windows, and then quickly hiding themselves so that invisible spirits would be blamed. The prankish "ghosts" justified the game as one that brought otherworldly good luck to the homes visited. Eventually the practice was formalized to also include the performance of lucky songs or recited rhymes offered in exchange for treats. Some groups carried pronged poles used to rap on windows, with the prong used to extract the reward, usually a bit of cake, doughnut, sausages, or cheese impaled by the homeowner on the barb. Knocks with padded hammers and broomsticks, or even handfuls of dried peas thrown against windows, were all used in efforts to startle homeowners.

At times the aggressive nocturnal visits and noisemaking led to confrontations, and a 1616 account from Nuremberg, where the custom was known as "*Bergnacht*," recounts that a girl was seriously injured by a tavern keeper who accused her of hammering on his establishment's door with particular violence. By the 17th century, after unsuccessful bans, the Church pushed to reform the tradition as a religious one. The house-to-house visits were now said to imitate the journey of Mary and Joseph seeking lodgings on the way to Bethlehem, or participants were dressed as shepherds associated with the shepherds of the Nativity story. Songs that had previously reflected the rustic humor of the tradition's pagan roots became Christmas carols. Possibly, at this point, the dates were shifted from the *Rauhnächte* to those before the Nativity to synchronize with Mary and Joseph's travels.

Knocking Nights in Tyrol once included figures borrowed from the Nicholas parades or costumed witches and devils, who engaged in rowdy antics. In South Tyrol, *Klöckeln* groups still raise a ruckus with clanging cowbells and discordant trumpets made of goat horns. The masked troupe is accompanied by two particularly rowdy figures—the *Zuslmandle* who bickers and fights with his wife, *Zuslweibl*, played by a male in drag.

Disguised *Berigln* in Styria's Ausseerland-Salzkammergut region go door to door during the "Knocking Nights." *Photo © Salzkammergut Presseagentur.*

The *Glöcklern*

In the Austrian state of Salzburg, and here and there in Styria and Upper Austria, the practice developed into something altogether different, the running of the *Glöcklern*, again from a Middle High German word for "knock." Here knocking itself became strictly incidental, as the event is much better known for the lighted "caps" worn by participants. These are actually colorful paper lanterns braced on performers' shoulders to support their large girth (sometimes measuring up to nine feet in diameter). Lanterns are decorated with intricate stained glass patterns created from colored tissue paper and punched cardboard covering light frames in the shapes of pyramids, crowns, crescents, suns, or stars. (During the Third Reich, there was an unfortunate one-off custom job sent to Berlin designed in the red, brown, and black color scheme of Nazi uniforms and decorated with swastikas.)

The lanterns did not become part of this Knocking Night tradition until the mid-1800s, competing with the region's traditional masked performers until winning out around 1900. Though the careful craftsmanship of the lanterns may suggest more elevated intent, the new *Glöcklern*—as with other masked processions described in this book—at times encountered bans and confrontations with civil authorities. It's said the all-white clothing the lantern-carriers wear was initially intended to help them disappear into snowy landscapes should trouble arise.

Glöckler from Ebensee, Upper Austria, first half 20th century. *Photo: Volkskundemuseum, Vienna.*

Now only remotely resembling other Knocking Night customs, the *Glöcklern* make their appearance exclusively on Twelfth Night. Given the date and their proximity to the *Perchten* tradition so strong in the state of Salzburg, their annual run is understood to represent the passage of benevolent *Schönperchten*. The bells they wear, like the patterns they follow in their run (circles, loops and figure eights—all signs for infinity), are said to repel evil and sustain and strengthen vital forces slumbering beneath the snow.

Pelzmärtel, the St. Martin Monster

The *Rauhnächte* or Twelve Nights could not contain all the sinister folkloric beings and malevolent spirits that roamed the Austrian and German winters. Appearing already in the first week of December, the Krampus himself demonstrates this. But even before this devil could swing his first switch or rattle his first chain, November had already seen the entrance of similar spooks.

Appearing on the eve of St. Martin's Day (November 11), the "*Pelzmärtel*" (also "*Belzmärtel*," "*Belzmärde*," "*Bulzermärtl*," etc.) combined the gift-giving function of St. Nicholas with the frightening antics of the Krampus. Wearing furs or ragged clothes, he roamed the villages of western Bavaria (Swabia and Franconia) scattering treats as bait for children, whom he would playfully strike with switches as they dove to retrieve them. The name is a compound of "Martin" (its diminutive

"Märtel") and "*Pelz*," from "*pelzen*" meaning "to beat." (Some etymologies relate it less reliably to the word "*Pelz*" for "pelts," as in the fur costuming.) While this practice largely died out in the 19th and 20th century, in the Bavarian town of Wassertrüdingen, it persisted up through World War II, and since 1972 has been taken up again as an annual tradition. Like the Krampus, the Wassertrüdingen characters rove about in groups, wearing bells and brandishing switches. Their costumes replicate those worn before the war, namely, long fur coats and caps, along with waist-length false beards half covering their blackened faces. The treats they toss to children have traditionally been nuts, hence the regional variation on the name: *Nußmärtel*, or "Nut Martin."

The similarity of all this to the Nicholas-Krampus customs is not coincidental. Along with the Nicholas play traditions, and those of the *Perchten*, St. Martin's Day customs represent another likely influence on the development of the Krampus. Of particular interest is the matter of the switches and why the *Pelzmärtel* applies them. Though the *Nußmärtel* in Wassertrüdingen follows somewhat closer to the Nicholas tradition in pairing moral admonishments with the playful blows, this may be a modern accommodation as the traditional *Pelzmärtel* beatings are not described this way. In most cases, his beatings were disbursed quite without regard to good or bad behavior. They were just administered as part of the seasonal sport and as "good luck."

Especially in their luck-transferring function, the switches wielded by the *Pelzmärtel* are generally understood to be identical to the *Martinsgerte* ("Martin's switches") presented on this day by cowherds or other herdsmen to their employers. As St. Martin's Day was the traditional day in Austria and Bavaria to bring livestock in from the fields for the winter, it was on this day herdsmen collected their earnings from those whose animals they tended. As a token of gratitude for the payment and good luck talisman, they presented their employer's family with the *Martinsgerte*. The bundled branches were said to bring good fortune if left hanging through the winter. In Bavaria, the *Gerte* protected the cow-stalls and stables, and in Lower Austria, it was hung indoors to bless the home. Usually cut from oak, birch, and juniper, the number of twigs and juniper berries were said to predict the number of cattle or loads of hay the farmer might expect in the following year. In some cases, the switches were presented to children. In the spring, the switches would be used to drive the livestock back out to pasture, instilling health and fertility in the animals as each was struck upon departure.

Wolfauslassen in Rinchnach, Bavaria. *Photo by Dengler Günther © Tourismusverband Ostbayern e.V.*

Release the Wolves!

Processions of herdsmen returning on St. Martin's Day from the fields in some areas of Austria and Germany evolved into particularly festive rituals. To provide a bit more fanfare for their seasonal march, the bells no longer required by the animals were worn by members of their procession. The clamor raised could simply celebrate completion of a season's work but might also serve as intimidating warning to any employer not ready and fair with his pay. Because a primary duty of the herdsman was to protect his animals from predators, and because it was the wolf feared above all, this procession with its noisy bells came to be called the *Wolfauslassen* or *Wolfablassen*, meaning "letting out the wolves," or, occasionally, the *Wolfausläuten* ("ringing out the wolves"). Whatever the name, the meaning was the same: wolves may now leave their forest hiding places and traverse the pasturelands.

The *Wolfauslassen* tradition began sometime in the 18th century, and was particularly associated with the easternmost Bavarian Forest. Its evolution is sometimes described as beginning with shepherds themselves wearing the bells, but as the tradition gathered momentum, tagalong village youths were recruited, either to wear the bells, or—it's sometimes said—to dress and act the role of wild wolves. Even today where the tradition lives on but is no longer enacted by actual shepherds seeking payments, groups of bell-wearing men called the "Wolf" still follow an appointed "Shepherd" door to door begging for food, drink, or money (now usually for charity). The Shepherd carries as a staff a version of the *Martinsgerte*, in this case, a large branch stripped of smaller branches at the bottom, gathered at the top into a sort of bush.

Since the years following World War II, the *Wolfauslassen* has experienced a rebirth, particularly in the Bavarian towns of Rinchnach and Bodenmais, where the event has become popular with tourists. In the process, *Wolfauslassen* groups competing for attention have abandoned the normal cowbells once used and adopted enormous custom bells, sometimes measuring nearly 3 feet wide and weighing as much as 80 pounds. It's no longer youths carrying these massive bells but hearty adult males, who each wear a single bell strapped to the waist and positioned like an enormous fig leaf. Stopping in front of each house visited, the Wolves form a tight, inward-facing circle, and ring their bells in a frenzy of hyper-masculine pelvic thrusting, a movement delicately described by local historian Jose Dengler as having "a certain aura."

Winter Comes Early

The peculiar *Wolfauslassen* ritual did not develop in all areas. In most, the young tagalong participants came to play a more prominent role than herdsmen in the door-to-door processions. Especially further north in Germany, participating youths began carrying candles in hollowed turnips or pumpkins, and this practice, in turn, gave way to parades of paper lanterns and St. Martin bonfires still seen today. As with the *Pelzmärtel* customs, St. Martin's Day became a rather child-centered holiday (similar to St. Nicholas Day).

This emphasis on children and the domestic sphere may have had something to do with the season's agricultural labors coming to a close. For centuries, this day was regarded as the traditional beginning of winter. St. Martin's Day marked the beginning of the indoor life, one lit by those lanterns and fires that came to symbolize the holiday. It was a day for settling business and settling in. Leases and other annual contracts ended on November 11. It was a day of slaughter and preparation of the St. Martin's Day goose, and St. Martin's Day beef. The first wine of the year was also drunk on this day, and it was generally a time set aside to enjoy the fruits of one's labors, domestic warmth, and conviviality.

Feasting on St. Martin's Day also made sense as it once marked the last day before the Church's 40-day Advent fast anticipating Christmas (formerly called the "St. Martin's Lent"). But the feasting customs associated with this date are clearly older than the Church's 5th-century creation of Advent. The custom of slaughtering (and feasting on) livestock at a time when seasonal changes no longer allowed grazing would be as old as any form of animal husbandry in that climate. In the case of the ancient Germanic peoples, it's assumed that at some point between mid-October and mid-November, near the date later settled upon by the Church as St. Martin's, this slaughter and feast occurred. It marked not only the start of winter, but for the Germans (like the Gaelic Celts), the New Year. Most historians agree that the significant body of customs accumulated around the feast of St. Martin in German-speaking lands point to an important pre-existing Germanic New Year celebration rather than any native fascination with the Church's otherwise relatively inconspicuous saint.

Halloween Leans toward Christmas

As St. Martin's Day jack-o-lanterns and the Celtic New Year we call Halloween have been mentioned, it's time to address something many readers might've been wondering since I first mentioned costumed Austrian youth begging for treats on nights the dead wander the earth, namely: Aren't all these winter-spook customs just a version of Halloween? Similarly, readers may have found themselves nagged by another: Why do St. Nicholas Day customs duplicate Christmas?

While bigger answers can certainly be found for these big questions, a shorter answer would simply be: "Hay." More specifically, it was advances in the agricultural technology during the Carolingian era that allowed meadows to produce more fodder for the winter, thus allowing animals to be kept longer and butchered later. This caused the major winter feast (and a portion of its customs) originally celebrated on St. Martin's (11/11), to be later moved to St. Andrew's (11/30), then to St. Nicholas' Day (12/6), and finally, St. Thomas' Day (12/21) during the week of Christmas. Similarly, it's possible that thanks to improvements in agricultural technology, Germanic year-end customs like those associated with the visiting dead were nudged forward from November later into the *Rauhnächte*. This would account not only for parallels between various *Rauhnacht* traditions and those of the Celtic Halloween, but also for Nicholas customs edging their way into Christmas, and a general blurring of customs of the late fall and early winter.

While all this is general and speculative, we have more definitive detail suggesting that old St. Martin's Day customs were transferred to St. Nicholas Day. The *Pelzmärtel* and his switches, and the child-focused emphasis of St. Martin's Day offer obvious parallels with St. Nicholas Day customs. Even the Krampus tradition, with its pairing of a pastoral bishop leading a wolfish pack of bell-ringing beasts, might be compared to the visiting shepherds and wolves of the *Wolfauslassen*.

Some even project the matter further, seeing in the bundled branches of the *Martinsgerte* a precedent for the Christmas Tree.

The slide of St. Nicholas customs into Christmas can partly be explained in terms of Protestant efforts to preserve those customs apart from any association with the Catholic saint. However, the influence of the agricultural shift cannot be discounted. Not only would the traditional slaughter of swine only four days prior to Christmas on St. Thomas Day encourage lavish Christmas Day feasting and merriment, but a generalized cascade effect caused by moving the first day of winter from November to December would inevitably tend to push any number of interconnected traditions later into the month.

Even after Advent was shortened to eventually begin the fourth Sunday before Christmas (instead of St. Martin's Day), Martin's association with Christmas and winter remained fixed in the German mind. As personified by the folksy *Pelzmärtel*, a figure with no pretense at representing an actual Catholic saint, Martin made a better Protestant gift-giver than the robed and mitered Nicholas. In Franconia, a Protestant-leaning region straddling Bavaria and Baden-Württemberg, the figure became associated with Christmas gift-giving. Horned and wearing a suit of pleated straw with bells woven to the chest, a peculiar version of the *Pelzmärtel* appears on Christmas Eve and Day in the town of Bad Herrenalb and around the Gais Valley. Imported by Tyrolean immigrants in the 17th or 18th century, this figure accompanies a *Christkind* (a costumed angel representing the newborn Christ), who offers small gifts to children in exchange for pious recitations. This *Pelzmärtel*'s straw suit, which takes roughly 100 hours to create, has been woven by the same family for decades, and the identity of its wearer is a "secret of the Gais Valley."

Wild Barbaras

Around nightfall on St. Barbara's Day (December 4) in the town of Sonthofen, and a few other communities in the Upper Allgäu region of the Bavarian Alps, there appear groups of strange figures known as Bärbele ("Barbaras"), or sometimes "Wild Barbaras."

Dressed in old-fashioned peasant skirts, aprons, and kerchiefs, they each carry switches and wear a cowbell or two belted to the waist. Their most distinctive trait, however, are their masks, each handcrafted and covered in weird mosaics of lichen, moss, bits of acorns, pine cone, or other forest materials. Behind the masks are young women, who are ideally over the age of 16 and still unmarried—traditional parameters for participation as they approximate the virgin martyr Barbara at the time of her death.

In Sonthofen, roughly 80 Barbaras annually sweep through the town's central pedestrian areas, administering light blows to those approaching too close and awarding apples, cookies, or nuts to well behaved children and their mothers. In a reversal of the macho Krampus tradition, the all-female *Bärbele* tend to target young men with sharper and more frequent blows to the lower leg, though these, like the blows of the *Pelzmärtel*, are not punitive and generally said to convey good luck or vitality. Blows often may continue until the victim begins to hop or dance to the satisfaction of the attacking *Bärbele*. In some other areas, the Barbaras may visit homes, using brooms to symbolically sweep evil from the home, into the yard, and out to the street. It is said that the more troubling evil spirits that can't be removed by the *Bärbele* must wait two days to be exorcised by the visits of St. Nicholas and his accompanying devils, regionally named *Klausen*.

The Barbara run or *Bärbeletreiben* ("Barbara drive" or "bustle") is of indeterminate origin, but is understood to be very old. The practice had lapsed and nearly fallen into obscurity when efforts to resurrect it began in the late 1970s. Since 1985, the event occurs annually in a growing number of communities. The area's special relationship to St. Barbara is further indicated by the fact that her day, rather than St. Nicholas Day, was formerly the local day for children to receive gifts.

The Allgäu *Bärbeletreiben* is not to be confused with the *Bärbelilaufen* of Upper Franconia, in which boys dressed in ragged disguises went out after dark with switches, striking any young woman who dared to show her face, calling her shameful names. The actions of the boys, called "Torture Fathers" (*Folterv

äter*), are said to allude to the martyrdom of the saint. Unsurprisingly, this less than charming custom has not survived into the 21st century.

A final bit of fortunetelling attached to St. Barbara's Day reminiscent of the *Rauhnacht* customs is that of *Barbarazweige* ("Barbara branches"). These are cut from a blooming tree brought inside on this day and placed in water. A flowering fruit tree, like cherry, plum, or apple, is traditional, but birch, hazel, or others may be used. Once indoors, the warmth causes buds or blooms to appear. These are regarded as bringing luck for the coming year. Their number can indicate the size of the year's crop; branches can be assigned by female hopefuls to various suitors to indicate a future groom, and systems have even been contrived whereby the buds might predict lottery numbers. References to *Barbarazweige* appear as early as the 13th century, and the tradition is supposed to be based on an incident during which the saint's robe caught on a branch as she was being dragged off to prison. She is said to have preserved the broken branch in her cell, standing it in a cup of water where it thrived, and at the hour of her execution, bloomed.

Opposite and above: "Wild Barbaras," masked for St. Barbara's Day in Sonthofen, Bavaria.
Photos © Sonthofen Klausenverein.

A Dark St. Lucy

On St. Lucy's Day (December 13) the *"schiache Luz,"* ("bad" or "ugly" Lucy), *"bluadige Luz"* ("bloody Lucy"), or *Lutzelfrau* appeared in Bavaria and Austria. The *Luz* bears a distinct similarity to Frau Perchta. She is described as ugly, ragged, and disheveled, and likewise equipped with a gutting knife or sickle, or sometimes a ladle wielded as a club. She may also sport an iron nose. Like Perchta, she regulated the craft of spinning, destroying all unfinished work left out on the night dedicated to her.

Around Wunsiedel, Bavaria, she was appeased with food offerings in hopes she would bless the fields. Like Perchta, she was sometimes impersonated by costumed villagers, who might appear wrapped in white sheets, usually veiled, masked, or even with face covered by a kitchen sieve. The *Luz* might creep quietly into homes, surprising occupants with frightful bleating sounds before disappearing, or she might boldly announce herself, holding her empty bowl and knife, and crying, "A bowl full of blood! A bowl full of guts!" In the Bavarian Forest, she might be costumed as a horned nanny goat or accompanied by the goat-like *Habergeiß* or other monsters. In the town of Tettenweis, she appeared in a straw robe and armed with a knife. In the area around Osterhofen, she wore a blood-red coat and pointed cap. Elsewhere she sometimes took the form of a swine.

In Landau an der Isar, she had a reputation for throwing disobedient children into the river. In Eisenstein she wound up the intestines of gutted children on her distaff. In Vilstal she appeared holding a bloody human head on a plate. And in Grafenau, she was said to scrape away the tongue or skins of naughty children with broken glass. Like Perchta, she might also show a benevolent side, handing out cookies, nuts, and dried fruits to obedient children. In some Tyrolean communities, she was the original gift-bearer for girls, while the gifts St. Nicholas brought were reserved for boys.

St. Lucy figures from Bohemia. Drawing by Karel Rozum for *Den se krátí, noc se dlouží* ("The Day is Short, the Night Lengthens") (1910).

The "dark Lucy" seems to be derived from the mythologies of Perchta, Holda, or the Slavic witch Baba Yaga. She's widely distributed, from Bavaria through eastern Austria, Hungary, the Czech Republic, Slovenia, Slovakia, and western Croatia. She also appeared in Scandinavia, particularly Sweden, where St. Lucy's wicked counterpart, the *Lussi*, was well known for haunting the *Lussinatta* ("Lucy Night"). On this night she flies through the skies like Holda, or the Wild Hunter, with her ghostly retinue called the *Lussen*, *Lussiner*, or the *Lussegubber*.

St. Lucy's night, though outside the *Rauhnächte*, was nonetheless similarly associated with prognostication and other supernatural happenings. At midnight, young men would scan the skies for the *Luzieschein*, a mysterious luminosity wherein were contained shapes of things to come. Young women were to find a willow tree, pull back the bark, and cut a small cross into the green wood below. Moistening the wood, they would then press back the bark to heal. Peeling it away again on New Year's Day would reveal new patterns from which the future might be read. Attacks from witches were particularly feared on this night, and prayers and incense were required in Lower Austria to fend off such dangers. St. Lucy's night also appears as a favored time for werewolf transformations and attacks, according to testimonies in werewolf trials. The *Drude* was also feared on these nights, and could only be barred by painting pentagrams on the doorstep of one's quarters.

Bloody Thomas   On the eve or in the night of St. Thomas Day (December 21), another monstrous figure appeared in the villages of Lower Bavaria and the Bavarian Forest. This demon or ogre went by the name "Bloody Thomas," rendered variously as "*Bluadige Dammal,*" "*Bluatige Thamerl,*" etc. He might also be "*Dammerl mit 'm Hammerl*" ("Thomas with the hammer"), referring to the large blood-drenched hammer he's said to brandish. Because December 21 was a traditional day of slaughter and sausage-making in the region, many believe the figure was inspired by the impressions made by blood-drenched butchers out and about on this day. According to a number of 19th-century sources, a popular St. Thomas Day's prank had a farmer drenched to the toes in blood after the day's slaughter frightening his children or young relatives. First banging on the cottage door and thundering out some threats about bashing children's skulls, he would then—with the children's full and fearful attention upon him—open the door a crack, and ever-so-slowly push one gory leg through the door. Apparently, this was all that was needed to clear the room, and no further disclosure was necessary.

It was said that on this night, St. Thomas would appear at midnight in a chariot of fire and fly to the churchyard to rendezvous with the dead. He would call from their graves all baptized in his name, and all these Thomas-souls would gather in prayer, thereby causing a cross set up over the graveyard to strangely luminesce. While stories like this circulated, few eyewitnesses would venture near graveyards on this night, most instead staying indoors directing prayers for protection to the saint and listening for the thunder of his passing chariot. The head of the house might, however, venture out to sprinkle the cattle with holy water or with salt blessed in the saint's name. Cattle might also be fed bread, salt, and bayberries consecrated to Thomas in order to stave off disease in the coming year.

Like customs related to the *Luz*, traditions associated with Bloody Thomas have fallen from practice. It is not clear how common it was to dress up as Bloody Thomas on this day, but there are 19th and early 20th-century surveys of folk customs describing this dark Thomas appearing "like a *Percht*," or a horned beast, or having "a devil's face." And there are also mentions of figures going by the names *Pelzthomas* ("fur Thomas"), *Kettenthomas* ("chains Thomas"), *Rumpelthomas* ("noisy Thomas"), and *Hollethomas* (possibly related to Frau Holle, or to *Hölle*, i.e., "hell"). Mysterious as all these may now be, one St. Thomas custom still survives in the Styrian town of Gams bei Hieflau, Austria. This is the "Thomas-Nicholas" (*Thomas-nikolo, -niglo, -nigl,* etc.) first mentioned in the 19th century. As the name suggests, this is really a St. Thomas Day version of the better known Nicholas customs, specifically, the costumed house visit. The costumed group includes, in lieu of a St. Nicholas, a St. Thomas dressed as a bishop, a second angelic "White Thomas" or "Light-bringer" (who carries a multi-tiered candlestick as a staff), the confusingly named "Nicholas-wife" (*Nikolofrau*), especially confusing here as there is no actual Nicholas, a couple Sack-carriers, an Old Man, several regular Krampuses, and the *Thomashutzn*. The last is represented by a performer wearing furs and an elongated beak. Looking something like a monstrous Kiwi bird, this creature is regarded as a sort of *Vogelpercht* (bird-*Percht*), and its role is largely limited to ominously, silently crouching in a corner during house visits, though it was once said to whisk away naughty children. The Krampuses here go by the local name *Rauchn*, from the old word for "fur." In this region, the *Rauhnächte* begin on December 21 and run the 12 nights to the New Year instead of Epiphany.

Bavarian Forest *Rauhnacht* Celebrations

The most prominent celebrations of the *Rauhnächte* today are the *Perchten* events to be discussed later. However, there are some notable exceptions focusing on other aspects and figures of the *Rauhnacht* mythology. Most of these events seem to have established themselves in the Bavarian Forest, the mountainous region of Lower Bavaria near the Czech border. The Waldkirchen *Rauhnacht*, the largest and oldest of these, at its peak drew roughly 7,000 visitors, but since 2008 has faced competition from similar events created by neighboring towns eager for tourism.

Staged by torchlight each Twelfth Night in the town square, the production includes dozens of masked characters and participation from folkloric groups from around the region. There are demonstrations of traditional whip artistry (*Goaßlschnalzern*), the firing of canons, or *Böllerschützen*—both forms of *Lärmbräuche* ("noise customs") used to frighten off evil spirits. There is also a performance of bell ringing by a *Wolfauslassen* group, even though this St. Martin's Day activity traditionally lies outside the calendric *Rauhnacht period*. The event becomes interactive with a crowd-jostling rumpus of costumed *Rauhnacht* spooks intended to represent the company of the Wild Hunt.

Though local *Rauhnacht* references date back to 1725, the public traditions practiced in Waldkirchen were interrupted by World War I and ended by World War II. It was not until 1978 that a local art teacher, Rupert Berndl, inspired by readings on the subject, crafted *Rauhnacht* masks and reignited interest in the custom, eventually receiving guidance from those who remembered pre-war practice.

This is not to say the Waldkirchen event is a literal revival of local folk custom. It is less folk ritual than presentation *about* folk ritual. The event weaves a narrative around masks Berndl created, giving these characters roles in illustrating and explaining seasonal superstitions. For instance, to demonstrate the notion that laundry must not be left out during the *Rauhnächte*, a drying rack is constructed in the town square, and the script calls for costumed ghosts and a Grim Reaper to hover close until driven off by a troupe of witches burning pots of incense. All of this is explained in voiceover, a duty at times assumed by a costumed Bloody Thomas. The program ends with the burning of a straw effigy. This effigy, Thomas explains (during a speech filled with satiric references to the sins of local politicians), represents "all the negatives of the old year." While witches may never have allied with man against the spooks of *Rauhnacht*, and Bloody Thomas was never a loquacious wag, the program makes up for its factual skew in sheer volume of masked and costumed characters. Among the 40-plus *Rauhnachtgeister* (*Rauhnacht* spirits) are various forest spirits like the *Schrazln* ("forest spirit") and *Moosweiberl* ("Moss-wife"), the *Drude*, the towering *Habergeiß*, devils beating drums, and the *Seelvögl* ("soul-bird") clapping its hinged beak at spectators.

Though some of these costumed figures are never mentioned in historical records as being part of seasonal customs and may be strictly modern interpolations intended to further the spectacle, at the heart of the production is a practice that is definitely known to be part of the region's history. This is the *Rauhnudelbetteln* or begging for *Rauhnudl*, a type of jam-filled doughnut named for the season. Over time *Rauhnudl* came to mean simply any small gift, sweets (or more recently, money) offered those going door-to-door singing a rhyme traditional to the season. Roughly translated, the most popular verse of this rhyme says:

> *Today is the Rauhnacht!*
> *Who summoned (or defied) it?*
> *An old man crawled down the stairs,*
> *Broke his bones, large and small.*
> *Doughnuts out! Doughnuts out!*
> *Or I'll bust a hole in your house.*

Perhaps more rhyme for rhyme's sake than anything else, the song, at least, leaves no doubt about the need for doughnuts. Traditionally, sweets provided by the homeowner would be stuck on a sharpened stick or similar contrivance held out by the singers. This practice is duplicated in the Waldkirchen event as the costumed troupe circulates through the town square serenading shopkeepers and collecting doughnuts hung on poles, pitchforks, horns, or other items handy to the *Rauhnacht* spirits. Troupe members distribute treats received to spectators, especially children. Participating merchants privately offer the *Rauhnudl*, brandy, and sausage. Following the *Rauhnacht* spirits as they move from shop to shop, spectators are invited to join the costumed troupe in song, and in this way, the event approaches the interactivity of an authentic folk ritual.

Rauhnacht celebration, Waldkirchen, Germany. *Photo © Tourismusbüro Waldkirchen.*

Similar Twelfth Night *Rauhnacht* events in the Bavarian Forest are held in St. Englmar, Rinchnach, and Lam. In Altreichenau the *Drude* is the focus, as Bloody Thomas is in Waldkirchen. She does not, however, fare as well as Thomas. The Altreichenau narrative has her captured and burned by the end of the evening. The Koishüttler *Lousnach* ("oracle night," a regional synonym for "*Rauhnacht*") is hosted by a scarecrow, Dodama, and features a Frau Perchta, Luzei (the dark St. Lucy), the glassworks-haunting goblin Durandl, and other figures straddling the worlds of history and legend. Those include ghosts of the wicked Chatelaine of Castle Rammelsberg transformed into the witch Wecklin, the doomy ghost of the "Forest Prophet" Mühlhiasl, and the half-man, half-monster cowherd Woidhaus-Mich.

The World of the Krampus

At first blush, the Krampus seemed to defy every American expectation of Christmas. He fit into nothing we knew about the holiday. But in this chapter, as we've cultivated his landscape and given him some family, he can hardly seem so inconceivable. His proper context is all these ghostly processions and monsters we've met haunting the nights from St. Martin's though Epiphany, the beastly bifurcations of St. Lucy and St. Thomas, the fur-covered St. Martin and his good-luck switches, the wild wolves let loose and hung with cowbells, the door-to-door performances of Knocking Nights and *Rauhnudelbetteln*. Only his closest cousins, the *Perchten*, remain to be examined in further detail, and this is the task we will next undertake.

Chapter Seven

THE PERCHTEN

A Parade in Gastein

From the waist up, he is a goat. Albeit a rather distended two-legged goat. Over perfectly ordinary boots and street clothes, he wears a shaggy fur coat, but where human head and shoulders should be, the figure melts into a long, attenuated neck covered in animal hides, stretching a yard or so over parade spectators, and surmounted by a wickedly grinning goat head. Though the neck may be more giraffe than goat, its purpose becomes evident as the creature craftily sways and dips, clacking its jaw and snatching the hat from an onlooker standing at some distance.

This is the *Habergeiß* (or in the dialect, *Habergoaß*). He is a well-known type of *Percht* as portrayed for decades in the Gastein *Perchtenlauf*. Looking at the weird assembly marching down the snowy streets on Epiphany Day, it's hard to draw any conclusions as to what exactly a *Percht* may be. I have spoken of the *Perchten* as historic forerunners of the Krampus, and indeed there is a subspecies that looks for all the world like a Krampus, but he's hard to find in this crowd of wildly diverse characters.

We might recognize Frau Perchta (or Domina Perchta as she's sometimes called here) by her Janus-like mask, greeting onlookers with a benevolent face, then spinning to show a bestial visage, twisted and snarling, with yellow teeth and skin dark as mummy leather. There are the witches we associate with Perchta with their gnarled wooden masks and twig brooms. There's the Gastein version of the *Schnabelpercht*, a hulking bearlike birdlike thing snapping its saw-tooth beak. There are men on a roof kicking cascades of snow down over laughing spectators,

Habergeiß wrangler and *Tafelperchten* at *Perchtenlauf* in Gastein, Austria.
Photo © Gasteinertal.com.

one covered in moss like some swamp monster, another encrusted in pinecones, and the third costumed as a chimney sweep and black with soot. There are grown men in 19th-century cavalry uniforms cracking whips and mounted on ridiculous hobbyhorses. There are ladies with distinct Adam's apples and unusually heavy eyebrows, stuffed into traditional folkloric dress, complete with aprons, starched collars, and dainty caps.

And there are these other figures. From the head down, they are rather straightforward examples of old imperialist pomp—uniforms decked with tassels, aiguillettes, and medallions, white gloves and drawn sabers at the shoulder. But the caps they wear erupt into strange surrealist spectacle. One wears a taxidermied ibex on his head, another the front half of a stuffed elk, a third balances a tableau of badger, weasel, and goat, the latter only a head, posed as if munching pine boughs framing the assembly.

Other caps shoot up impossibly high into ornate wedding-cake structures configured as pyramids, cones, and onion domes. These are exuberantly ornamented with glittering mirrors and more mirrors, flowers, ribbons, feathers, foliage, crosses, heraldic devices, and other talismans.

Even more confusing perhaps is the random array of figures trailing behind—a man in a bear suit, some figures dressed in Biblical costume, a clown, a theatrical vendor of tonics and elixirs, another selling bras.

Finding a Pagan *Percht*

Where is the genuine pagan folklore in this jumble of carnivalesque frivolities? Gastein's *Perchtenlauf* is the oldest celebration of its kind, so one would expect to find pagan elements here if anywhere, but many scholars now question the extent to which pre-Christian folklore actually plays a role in the proceedings. The masked figure of Frau Perchta is present, but she is not particularly prominent in this horde. We may recognize the witches as Perchta's subjects, but they do not necessarily march aside her, or perform in a way that clearly associates them with her.

There are no parade figures representing the *Heimchen* or other departed spirits most prominently associated with Perchta. The devils Christian teaching associated with Frau Perchta are barely represented. While folklore around the Gastein *Perchtenlauf* speaks of demonic *Schiachperchten*, the parade does little to highlight or articulate the role of such diabolic beings. In the procession, these

Frau Perchta at Gastein Perchtenlauf. *Photo © Gasteinertal.com.*

Percht from Barmstoana Perchten, Hallein, Austria. *Photo © Roland Käfer.*

horned characters are called by the same regional names used for the Krampus (*Kramperl, Klaubauf*) and are costumed more or less identically. What's more, there are only a handful of these figures compared to the more than roughly 30 *Tafelperchten* outfitted in their monumental caps.

While benevolent *Schönperchten* may be the focus of Gastein's celebration, the appearance of these figures in the parade dates only to the middle of the 19th century. Even though early folklore may have sometime associated *Perchten* with good fortune, the name and probably concept of *Schönperchten* first appears contemporaneously with the emergence of 19th-century *Tafelperchten*, so we are hardly encountering pre-Christian mysteries here.

"Das Perchtenlaufen im Salzburgischen" by Oskar Gräf for *Die Gartenlaube* (1892).

The *Habergeiß*

If we return to the figure first mentioned in this chapter, the *Habergeiß*, we gain a better foothold in the *Perchten's* mythology. Though the word *Perchten* tends to refer rather loosely to an undifferentiated group of Alpine winter demons, this *Percht* offers a uniquely well-defined body of folklore.

The two-legged Gastein embodiment of the creature is only one of many ways the *Habergeiß* is represented. He often appears as an immense four-legged beast impersonated by two performers hidden under hides or blankets. Sometimes there are four men, with the foremost operating the head (carved from wood or crafted out of other materials, sometimes even an animal skull). Occasionally it's just one man hunching forward, clutching wooden canes, sticks, or brooms to simulate legs. Sometimes the long neck is even done away with, and the performer wears an outfit similar to the Krampus but with a mask carved to look like a goat.

Along with appearing as a *Percht* in *Perchten* events, the creature is associated with the Wild Hunt, and would show up in Nicholas plays or processions. Less frequently it's a figure in Carnival parades, and in earlier times, it would even make appearances at weddings to convey a blessing upon the couple.

As with any creature of the imagination, the *Habergeiß*, before it came to be embodied as a costumed figure, was of more ambiguous form. Though most often

described as a sort of goat, it sometimes possessed only three legs, two hind and one foreleg, or it might be imagined as a goat with ponderous horse hooves, or a goat with wings. This birdlike nature is often mentioned. Sometimes it's a great and loathsome bird with three legs. Or is half-bird, half-goat. In Tyrol it could be a bird that somehow looked like a man. In Styria and Carinthia, it could even be a winged dragon, or the embodiment of the Devil, or the Dark One's mount. Sometimes it was said to visit sleeping victims at night and press its weight upon them like the *Drude*, causing what we now call sleep paralysis.

In Styria, one legend identified the *Habergeiß* as the ghost of goat that plunged from a cliff with its master during a flight from a creditor eager to seize the animal. Other stories describe it as a departed soul in the shape of a goat haunting the fields around a home in which someone lies dying.

While it was not easily seen, it was often heard. Its voice was sometimes like the bleating of a goat, at others, the cackling of a goblin, the shriek of an owl, or the croaking of a toad. Woe to any who would dare to imitate its hideous call; the *Habergeiß* would come by night and attack him. The cry of the *Habergeiß* usually heralded misfortune, particularly if it followed the ringing of the Ave Maria. Should its call precede the bells, however, good fortune might follow. Hearing its call in the autumn foretold a long and grueling winter, though sometimes its call, like the cuckoo's, could announce the coming of spring.

The *Habergeiß* particularly bedeviled farmers. Its appearance caused cows to go dry or grow thin and turned milk sour. It was particularly destructive to crops. It would come amidst hailstorms that battered the plants, trample or cut the grain, or scatter ordered piles of cut grain into neighbors' fields. Sometimes it appeared in the company of, or was ridden by, the *Pilwiz*, an evil spirit that walked or rode through fields with sickles at its feet, leaving swathes of destruction.

A Spirit of the Fields

The *Habergeiß* has often been said to essentially represent a spirit of the fields, one identified with grain. The word *Haber*, after all, is an Austrian word for "oats" and "*Geiß*" a dialect word for "female goat." However, this etymology has been widely disputed by those deriving "*Haber*" instead from the Proto-Germanic "*Hafr*" used for male goats, making the creature a sort of male-female enigma. Others have suggested that "*Geiß*" is in fact a corruption of "*Geist*" (spirit).

Habergeiß mask from a NIcholas play. Pustertal, South Tyrol. ca 1900.
Photo: Christa Knott © Volkskundemuseum, Vienna.

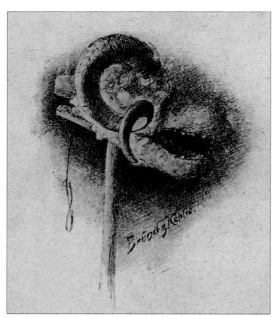

Left: *Habergeiß* from German-settled German Bohemia. Drawing by Karel Rozum for *Den se krátí, noc se dlouží* ("The Day is Short, the Night Lengthens"), 1910.
Right: *Habergeiß*, Buchbach, Lower Austria (ca. 1900). *Photo © Volkskundemuseum, Vienna.*

Habergeiß at Nicholas play in Tauplitz, Austria. *Photo © Wolfgang Böhm.*

Whatever the source of this mysterious name, there is an association between the name and folk customs associated with grain harvest. In a 1905 volume on "forest and field cults" by Wilhelm Mannhardt and Walter Heuschkel, many of these are detailed. In Straubing in Lower Bavaria, the last grain to be cut was called "the *Korngeiß, Weizengeiß,* or *Habergeiß.*" (corn-, wheat-, or oat-goat), and on the gathered sheaves, two horns were placed. In Upper Austria, "*Habergeiß*" could be a name for the last bit of stubble cut. In Swabian Germany, reapers created from wood and oat sheaves the figure of a goat, which was decorated with flowers and set out to honor the field, and they called this a *Habergeiß*. Or it could be a straw goat left as a taunt to the neighbor slow to finish his harvest, or as mockery for any competition lost.

Cave of the *Habergeiß*

The often-questionable tendency to interpret folk practice in terms of ancient and forgotten fertility rites was in vogue at the time of the above-mentioned volume's publication. Many peasant customs were assumed to be of much older provenance than researchers believe today. Near Bad Griesbach in Bavaria, there is even a boulder that is said to bear a carving of a *Habergeiß* dating to the Stone Age. The carving, whatever it truly represents, can be viewed in a small cave formed by two curiously placed boulders leaning together. The area is long assumed to be haunted, and the boulders are said to have been deposited there by the Devil, who was startled by church bells while on his way to drop the stones on the nearby Tettenweis monastery. The carving is believed to depict a meter-high *Habergeiß* (also simply identified as the Devil). It appears to be dancing with small horses and other characters. The style of the carving, and stone-age artifacts recovered around the site, have suggested to locals a prehistoric origin.

The cave and its reputation have even served as inspiration for a contemporary *Perchten* group in nearby Rottal, the *Brauchtumsverein Rottaler Habergoaß, Hexn und Rauwuggl,* whose members costume themselves as the *Habergeiß* as well as witches and *Rauwuggl,* an obscure monster resembling a Krampus without horns. Beginning in the 1700s, the cave also served as the headquarters or "church" of a secret society known as the *Haberfeld* movement. The *Haberfelder* were a masked vigilante group expressing community outrage at certain transgressions (especially adultery and extramarital pregnancies) through intimidating nocturnal visits to the homes of those accused. Similar to the charivari in France, the *Haberfelder* used guns, firecrackers, whips, drums, horns, and other noisemakers to frighten the victim and possibly force them from hiding to offer a confession.

The society's name comes from the word for "field" (*Feld*), and "*Haber*," which can be taken here to mean "fellow" or, some say, "goat," as goat skins were often part of the *Haberfelder's* disguise, along with masks, dark clothes, and blackened faces.

Goats Everywhere

We've defined the *Perchten* as winter spirits of the Austrian and Bavarian Alps somehow associated with Frau Perchta or with the eve of Epiphany, "the shining night," "*giberahta naht.*" Along with the manlike *Percht* known in Gastein as the *Kramperl*, the goat-like *Habergeiß* is the only well-articulated representative of the genus.

What is surprising about the creature is the number of similar figures that appear in Christmas and New Year's traditions far removed from the *Perchten's* home. In the introduction to this book, I've already mentioned the Welsh *Mari Lywd* represented during the Twelve Nights as a horse skull paraded on a pole by draped performers. While this might be dismissed as chance resemblance, there are other geographically closer instances where a direct borrowing or common lineage seems more possible.

Though once more widespread, the Swiss *Schnabelgeiß* ("beak-goat") still can be found around Christmas in the area around Zürich. Like the *Habergeiß*, this creature is represented by a draped performer holding a goat-head with a hinged jaw. It was one of the *Spräggelen*, frightening spirits who visited homes to ensure good behavior among children and young women working as spinners. In the Italian South Tyrolean town of Termeno, the Egetmann Carnival parade features similarly contrived but particularly large creatures known as *Schnappvieh* ("snap-beasts") or *Wuddelen*.

Oddly enough, most of these *Habergeiß* lookalikes are found far to the North, nearer the North Sea and especially the Baltic coastal regions that were once part of the German Empire. In old Pomerania, now divided between northeast Germany and Poland, the *Klapperbock* ("snapping buck") also consisted of a hidden performer and snapping head on a stick. It would appear at Christmas to frighten children who had neglected prayers and other duties, and was usually accompanied by someone costumed in straw as a "bear," and another costumed as a stork, though exactly how a stork costume was realized is not clear.

A fourth traditional companion in this troupe might be the *Schimmel* (a gray, white, or ghostly horse). While the figure might be represented by a crouched, draped performer with puppet head, the phantom horse might also appear as a hobby-horse ridden by a ghost rider, the *Schimmelreiter*. The folklore of the *Schim-*

melreiter is also found west of Pomerania in the northern lowlands of the German state of Schleswig-Holstein. The *Schimmelreiter* is probably best known to most Germans through Theodor Storm's 1888 novella of that name, in which tales of the phantom rider frame hard-edged depictions of life on the windswept heaths and shorelines of Northern Frisia.

In the Prussian Empire's more Polish regions, where the goat was often known as the *Turoń*, similar animal mumming customs thrived. In Silesia a larger version of the *Schimmelreiter* might consist of three or even four youths hidden under draped sheets, and a rider, who might also be veiled. Sometimes the rider would wear atop his head a pot filled with burning coals cut like a jack-o-lantern with glowing eyes and mouth. In Lithuanian East Prussia, the *Schimmel's* head was sometimes a horse skull with lights installed in the eye sockets. Here too, the horse was accompanied by traditional straw bear, stork, and a goat with snapping jaw.

A Scandinavian Connection

Across the Baltic Sea in Finland, there is the *Joulupukki* or "Yule buck," also once represented by a draped performer holding or wearing what looked like a goat head. This sometimes frightening gift-bringer over the years became strangely intermingled and finally more or less replaced by a figure mostly identical with the more benevolent American Santa Claus. A sort of fanciful hybrid of the monstrous character and the modern St. Nick was amusingly depicted in the 2010 Finnish movie *Rare Exports*. A similar figure, *Nuuttipukki*, also once visited homes in Sweden and Finland on January 13, St. Knut's Day. From the 11th century, we also have reports of Holy Innocents' Day celebrations involving a man costumed as a goat led by St. Nicholas. Related mumming customs continued throughout the 19th century and into the early years of the 20th. Sometimes the Krampus is compared to these figures.

There is also a Scandinavian harvest tradition similar to that mentioned above. The last sheaf of grain was sometimes described as a goat or as a "Yule buck" (*Julbock*) and kept through Christmas as a magical token. As a seasonal prank, straw or wooden effigies of a goat were likewise secretly hidden on neighbors' property with tradition demanding the object be returned in like manner.

Origins of the *Habergeiß*

My reasons for so thoroughly enumerating these figures is that their geographic dispersion might be taken to indicate historical diffusion of the *Habergeiß* figure, and by extension, the whole *Perchten* mythology.

Having preserved pagan beliefs and practice long after Christianity had been assimilated into the rest of Europe, Scandinavian tradition has always represented an enticing model of pre-Christian Germanic custom in regions to the south. If we are searching for ancient and unadulterated pagan elements within the *Perchten* folklore, this connection between the Alpine *Habergeiß* and Nordic traditions seems particularly interesting. The presence of the *Klapperbock* and similar figures near the Baltic and North Sea coasts of the old German empire hints at a southward diffusion from Scandinavia, one which parallels that first wave of migration that brought Germanic peoples south into the region between Germany's Oder and Elbe rivers around 1000 BC.

However, there are immense gaps—both chronological and geographic—between the appearance of the *Habergeiß* and its fellow *Perchten* in the Alps during the Christian era and what little is known of the beliefs and practices of pre-Christian Germanic tribes. While there are similarities between the folklore of the Alpine regions and Germanic beliefs further north (e.g., those between Perchta and Holda), there is a geographic missing link when it comes to the *Habergeiß*. Figures resembling the *Habergeiß* are difficult or impossible to find in those central regions between the Alps and the remote northernmost edge of the old German Empire.

Ultimately, the possible diffusion of folkloric influences from Nordic sources requires an examination of tribal migrations supported by archeological and linguistic evidence far beyond the scope of this book. While this topic would seem fruitful for investigation, any theories connecting southern German traditions with Nordic beliefs are now subject to particularly skeptical scrutiny thanks to the wildly speculative scholarship of Third Reich scholars bent on discovering "pure" Nordic roots for any and all folkways present in German-speaking lands.

Roman influence or Romanized Celtic influence on the *Perchten* can also not be ruled out when considering figures, which—like the *Habergeiß*—appear in far-flung locations once under Roman control. In Chapter Two, we have already encountered a possible common thread in the similarly widespread processions of men costumed as "horned beasts" during the Roman January Kalends.

Traditions of the Late Roman Empire tended to be particularly well-preserved by the Eastern Church and its associated folk culture. Not surprisingly, traditions of New Year's and Christmas animal masking (similar to that of the Roman Kalends) is quite prevalent in lands dominated by or experiencing significant contact with the Orthodox Church. The word "Kalends" itself is preserved in the names for these customs in these regions, i.e., "*koliada*" in Russian and Ukrainian, "*kolęda*" in Polish, and "*koleda*" in Czech, Slovak, and Croatian. In most of these traditions, figures similar to the *Habergeiß* have been or are represented.

Disciplined by a Goat   The function of the *Habergeiß* in Alpine culture is to enforce the social order. A visit from a costumed *Habergeiß* blessed those who perpetuated that order through marriage, and at the same time represented, according to Mannhardt and Heuschkel, "a hand of justice by pursuing, for example, sinners," and frightening the disobedient including "children who torture animals and lazy maids." It attacked troublemakers who dare to wander into the grain fields or forests where they do not belong. This association with reward and punishment is most prevalent in the many instances of the *Habergeiß* appearing alongside Nicholas.

The authors even cite a practice from Bavaria's Bohemian Forest in which the *Habergeiß* is made to explicitly play a role like that of the dark St. Lucy, describing a creature represented "as a goat with a spread-over sheet and horns poking through but with the name 'Luzia' as it personifies that saint's day." Like Perchta, the figure "exhorts the children to pray, bestows upon them tasty fruit, and threatens the wicked with the prospect of having their bellies slit and stuffed with straw and pebbles."

Magic Rite or Playful Celebration?   Though we often discuss folkloric entities in terms of peasant superstition, as beings greatly feared and respected by rural populations, it should be recognized that more often than not, when the *Perchten* appeared as costumed figures, it was understood as a distracting entertainment for adults or edifying game for children. The same must be said of the Krampus. Too much can easily be made of a possible magic function in driving off evil, awakening the spring, or blessing field. Though magical thinking might have been more at home in remote Alpine villages of the 18th and 19th century than our world today, looking for magical intent every time a farmer dons a pair of goat horns can be as ridiculous as regarding the appearance of a costumed Uncle Sam parading on July 4th as a ritual to ensure American military victory.

One of the earliest records of a procession in which the Holda-Perchta folklore is represented describes something closer to a civic festivity than magical ritual. Though it is Eckhart rather than Holda herself mentioned, it seems to be the same horde of wandering souls referenced. In 1688, Lutheran minister P.C. Hilscher describes the custom then extant in Frankfurt:

> Every year a number of youths were paid to take a large cart covered with leaves from door to door, to the accompaniment of songs and predictions which, to prevent errors, they had been taught by experienced people. The populace asserts that in this way the memory of Eckhart's army is celebrated.

Witchcraft scholar Carlo Ginzburg, in his *Ecstasies: Deciphering the Witches' Sabbath*, points out that in this case, the performers were paid actors rather than earnest petitioners of the spirits. While perhaps the more superstitious might believe that secrets of the future could be discovered within Holda's Venusberg, here the prognostications would have been mostly offered in the spirit of fun, or as a commemoration of a time when such things were widely believed (before the relatively early date of 1688, it should be noted). If anything, the description seems to hint at something a bit cynical, with "experienced people" teaching the youths how to "prevent errors" in their fortunetelling, perhaps by keeping pronouncements extremely general, ambiguous, and hard to verify.

The Wild Hunt of Untersberg

Aside from the handful of events in Austria's Pongau region (where Gastein is located), the oldest *Perchten* events date only to the years after World War II. The Wild Hunt of Untersberg, held annually in the shadow of the Untersberg Mountain on the southern outskirts of metropolitan Salzburg, is one of these. While the *Perchten* are most strongly associated the *Rauhnächte*, the Untersberg event brings them out earlier in December, on the second Thursday of Advent. Likely the date is borrowed from local "knocking" customs (*Anklöpfeln*) occurring on Thursdays in Advent. Though it was only organized in current form in 1949, thanks to its incorporation of older elements of local customs like *Anklöpfeln*, it's sometimes said to have roots in the 1880s. The event is rather meticulously anchored in regional folklore, particularly tales of phantoms said to pass over the swamplands of the now-dried Leopoldskron Moor or spirits associated with the Untersberg Mountain.

Accompanied by torchbearers, the maskers, all hung with jangling bells, march to the beat of a drummer costumed as Death. The troupe is limited to twelve performers, a number often traditional for *Perchten*, and also includes the Moss-wife often mentioned as prey pursued by the Wild Hunter, a *Baumpercht* (a tree spirit covered in bark and fir branches), a costumed bear and his wrangler, a witch, the boar *Saurüssel*, the two-man, four-legged *Habergeiß*, the rooster *Hahnengickerl* symbolizing vigilance and fertility, the benevolent giant of Salzburg lore Abfal-tersbach, and the Raven, a bird said to eternally circle the Untersberg mountain and tasked with awakening on the last day the king and his armies slumbering within (usually Charlemagne, but sometimes Frederick I or Charles V).

As each house is reached, the *Perchten* begin a circle dance accompanied by fife and drum. The monsters bob, crouch, twirl, and change direction. Every third step is a hop and clatter of cowbells. At the sound of Death's drumroll, all freeze in their circle. All bells fall silent. With the next drumbeat, the ring bursts, and the dancers charge the crowd. At the crow of the *Hahnengickerl*, the melee stops, and all *Perchten* drop to their knees. The witch steps to the center. With her broom she sweeps out a large cross upon the ground. The Chief *Percht* then declares:

> "*Glück hinein, Unglück hinaus,*
> *es ziagt des wilde Gjoad ums Haus*"
> ("Fortune in, misfortune out,
> The Wild Hunt goes round your house.")

Again the *Hahnengickerl* crows. The dancers, accompanied by fife and drum, again perform the *Perchtentanz*. As the song concludes, the Raven crows, and all figures kneel one last time, prostrating themselves as if to transfer energies accumulated in their dance into the earth. This concludes the visit, and they depart.

The Kirchseeon *Perchtenlauf*

The Bavarian town of Kirchseeon, about 30 minutes east of Munich, also hosts a well-known *Perchtenlauf* created in the winter of 1953-4 under the direction of Dr. Heinrich Kastner, a cultural preservationist who also headed the town's local *Trachtenverein* (a club devoted to traditionalist culture and folkloric costume specific to the region).

The event reflects a meticulous, if idiosyncratic, attention to detail in its costumes and choreography, all intended to reinforce an interpretation of the folklore internally consistent if slightly out of step with recent scholarship. The *Perchtenlauf* is visually rich with roughly two-dozen *Perchten* featuring unique,

Death as drummer at The Wild Hunt of Untersberg, Salzburg. *Photo © Jung Alpenland.*

richly ornamented masks, and colorful costumes. It incorporates traditional songs, complex dances, and music on a variety of instruments including a wheeled Glockenspiel with tuned bells arranged on a decorative tree-like structure.

At dusk on Saturdays and Sundays, between the last weekend of November and Epiphany, performers gather at a different spot each day. Their torchlight procession begins with three crashing, jangling thumps produced by a strange instrument held by the Chief *Percht*, his *Teufelsgeige* ("devil's violin"), a staff cluttered with cymbals, bells, and topped by a grotesque, carved head. As the assembly moves out, masked drummers set a beat and others crack whips.

The drummers and musicians manning the Glockenspiel are Kirchseeon's version of the *Schönperchten*, one of the five classes of *Perchten* here called "Passen." Their masks represent human faces crowned by decorative helmets adorned with magical talismans, mirrors, musical symbols, heraldic devices, and shellfish representing fertility. The figures go by strange names including Harp, Bard, Hexagram, and Pentagram, Indian, and Firebird.

Frau Perchta assumes a central position in the *Perchtentanz* performed by Kirchseeon's *Schiachperchten*. These consist of two *Passen* with the names *Klaubauf* and *Holzmandln* ("Wood Folk"). Perchta carries a staff topped by a pentagram and wears a peculiar mask with a male devil facing forward and a backward female visage set in a burst of sunbeams.

Interestingly, the design of the feminine face is believed to have been influenced by a mask created for the 1934 film, *The Prodigal Son*, by South Tyrolean director Luis Trenker. In the film, the protagonist encounters folk rituals featuring the *Perchten* along with an interestingly staged scene emphasizing a relationship between the awakening of natural forces and the *Perchten* (who appear rising from under the winter snows). The film's *Sonnenpercht* ("sun Percht") mask with its sunbeam halo, a design unprecedented in actual folk traditions, reflects the mythology embraced in the Kirchseeon festivities, identifying Perchta as an all-powerful goddess of "an old sun cult." Her peculiar male visage is explained by her dominion over all dualities, "male and female, life and death, past and future."

A number of dances are performed over the course of the *Perchtenlauf*, usually accompanied by drums, Glockenspiel and traditional lyrics chanted or sung. There are round dances executed in patterns—circle, square, and star formations—said to have magical significance. Most striking is the *Drudenhax* ("Pentagram"), a dance in which the Wood Folk circle, chant, and form complex patterns with the long hazelwood staffs they carry. At the close, they interlock these, forming the shape of the pentagram, which is raised skyward.

The names and masks of these dancers are noteworthy. The *Klaubauf* faces are carved in a grotesque rounded style resembling those of East Tyrol, the region most associated with that name. They represent the malevolent Luz, Boar, Bat, Werewolf, Dragon, Devil, a froglike Wasserman ("Water Man"), an evil-looking Hare, and a raptor-like Bird. The masks of the Wood Folk incorporate forest elements: a pinecone for a nose, a fern branch for an ear, a snail shell for a wart, and a hat modeled on a mushroom cap. One named Snapdragon is modeled on the dried seedpod of that flower, which itself resembles a human skull. While some traditional animal fur is incorporated into the clothing, most of the *Perchten* instead wear coveralls decorated with layers of colorful yarn strands suggestive of fur.

At each stop along the route, these dances, songs, and chants are performed, and the visit concludes with the *Habergeiß* symbolically offering a rhymed blessing. He is then repaid with coins deposited into his hinged jaw and "swallowed" into a hidden bag. While the Kirchseeon *Habergeiß* is surprisingly atypical and utterly lacking in goat-like ears, horns, or other traits of the animal, there are figures

***Tresterer*, Zell am See, Austria.** *Photo by Johannes Schwaninger © Steinerwirt, Zell am See.*

***Krapfenshnapper* from *Tresterer* group, Zell am See, Austria.**
Photo by Johannes Schwaninger © Steinerwirt, Zell am See.

closer to the traditional *Habergeiß* in the final *Pass*. These are the *Schlenzer*, consisting of the familiar draped performer holding a rod topped by a puppet head with flapping jaw. The *Schlenzer* are known for sneaking up on spectators otherwise absorbed in the performance. Their most notorious prank involves scooping up mouthfuls of snow and dropping them down the collars of the unwary.

The Kirchseeon *Perchtenlauf* has received extensive coverage: local, national, and throughout the EU via print, TV, radio, and online media. Unlike the secretive modus operandi of organizers of the Wild Hunt of Untersberg, Kirchseeon event producers post routes, festival information, and advertising throughout the city, drawing spectators to line the streets hours in advance. Though eschewing appearances at "some of the more commercial Christmas Markets," the desire to expand the audience is clear and seems fueled by a sense of righteous duty coloring Kirchseeon's *Perchten* mythology—as in this quote by H. Reupold, Jr., son of the event's founder:

> "Perchten, in the broader sense, are those who, with their entire thought and actions, set an example in both private and public life. They are committed to social needs as much as the cultural. Finally, as the translation of Percht is 'bright, shining,' we must, as the saying goes, 'be a shining example.'"

The Pinzgau *Tresterer*

A *Perchten* tradition with genuinely old roots is that of the *Tresterer* dancers found in the Pinzgau region of the state of Salzburg. The practice has been preserved in five municipalities (Bruck, Stuhlfelden, Unken, Zell am See, and the city of Salzburg) and takes place only during the twelve days of Christmas, except in Zell, where it also occurs on St. Thomas Day.

Classed as benevolent *Schönperchten*, the dancers' elaborate costumes are unlike those worn by *Perchten* in any other region but may represent a style more typical in the past. Particularly striking is the crown surmounted by white rooster feathers and hung with several dozen colored ribbons dangling to the dancer's hips. Partially obscuring the face, the ribbons are thought to have functioned perhaps as a disguise during the years when *Perchten* events were banned and carried out in secret.

The cut and rich brocade of the clothing recalls costume of the 18th century and is restricted to a symbolic color scheme: red for defensive power and white for purity. An embroidered belt and handmade shoes with hobnailed wooden soles complete the outfit. In the right hand, the dancers also carry and occasionally wave a handkerchief, as do the Morris Dancers of England. The dance is executed in a combination of light jumps, grinding spins, and heavy stomps, commonly said to awaken the earth's dormant energies. It is intermittently accompanied by music performed by pipers, dressed in folkloric costume.

The *Tresterer*, like other traditional *Perchten*, roam from home to home giving their performances and are accompanied by other figures including *Schiachperchten* and a *Habergeiß*. The master of the procession, whose duty it is to offer rhymed blessings to the host and symbolically sweep open the spot where the *Tresterer* will perform, is a figure called *Hanswurst*, the name for a traditional Carnival fool throughout German-speaking lands. Here he wears a tall feathered, beribboned hat and white suit adorned with jingling bells. He carries a leather club or "sausage" (*Wurst*) used to clear the performance space and to threaten any misbehaving *Schiachperchten*.

Also accompanying the troupe are the bufoonish husband and wife Lapp and Lappin, both played by men. Carrying a rag-doll "baby," Lappin is a figure of low comedy, one constantly and indiscriminately pregnant. Her antic attempts to hand off the doll to spectators are said to convey to them the gift of fertility (whether desired or not!) A *Zapfenmandl* ("pinecone man") and the lichen-covered *Werchmandl* also appear with the *Tresterer*. Their presence is intended to bestow symbolic protection upon woodcutters and forest workers, and guard their trees from fire, wind, disease, and infestations.

Finally come two *Perchten* in animal form. The *Hühnerpercht* (chicken *Percht*) is outfitted in feathers and mask more reminiscent of a hawk than chicken, and is said to bless the family poultry, protecting them against birds of prey. At the end of the *Perchten's* performance, she lays an egg symbolizing renewal. Guarding the henhouse against other predators is the *Krapfenschnapper* with foxlike mask and suit crafted from roughly two-dozen fox pelts. The *Percht's* name comes from its secondary function of collecting gifts from the householders. Traditional tokens of appreciation are brandy, bacon, or donuts (*Krapfen*). The last is represented in the creature's name, which has nothing to do with foxes, but instead means "donut snapper."

Contemporary *Tresterer* groups are the result of revival of the practice in the decades after World War II, but the tradition's origin is undoubtedly much older. The name, at least, appears in ethnographic surveys as early as 1841, but the form may have existed under another name before this as similar dances and elements of the costume can be found in much older records. Since the word "*trestern*" means "to mash," a time-honored explanation for the custom derives the dancer's

The Klaubauf Pass at *Perchtenlauf*, Kirschseeon, Germany. *Photo © Manfred Kornherr.*

Percht nicknamed "*Baumschwammerl*" ("Mushroom") at *Perchtenlauf*, Kirchseeon, Germany.
Photo © Manfred Kornherr.

stomping movements from the rhythms of the threshing floor, and connects this with the spirit of fertility the ritual is supposed to awaken. But modern scholars point to the Italian style of costume, seeing in it the highly decorative dress of the Venice Carnival. As the verb *trestern* is more commonly applied to the crushing of grapes in wine-making, it seems likely that not only the *Tresterer's* costume is of Italian origin, but that the movements of the dance itself are originally inspired not by milling in Austria but wine-making in Italy.

Opposite: *Habergeiß* at Kirchseeon *Perchtenlauf*. *Photo © Manfred Kornherr.*

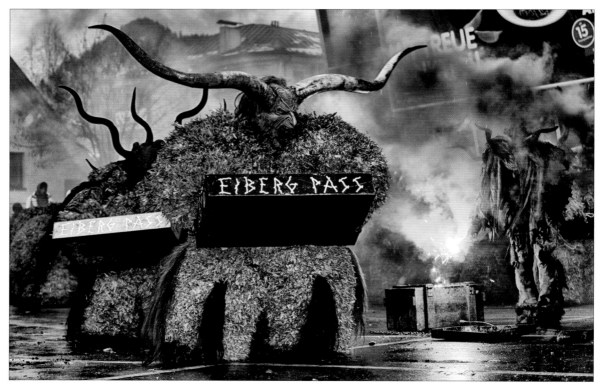

Tyrolean Unterland-style *Perchten* from Eiber Pass, Schwoich, Austria.
Photo © Martin Guggenberger Photography (2015).

Perchten in the Tyrolean Unterland

A *Perchten* tradition worth mentioning not for its antiquity but for its unique style is that of the Tyrolean Unterland, along the Lower Inn Valley in the district of Kufstein. *Perchten* there are outfitted in immense, voluminous suits made of cornhusks.

In this region with no deep-rooted *Perchten* customs, the style seems to have evolved over the last few decades, beginning in Breitenbach am Inn, and spreading to other nearby towns, notably Wörgl, and Angerberg. To what extent the suits may have been inspired by earlier, similar uses of straw is unknown, but there are plenty of precedents, dating back to 1522 with Luther's reference to "fraw Hulda," costumed in "straw armor."

Work on the suits, which are made anew every year, begins as early as August with the husking of corn. Husks are stitched into bundles, combed over nails set in a board to make them bushier, then sewn over old clothes. Up to 1000 bundles are needed to make a single suit, which can weigh well over 200 pounds. Even more daunting is the fact that the husks aren't always plentiful on local farms, so troupes have been known to drive as far away as Northern Italy to obtain them. Though the local term for *Perchten* is "Peaschtln," and this word is often used, the figures are also sometimes called *Bratschinger* from the word for cornhusk (*Bratschen*). The *Bratschinger* wear more traditional masks usually topped by particularly long and impressive horns, either resin replicas or real specimens from the African kudu.

The Unterland *Perchten* wear not only the usual bells but also produce an impressive din with synchronized drumming on old gas tanks carried on chains hung over the shoulders. Each troupe composes a distinct rhythm by which it is recognized. Sometimes the tanks are even rigged to spew evil-looking smoke when played. Discordant horns contrived from old car horns also contribute to the cacophony. Each member of the troupe is identified by his role in raising this hellish din, either being a *Damperer* (drummer), *Glockinger* (bell ringer), or *Bläser* (horn-blower).

While the *Bratschinger* handle the noisemaking, they are not the only type of *Percht* in the troupes. They are accompanied by the *Fellteufeln* ("fur devils") costumed, as the name suggests, in the traditional animal hides. Infinitely more mobile than their corn-clad cousins, the *Fellteufeln* are also called "runners" (*Läufer*). The leader of the troupe is the Witch, played by a man dressed in black rags and with face blackened.

To begin a performance the Witch prepares a fire in a cauldron in a central area. For this reason the *Perchten* events here are less mobile, and processions tend to revolve around this staging area. The fire is usually rather smoky by design, and throughout the performance, the Witch will often enhance the infernal miasma with smoke bombs or other pyrotechnics.

The ritual begins with the *Bratschinger* entering and forming a circle around the cauldron, beating their tanks as accompaniment to the Witch. Throughout her routine, she uses her broom to symbolically sweep evil spirits inward toward the central fire where they will be destroyed. The *Fellteufeln* assist in the sorcery by circulating outside the drummers' circle, searching out additional troublesome demons and wrangling them inward. Though only decades old, this spectacle, with its monstrously oversized *Perchten*, soot-black witch, thundering gas-can percussion, and ample use of fire and smoke, does more perhaps than any to conjure for the modern imagination the notion of a supernatural battle with infernal forces.

The Gastein *Perchtenlauf*

History

With centuries-old roots deeply intertwined with the Krampus tradition, the Gastein *Perchtenlauf*, founded in 1898, is the oldest and best known in the world, and in 2011 became an Austrian addition to UNESCO's list for Intangible Cultural Heritage. The Gastein event takes place every four years (most recently in 2014) on Epiphany Day and on the Sunday preceding. The 9-hour procession visiting Bad Gastein, Bad Hofgastein, and farms and

Chimney sweep and *Zapfenmandl* ("Pinecone Man") at *Perchtenlauf*, Gastein, Austria.
Photo © Gasteinertal.com.

homes in outlying regions covers approximately 10 miles with different routes both days. On years the event is not held in Gastein, the nearby Pongau towns of Altenmarkt, St. Johann, and Bischofshofen alternate hosting duties, with the entire four-year cycle sometimes referred to as the "Great Pongau *Perchtenlauf.*" The parade in Bischofshofen dates to 1912, St. Johann to 1952, and Altenmarkt to 1959. While the Gastein's *Perchtenlauf* is first documented in its current form in 1898, less organized forms of *Perchten* activity in the Pongau occurred long before this.

On the Roofs

Before the parade has even begun, forest *Perchten* represented by the mossy *Baumwercher* and pinecone-studded *Zapfenmandl* have begun their ascent of overlooking roofs and balconies. They are joined on their perches by the Chimney Sweep. Here—as in England, Germany, Poland, and the Czech Republic—the sweep is regarded as a good-luck symbol, one particularly associated with the New Year in Austria and Germany, where they appear as small marzipan figures or as ornaments attached to floral bouquets given on the holiday.

Opposite: "*Schiach*" ("Ugly") Cap Wearers at *Perchtenlauf*, Gastein, Austria.
Photo © Gasteinertal.com.

The Horsemen, Lead-Devil, and Bell-Carrier

Leading the parade are the *Rösselreiter*, hobbyhorse riders dressed in old imperial cavalry uniforms and armed with whips. Their whip-cracking reflects the tradition of *Aperschnalzen*, a form of synchronized whip-snapping performed at certain Carnival and *Rauhnacht* events. *"Aper"* is a (very Alpine) adjective for "snow-free," and the noise of their whips is said to drive back the winter and its snows. The whip-crackers are followed by a single *Vorteufel* ("Chief Devil") costumed like a Krampus but carrying a pitchfork rather than switches. After him comes the *Glockenträger* ("bell-carrier") who wears upon his back a wooden frame hung with cowbells and decorated with both wintery pine boughs and flowers representing spring.

The Captain and Band

The Captain of the *Perchten* (*Perchtenhauptmann*) enters next, dressed in the green tailcoat, long lederhosen, and tall felt hat traditional to the Gastein Valley. It is his duty to deliver the rhymed blessing upon each location visited, and certain touches such as his white gloves, medallions, and saber emphasize the dignity of this role. Formerly, he appeared in military uniform and sported a long dignity-enhancing beard made of wool. He is usually in the company of a small band of folk musicians, performing on trumpet, clarinet, and accordion.

The *Perchtenhauptmann's* duties go far beyond the ceremonial. He must ensure that all participants are over the age of 16, do not make excessive use of alcohol before or during the parade, and that masked performers do not remove their masks within view of spectators. He also presides over planning meetings, and is tasked with ensuring the success of the parade in all of its logistical detail, from the selection of the route down to the food served during the midday break.

The Cap Wearers

Following the Captain and musicians is the core of the *Perchtenlauf*, the 30 *Schönperchten* known as *Tafelkappen* ("board caps") thanks to their flat surfaces, which are adorned primarily with mirrors and flowers. A variety of other decorative materials may supplement this, including garlands, decorative chains, dolls in folkloric costume, Christmas tree ornaments, and collections of old jewelry. Many are topped with scaled-up versions of the *Gamsbart*, that tuft of fur resembling a shaving brush found on Alpine hats and traditionally cut as a hunting trophy from the beard of the alpine chamois.

More wearable parade-float than hat, these structures (which can tower up to 8' overhead and weigh over 100 lbs.) are supported by special neck and back braces mostly hidden under the wearer's coat. These braces facilitate the dangerously deep ceremonial bow executed by these figures at certain points along their parade route. This bow follows the rhymed blessing delivered by the captain and a slow, twirling dance that sets the caps' mirrors flashing in the Alpine sun.

Schnabelpercht ("Beaked *Percht*") at *Perchtenlauf*, **Gastein, Austria.** *Photo © Gasteinertal.com.*

There is a fair amount of variety among the 30 caps. An unusual specimen covered in black velvet, flowers and glass crystals pays tribute to the local mining industry, displaying miner's pick and hammer along with the heraldic seals of the area's five prominent mining families.

Of the five caps displaying stuffed animals, the most noteworthy perhaps is one first worn in 1830, before the *Perchtenlauf* was organized into its current form. Periodically repaired and remodeled, it now displays the head of a deer, arrays of antlers, two species of mountain goat, a fox, marmots, and weasel. While most caps do not have a lineage so old, many tend to be kept within certain families, and are therefore sometimes called *Hauskappen* ("house caps").

A particularly interesting *Tafelkappe* represents a *Schiachpercht*. In times gone by, this was covered in dead rats, birds, and snakes, though today it's sadly toned down, displaying only moderately distasteful items like mousetraps, mire-stained stable shoes, and other debris. The saber carried by the wearer is rusted, and he and his feminized partner are also dressed in patched, ragged clothes adorned with straw and chicken feathers suggesting farmyard filth. His partner wears a necklace of potatoes and clothespins.

The "women" accompanying the cap-wearers tend to be the junior members of the *Perchten* community, apprenticing in the role while their features are still less noticeably masculine. They are picked by the wearers of the caps not only as dance partners but also as assistants to help them don and secure the immense structures worn on their heads.

Perchtenlauf, Gastein, Austria. *Photo © Gasteinertal.com.*

Bears and bear wrangler at *Perchtenlauf*, Gastein, Austria. *Photo © Gasteinertal.com.*

Bear and Clowns

A bear costumed in furs and carved mask "controlled" by a rustically dressed wrangler follows the *Tafelperchten*. The wrangler's beastly companion and the long chain connecting the two serve as a sort of barrier to keep distance between spectators crowding in to see the cap-wearers. The bear—who's sometimes said to represent the winter and its terrible powers—was joined in 1978 by a *Schnabelpercht* (the "beak *Percht*" mentioned previously), and a *Habergeiß* in 1982.

Other clownish characters trail behind mingling with and entertaining the crowd. Among them, a fool, who may be called either Hanswurst or Bajazzl, an Austrian version of an Italian Carnival clown name "Bajazzo." There are two differently costumed versions of this figure, a *schön* and *schiach*, both carrying a doll on a rope like the Lapp and Lappin accompanying the *Tresterer*.

The Tradesmen

The other roving performers taking part represent caricatures of old-fashioned tradespeople who engage spectators with well-worn routines and comic business employing prop tools of their trades. While mostly added in the last decades, some of them, like the quack doctor, make similarly comic appearances in Nicholas parades dating back centuries and reflect the peasant humor of the "Everyman" scenes from those plays. They are not really *Perchten*, and their presence may seem strange, but such itinerant merchants and handymen were a sort of traditional entertainment in old Gastein, bringing news, gossip, and perhaps comic stories and jokes intended to drum up business. Coming from other regions in Austria, Germany, and Italy, their accents and curious customs would also be a source of local humor.

Perhaps the most mischievous of these would be the Tailor, who—like the Blacksmith nailing shoes to the floor in old Nicholas plays—will sometimes set about stitching together unwary parade-goers. More commonly, he is now equipped with a toy called "stretch scissors," an arrangement of wooden slats hinged to extend deep into the crowd and grasp or knock off spectators' hats.

A Knife Sharpener equipped with a replica grinding stone roams about, distributing small foil razor blades inscribed with a pentagram for good luck. A traveling junk salesman and handyman similar to a tinker called a *Rastelbinder* (from "binder or pieces") hawks old mousetraps, bras, and other items offering gag potential. A Postman in old imperial uniform delivers random and misdirected letters, and a Hunter and Poacher act out a comic rivalry complete with guns firing blanks.

Biblical Figures

Also interacting with the crowd are figures from the Biblical world. At the event staged on Epiphany, "Three Kings' Day" in German, these figures join the parade, singing in four-part harmony and carrying a wooden reproduction of the Bethlehem star atop a pole. They are *Sternsinger* ("star singers"), carolers who around Epiphany go door to door with their star in imitation of the Three Magi. The tradition, which dates back to the 16th century, is widespread not only in Austria and Germany but is also found in Poland, Slavic Europe, Scandinavia, and in the UK, where they are called "star boys."

The Biblical King Herod, who solicited from the Three Kings the location of the infant Christ, is also represented, as is his wife. Likely inspired by the figure in the medieval plays, Gastein's representation of Herod deviates from the usually monstrous characterization, instead making comic use of the king. He presides over mock trials of locals he accuses of various "crimes." Offenses, for which token fines are demanded, might include stinginess toward employees, price gouging, bragging, whining, or watering down drinks in a tavern.

Schiachperchten, Witches, and Perchta

Though today they march with their brooms and wooden masks alongside the *Tafelperchten*, until the 1950s, it was the witches who served Herod by rounding up miscreants. Today that duty falls to Krampus-like *Schiachperchten*. It's noteworthy that unlike the modernized *Perchtenlauf*, consisting exclusively of large mobs of these devils, the number of *Schiachperchten* in Gastein is limited to four.

Finally, there is Frau Perchta. She also holds a doll as a symbol of fertility. Along with several witches, she tends to wander in the shadow of the eye-catching *Tafelperchten*. That she is relegated to this peripheral station seems to conflict with the historical importance the character's assigned elsewhere. Stranger still, the figure of Frau Perchta is missing from the earliest accounts of the Gastein parade. She was, in fact, not added until 1982. Being without precedent in the local folk-art tradition, the mask Perchta wears is likely inspired by the 1949 Kirchseeon model or perhaps even the studio-created mask for the 1934 film *The Prodigal Son*.

This again raises the question of Frau Perchta's place in the established *Perchten* mythology or within the history of the *Perchtenlauf*. In the following chapter, we'll examine the history of the *Perchtenlauf* for some clues to these questions as well as the ultimate roots of the Krampus tradition itself.

Witches at Gastein *Perchtenlauf*. *Photo © Gasteinertal.com.*

Chapter Eight

PAGAN ROOTS AND FINAL QUESTIONS

Too Bright to See

In the Introduction, I wrote about the darkness being essential to whatever magic is in Christmas. As I researched the *Rauhnächte*, each book or article I read described those long winter nights by the hearth, the moaning winds, creaking pines, and dancing shadows filling the imagination with ghosts and witches. I knew this was where the Krampus lived, before all the entanglement with St. Nicholas and his pious nagging. I found the *Perchten*, and dug for dark and pagan roots beneath the Hollywood-inspired masks and posturing of the modern *Perchtenlauf*. But what I found in Gastein, somehow, belonged to the daylight. It wasn't there in all the wedding-cake finery and natty craftsmanship of the *Tafelkappen*. This was unrelated, a civic exercise closer to the Rose Parade than anything I'd imagined.

When I spoke with my friend Matthäus Rest from the Gastein Valley about this difference between the Krampus and *Perchtenlauf*, he seemed to understand. "That's part of the charm and mystery of the Krampus, that it only happens at night, that there hasn't been compromise by having the event during the day when it might be friendlier to photographers." The *Perchten* events in Gastein, he says, were once only nocturnal, "but this was part of its institutionalization, dragging it out of the night into broad daylight."

Another influential moment in the event's history transposed it seasonally. "What really contributed to that institutionalization was the one time they did it

Schnabelpercht (**"Beaked *Percht*"**) from Rauris, Austria. *Photo: Florian Bachmeier © TVB Rauris.*

in the *summer*. It was in 1837 for the Kaiser. He never came in the winter, only the summer. Tourism then was all about the spa; no one came in winter."

The curiosity expressed by Kaiser Ferdinand I, which led to the organization of this out-of-season entertainment, did much to encourage local pride in a tradition more urbane tastes previously dismissed as hopelessly rustic. It also ignited a competitive spirit that drove participants to create *Tafelkappen* of then-unprecedented scale and ornamental richness. In the years that followed an increasing number of visitors arrived in the valley to see the wonders worthy of the emperor.

Rest begins chuckling and asks me if I know about the Eurovision Song Contest. It's the world's longest-running broadcast competition, an over-the-top spectacle selecting a winning song from among member nations of the European Broadcasting Union. First televised in 1956, it is widely watched and just as widely reviled for its cheesy pomp and vacuous entries, with winning titles like 1969's UK entry "Boom Bang-a-Bang" or Spain's 1968 winner, "La, La, La."

"Just a couple weeks ago," he says, "there was this new story about the contest that's going to be held in Vienna this year." As a sort of distinctly Austrian diversion between songs, the Gastein *Perchten* were invited to perform.

"You should have heard the response!"

"Never!" he cries, imitating the shrill of moral outrage. "*No* amount of money will bring us there! This tradition belongs only here, in Bad Gastein, in Hof Gastein. Only here, and not on command! Only on the date that is traditional, and only once every four years! It is not for sale and not for tourism."

"Well, you know, the history, now. How it grew. Staging the whole thing in summer for the Kaiser. But that's all now forgotten."

Later I discover that the Kirchseeon *Perchten* agreed to perform on the very first Eurovision contest. Perhaps that didn't go over well in Gastein either.

A Devil's Cross

Just west of Bad Gastein, about three miles down the road from Rauris heading toward Goldegg, just after you cross the River Ache, you'll find an ancient granite cross. It's carved with the year 1550, believed to be the year of its erection. For unknown reason the year 1853 is inscribed below. First mentioned in the historical record in 1576, it was described in rather remarkable terms. It's said to be the grave of a *Percht*.

Two legends attach themselves to the site. The first relates that a group of costumed *Perchten* was traveling along this road during the *Rauhnächte*. Though they had left their village with 12 members, they discovered upon counting that they now numbered 13. Terror seized the group as they suspected their party had been joined by an actual *Percht*, or the Devil himself, and in their panic and ensuing arguments, one of their party was killed and buried on the spot to cover the crime.

The second tale is more prosaic. It says that two costumed troupes from rival towns met on that narrow road and fell into a violent altercation during which one of the travelers was killed. Knowing that a man who dies while dressed as a *Percht* cannot be buried in hallowed ground, they buried him there at the site of the murder.

The Beautiful Ones Arrive

Whatever the truth in any of this, we know that early *Perchten* outings were regarded as unruly affairs, occasionally resulting in violence, and sometimes even in deaths. As with activities related to the Nicholas-Krampus troupes, our earliest knowledge of the *Perchtenlauf* often comes from official complaints and prohibitions.

The first reference to such things appears in 1668 in the court records of Lienz, Austria, where we find a complaint alleging a man dressed as a "*Perchtln*" had beaten the plaintiff, one Peter Ackherer, severely. We know that *Perchten* often came well equipped for such mischief, as they are described in 1796 by Lorenz Hübner, editor of Salzburg's first daily newspaper, as dancing about "in absurd masks *and armed with all kinds of weapons*." Long sticks are often mentioned, as are whips, though these were ostensibly used only as noisemakers. Even a form of air-gun used to fire ashes appears in one report from 1857.

Perchten activities were often prohibited under bans intended to prevent masking associated with St. Nicholas Day, Christmas, or Carnival, but were also increasingly the subject of more explicit bans. In 1773 Prince-Archbishop Sigismund III, calling for strict enforcement and punishment of those engaged in *Perchten* activities, urged citizens not to "support them with food and drink," and in 1741, Prince-Archbishop Leopold Anton Freiherr von Firmian likewise prohibited "masking, costuming and going about as *Perchten*."

Where overt bans failed, other influences succeeded. We have already seen in the birth of the Krampus tradition how a force for social control came in the form of St. Nicholas. In the same way the *Schönperchten-Schiachperchten* duality seems to have evolved in a society likely tired of the havoc wrought by the costumed ruffians. Before the 19th century, neither the terms *Schönperchten* or *Schiachperchten* appear in the record. There were only *Perchten*, and at the time, they were all likely more *schiach* than *schön,* costumed in rags and animal skins from the farm

rather than neatly crafted finery. Their outings took place exclusively by night, partly because this had become traditional and partly to evade enforcement of the bans. They were known to move swiftly. Before policing parties could mobilize, they had disappeared, taking routes inaccessible to horseback patrols, moving over streams and difficult terrain with the aid of long poles also employed in vaulting leaps once part of *Perchten* performances. The curious choice of the word "*Lauf*," usually meaning "run or race," to describe the slow-moving *Perchtenlauf* or *Krampuslauf* of today might be explained by this historical stage where speedy movement was called for.

We first begin hearing of the *schön-schiach* dichotomy somewhere in the mid-19th century. By the time the *Tafelperchten* appear in the last decades of that century, the duality was more commonly recognized. The arrival of such heavy, awkward headdresses naturally changed the pace and feel of the *Perchtenlauf* from earlier surprise attacks by roughly costumed devils to what a chronicler described in 1892 as "measured and dignified." This newfound dignity can also be associated with economic class, as pointed out by Salzburg folklorist Karl Adrian, who in 1908 noted that only the wealthier farming families could really afford to produce the elaborate *Tafelkappen*. The visual appeal of the caps naturally also helped mold the tradition as one associated with the daytime as such intricate handiwork would be wasted in the darkness.

The Swiss Version   A similar evolution occurred in Switzerland with the *Silvesterchläuse* or "New Year's Nicholases" still found in the hinterlands of the Canton of Appenzell-Ausserrhoden. The *Silvesterchläuse* are men and male youths wearing huge bells and ornate costumes who go door to door around the New Year to offer seasonal blessings and yodel traditional songs characterized by mesmerizing slow-shifting harmonies.

There are three styles of *Silvesterchläuse*, the "beautiful" *Schöchläus* wearing doll-like masks, baroque handcrafted headgear decorated with scenes of peasant life, elaborately embroidered folkloric dress, and simple, doll-like masks. The *Schö-Wüeschte* ("pretty-ugly") wear similar, though slightly less ornate headgear and are costumed in massive suits assembled from evergreen boughs, moss, and ivy, and sometimes featuring mosaic panels assembled from pine cones, bark, acorns, and

Moosmandl ("Moss Man") from Barmstoana Perchten, Hallein, Austria. *Photo © Roland Käfer.*

Schöchläus ("Beautiful") *Silvesterchlaus*, Hundwil, Switzerland. *Photo © Bischof Médard (2014).*

snail shells. The *Wüeschte* ("ugly") wear more voluminous costumes of wilder appearance along with mask and headpieces but of the same natural materials.

The elaborate craftsmanship lavished on the "beautiful" *Schöchläus* and their benign appearance can be compared to that of Gastein's *Tafelperchten*. As with the latter, this elaborated form of the *Silvesterchläuse* is a later development appearing only in the mid-19th century. Previously, the figures were only represented in the form of the more primitive and fearsome *Schö-Wüeschte*. Created of simple forest materials, these costumes require far less time and financial capital to create, and their countenance is also decidedly more demonic. We might even imagine these suits in their earliest versions as a simple form of woodland camouflage providing cover for a tradition celebrated under the cover of darkness and with greater mischief, like that of the early *Perchten* in their rough animal skins and rags.

Like the Austrian tradition, the *Silvesterchläuse* tradition also encountered bans by church authorities throughout the 17th through 19th centuries. It's believed that the unruly nature of the celebrations is responsible for the strange name assigned the figures, the first half of which references December 31, St. Sylvester's Day, and the appended "*Chlaus*," pointing to St. Nicholas Day when the figures originally

Schö-Wüeschte ("Pretty-Ugly") *Silvesterchlaus*, Hundwil, Switzerland. *Photo © Medard Bischof (2014)*

appeared. Presumably because of the custom's pagan origins and the performers' indecorous behavior it was deemed inappropriate to Advent and shifted in the 17th century to New Year's Eve. Because the Gregorian calendar had still not been universally accepted throughout the independent-minded valleys of the Swiss Alps, the tradition was celebrated both on the Gregorian and Julian New Year. Today it is still celebrated on the Julian date, January 13, as well as the modern New Year's.

How Perchta Grew a Second Face

Discovering that the *Schönperchten*, like the "beautiful" *Silvesterchläuse*, are a relatively recent creation makes implausible the notion of Perchta as an ancient Janus-faced goddess commanding *schön* and *schiach* spirits. Her absence from early descriptions of *Perchtenläufe* and late addition to the Gastein procession in 1982, roughly a century after the first mention of *Schönperchten*, could even suggest that rather than embodying spirits of an indigenous folklore, parade figures themselves were the source of a *schön/schiach* mythology requiring Frau Perchta to be reconceived in a way not representative of the original folklore.

While certainly the two-faced masks used in Kirchseeon and Gastein are unprecedented in the traditional folk art or folk customs, the notion of Frau Perchta as a goddess of dualities may predate the *Schönpercht* figures appearing in the mid 19th century—but only by a decade or so. Primarily responsible for this conception is Jacob Grimm. Consolidating Perchta with Holda, his 1835 *Deutsche Mythologie* spins from a few dozen tales of lucky and unlucky encounters with a fairy-like being, what seems to me an exaggerated image of a life-and-death-bringing cosmic Ur-Mother. Something in the mid-19th-century zeitgeist seems to have hungered for this rising mythology of feminine omnipotence. It was most famously articulated by a contemporary of Grimm's, Swiss philologist and anthropologist Johann Jakob Bachofen, in his theories of ancient matriarchies. This in turn inspired the mythologizing of fellow Swiss psychologist-mystic Carl Jung whose discussion of the eternal Magna Mater had trickled into popular consciousness by the first half of the 20th-century. It is at this point Frau Perchta is reborn as the Janus-faced parade figure.

Influences from Venice

Another bias of Grimm's that seems to have skewed our understanding of the *Perchtenlauf* is his active involvement with the Pan-Germanic movement that gave birth to a unified German state in 1871. An overt goal of his inspiring compilation of German folklore was to solidify a common mythology defining a common *Volk* deserving unification. This may partially explain the manner in which he seems at times to press fairy-like beings like Perchta and Holda into molds more fitting to the religions of the empire-building cultures of the Greek and Romans. His treatment of folklore of the Austrian Empire largely ignores potential influences of Slavic, Italian, and other cultures in favor of Germanic, even Nordic models. For this reason, the *Perchtenlauf* of Salzburg and Tyrol, particularly in the late 19th and early 20th century, was inevitably read against a background of fancifully ancient Germanic nature cults.

In a previous chapter, we looked at influences on the Nicholas celebrations from outside the German-speaking sphere. A primary source of this was the archbishop's 1731 expulsion of Protestants and selective repopulation laws favoring farmers and craftsmen from Catholic Bavaria and Tyrol. This influx, containing a number of Italian South Tyroleans, brought not only Nicholas customs but also those of the Italian Carnival, an undeniable influence on the Salzburg-area *Perchtenlauf*.

Both the working and aristocratic classes in Tyrol were fascinated by the Venetian Carnival. German Emperor Maximillian I, ruling from his court in Innsbruck, was known to have purchased costumes from Venice for masked festivities, illustrating these in his illuminated Freydal book between 1512-15. The Carnival influence on Salzburg nobility was also strong. Situated midway on trade routes between Europe's two major centers of Carnival (Venice and Nuremberg), Salzburg would be influenced by those festive customs from both North and South.

Carnival customs, like the rich brocaded fabrics distinguishing the costumes of the *Tresterer*, arrived with merchants traveling North from Venice through the mountain passes of the Pongau and Pinzgau areas of the state of Salzburg. The region lies in the High Tauern Mountains named for the "*Tauern*" or narrow roads and pathways cut through the mountain ranges. The merchants who traversed these routes with their pack animals were known as *Säumer*, and transported primarily salt from the Salzburg area and wine from Italy. The *Saumhandeln* ("business conducted by the *Säumer*") greatly contributed to the wealth of the region, in turn facilitating the evolution of uniquely lavish *Perchtenlauf* traditions. The itinerant tradespeople parodied in the Gastein *Perchtenlauf* were part of the *Saumhandeln* that shaped the culture of the region.

In an address given at the opening of the *Perchtenlauf* headquarters in Bad Gastein in 2012, professor Ulrike Kammerhofer-Aggermann, of the Salzburg National Institute for Folklore, described the Venetian tradition that would be reimagined in the *Perchtenlauf*.

The Carnivals caricatured societal hierarchies and norms with exaggerated glittering, elaborately outfitted pairs of figures and their servants as well as caricatures of craftsmen and the poor. The foolishness of the world was burlesqued to illustrate the vanity of all earthly things.

The imperial uniforms comically festooned with medallions worn by the *Tafelperchten*, Postman, and *Rösselreiter*, the feuding Hunter and Poacher, the lying Quack, the roguish Tailor and *Rastelbinder*—all are part of the image Kammerhofer-Aggermann describes as a "funhouse mirror reflecting society and its hierarchies."

With a history of over 600 years, the oldest and most essentially carnivalesque of those figures is Hanswurst. In the doll, or "Poppin," thrown by the Lappin, Kammerhofer-Aggermann sees direct reference to the social predicament of the young servant woman being "too open-minded," regarding men, and without adequate resources "brought into the world illegitimate children without a future." This interpretation of the gesture in terms of the bawdy social satire of Carnival obviously parts ways with the notion of the doll as the fertility blessing preferred by those looking for remnants of a Germanic nature cult.

Between Carnival Amusements and Folk Ritual

Retrofitting the *Perchtenlauf* with a mythology that smacks of Nordic sagas and worship in sacred groves can seem rather absurd, even distasteful given the Nazi's propensity for such things. But can we really write it all off as a regional extension of activities in Venice? Some early 19th-century ethnographers rather broadly identified the *Perchten* celebrations as mere "Carnival amusements." Though rarely celebrated as such, Epiphany is after all the official start of Carnival season in many regions. Others have seen the *Percht* as nothing more than the name for a seasonal masker.

It seems undeniable that some elements of Carnival have bled backward in the calendar into *Perchtenlauf* customs. In the same way, we might see customs of the *Perchten* themselves transferred to celebrations earlier in the year. This notion is nicely expressed by Ignaz Zingerle, in his 1871 survey of folk customs in Tyrol. Deriving *"Percht"* strictly from the Bavarian word for Epiphany, he comments that those maskers celebrating on this day "receive from this the name *Perchteln* or *Perchten*; from here outward, the name is expanded to the whole period of the Twelve Nights, yes, even to the time of Advent."

Zapfenmandl ("Pinecone Man") from Barmstoana *Perchten*, Hallein, Austria. *Photo © Roland Käfer.*

We should also consider that customs associated with Advent and even St. Martin's Day could migrate *forward* in the direction of Carnival landing on Epiphany and becoming associated with the *Perchten*. We have already seen this forward calendrical shift with the Swiss *Silvesterchläuse* tradition moved toward Carnival season. We've also seen St. Martin's customs transferred into those of St. Nicholas Day several weeks later. As the focus in all this is the Krampus, the most important of these migrations are St. Nicholas Day traditions borrowed from Epiphany. Chief among these are the obvious parallels between Frau Perchta's annual review of work done by young female spinners and domestics and the review of children's behavior undertaken by Nicholas and the Krampus.

In examples in Gastein or those of the *Tresterer* as early source-forms of *Perchten* tradition, we may find the mythology of Frau Perchta irrelevant and lean toward a demythologizing view of the whole as "Carnival amusements." But outside the Venetian-influenced sphere of the *Saumhandeln*, there have been many *Perchten* customs more intimately bound up with the Lady Perchta and her mythology.

Where Perchta Lived On

I've already mentioned the 19th-century Bavarian figure "Iron Bertha" (i.e., "Perchta of the Iron Nose") roaming Middle Franconia disguised in hides and horns and frightening ill-behaved children and rewarding others. We've also seen the soot-blackened *Butzabercht* going about in rags performing similar duties alongside a Nicholas ("Kläs") in Oberhausen, Germany of the 19th century.

The ongoing annual visits by *Schnabelperchten* in Rauris, Austria, represent female "beaked *Perchten*" who carry brooms and inspect homes for cleanliness and order, as did the mythic Perchta. Here her belly-slitting threats are even imitated by performers carrying a pair of oversized wooden scissors. Somewhat reminiscent is the Upper Bavarian custom of the late 1800s known as *Berchtengehen* ("going as Perchten"), again involving apparently female *Perchten* figures represented by males in drag. Wearing hood-like masks, they visited homes equipped with symbolic instruments of domestic order (brooms and hoes) and collected small snacks from homeowners. Edibles like this provided to roaming *Perchten*-maskers folklorist Max Höfler connects to food offerings (e.g., *Perchtenmilch*) set out on the *Perchtentisch* first mentioned in medieval documents.

On either side of Austria's Carinthian border with Slovenia, up into the 1930s, a female-dressed boy portraying "Pechtra" or "Pechtrababa" would be chased in the Twelfth Night custom known as *Perchtenjagen* ("*Perchten* hunting"). Here,

Schnabelperchten ("Beaked *Perchten*") from Rauris, Austria. *Photo: Florian Bachmeier,* © *TVB Rauris.*

where the welfare of dairy cattle was the primary concern, Perchta's dark side and her maleficent influences as a witch controlling elemental forces that might harm the herd are emphasized, chased from the area by young men wearing noisy bells.

With practices such as this very explicitly referencing the folklore of Frau Perchta, it seems that we cannot entirely disconnect the earlier mythology from *all Perchten* practices, writing them off as simple "Carnival amusements." While the *Perchtenlauf* in the Salzburg area may have much more to do with relatively modern traditions from Venice, some customs still hint at Frau Perchta's medieval identity as a witch, later embraced as a sort of ogress enforcing domestic order.

Healthy Skepticism

Discussing the symbolic import assigned to Perchta and the *Perchten* reminds me of a certain discussion I had years ago in Austria, one mainly noteworthy because I seem to keep having it.

I recall standing in the snow in Bad Gastein talking to some older Bavarian visitors to the area during the Krampus season. They were obviously better acquainted with the frigid weather and interested in continuing the conversation despite the fact that the Krampuses had long departed and my feet were icing over.

I was happy they seemed impressed with the little bit of Krampus knowledge I could show off at the time, but when I alluded to the punishment of naughty children, the husband cut in. He wanted to tell me what it all really meant, that is, the real meaning before St. Nicholas came to muddle things.

He formulated his explanation something like this: It is about driving out the winter and the bad influences of the old year and bringing in spring and good luck for the new.

Since then, I've heard or read something like this dozens, maybe hundreds of times. Years later I repeat the conversation to Matthäus Rest, to see how a cultural anthropologist from the area might respond.

"About good luck?" He repeats. "Yeah, some people say that." He sips his coffee and sets it down with a hint of weariness.

"I also think this is a very bookish explanation. I think people who mainly have just read about it, and want to think about it in these terms, this is what they would say."

Then he offers me the big-picture origin story I'd been hoping for.

"I would just assume that the whole complex of customs, the Krampus and *Perchten*, evolved simultaneously, so there are all these things happening at the same time—different people coming up with different, very localized traditions, all these kinds of rural entertainments going on over the winter. People would just meet and play cards and drink and just try to entertain themselves, put on these plays for each other. These were probably the only weeks during the year they really had time for a bit of fun, so I think something like this is a much more logical explanation than to say it was about fear of the winter, and the long nights, and driving out the devil by dressing up as the devil, all that."

I liked this. It was skeptically no-nonsense. I am not an anthropologist, and did not quite follow the critique of structuralism that followed, but what I appreciated in his origin story was the spirit of fun.

Nineteenth century theorists, and those regurgitating them, seem not to recognize the human capacity for fun. Or they believe it is something that evolved within the last 50 years. In the miserable little world they build for their inferiors, whether in the past or in some distant rural community, everything proceeds from want, fear, and ignorance. This version of the story especially surprises me when it is the tack taken in dubious histories of the tradition provided on the websites of contemporary Krampus or *Perchten* troupes. How can our modern Krampuses imagine that their historic forerunners would be immune to what is so vital —the simple fun of dressing up and smacking people?

All this being said, for the sake of the broader picture, some talk about this magical fertility stuff would still seem useful.

Percht **from Barmstoana Perchten, Hallein, Austria.** *Photo © Roland Käfer.*

Lucky Strikes

One reason the idea of the luck-bringing blows is so popular is that it conforms to a beloved narrative, namely the corruption of the pure Pagan by civilization and its ills (i.e., the Church). Regarding switches, this translates as: happy luck-bringing ritual corrupted to cruel punishment. The power of this narrative was demonstrated to me recently when someone (who is in fact involved in producing Krampus events in the US) explained to me that the Krampus was a kindly folkloric figure known to the pagans but misunderstood by Christians and perverted into something evil.

However, there is a problem with those benevolent beatings as a relic of the misty pagan past; namely that there is nothing in the historical record matching this. No matter how many old accounts we read of *Perchten* storming noisily about or scuffling amongst themselves—or scuffling with spectators—we do not find switches or whips swung by anyone like this until we begin looking at the Krampus.

In the most detailed account available of an early Gastein *Perchtenlauf*, folklorist Marie Andree-Eysn in 1904 mentions a sand-filled cow's tail used as a sort of whip, but it's not in the hands of a fur-wearing devil. It's used by one of the clowns, the Hanswurst character borrowed from Carnival along with his traditional stuffed leather "sausage" used as a club.

I would instead suggest that the use of the whip by contemporary *Perchten* simply represents the previously discussed migration of customs from one celebration into another. Quite the opposite of what is assumed, I believe the *Percht* has borrowed his whip from the Krampus and retrofitted its use with new meaning.

The *Perchten* run as it exists today, a mob exclusively consisting of fur-wearing devils, is a phenomenon only really appearing in the last two decades of the 20th century, one which grew up apace the urban Krampus run. Connecting the ubiquitous use of whips here with the isolated use of a whip by a clown in Gastein around the turn of the century hardly seems a sensible explanation for the usage today.

The *Perchten's* modification of the Krampus' potentially injurious bundle of switches to softer horse-tail whips also fits nicely with the narrative of the friendlier pagan world. Not surprisingly the same preference is shown by liability-minded city officials increasingly compelling Krampus as well as *Percht* to only employ the horsehair whip in public events. Likewise conforming to the narrative is the insistence on the *Percht's* multiple horns, which is cited as the breed's identifying trait, despite early and ongoing use of multi-horned Krampus masks in Gastein when representing Perchten. Widely recognized as a symbol of virility, sexuality, and fertility, the additional horns comply with the image of the pagan *Percht* and his more life-affirming and positive mission.

Though the action itself and the instrument wielded by the *Percht* may have been borrowed from the Krampus, the meaning assigned, those luck-imparting strokes, needn't have come from thin air. Other historical examples may have suggested the interpretation, and there seems to also be some intuitive connection between being struck and thriving. Some might even point to the obstetrician's slap that kick-starts the newborn infant, but we don't have to dig that deep. Americans should recognize this concept from the birthday spankings administered "for luck." The English wassail tradition enacts it in the beating of trees in an apple orchard to stimulate their growth. And many will be familiar with an example from the classical world—the use of goat-hide thongs to strike women and impart fertility in the ancient Roman festival of Lupercalia.

"Life Switches" and "Smacking Easter"

Closer to the *Percht's* world, we can find other traditions in which switches figure positively. Already mentioned were the *Martinsgerte* ("Martin's switches") brought in at the end of the pasture season and presented by herdsmen to their employers as a token of the life-giving properties of the fields. Though they were not employed to strike people, they were used to drive the cattle back to pasture in spring, and that contact was said to help the animals thrive.

Folklorists use the term "*Lebensrute*" ("life switches") to describe symbolic items like the *Martinsgerte,* and more than a few other examples are found among the folkways of the German-speaking peoples. Traditions involving lucky or life-giving switches are occasionally associated with St. Steven's Day (12/26) and New Year's, but most frequently Holy Innocents Day (12/28). These occur mostly in Catholic regions of southern Germany and south-central Austria and involve children as the wielder of the switches. The German custom, widely known as *Pfeffern* ("peppering"), is preserved in Bavaria's Franconian region, where children wander house to house hitting other children and adults, usually on the feet, and reciting a rhyme typically involving the phrase "*frisch und gesund*" ("fresh and healthy") and the question "Does the pepper taste good?" The beating would continue until the recipient agreed, "Yes, it tastes good!" and offered a small gift of nuts, fruits, or coins. Sometimes only boys would *pfeffern* on Holy Innocent's and the girls would reciprocate two days later on New Year, asking, "Does the New Year taste good?" The switches were either used by children to strike adults or on children of the opposite sex.

The Austrian version of this tradition, known as *Schappen* or *Pisnen*, also occurs on Holy Innocent's and is most associated with Carinthia, where it survives in certain town and villages today. The practice is similar, but is also combined with singing and dancing performances. The branches used are less like bundled switches than decorated evergreen boughs. *Schappen* visits, if generously rewarded, are said to bring success, luck, and abundant crops. Here, the switches may also be applied to trees in the orchards for increased yields.

Lebensrute practices, with their suggestion of fertility and stirring life, are also found in the spring, on Palm Sunday, or most widely in the tradition of "Smacking Easter" (*Schmackostern*) during which young women were usually targeted by young men. Use of some form of the *Lebensrute* was once traditional even at weddings where its association with fertility and mating would be particularly inescapable.

Battles in the Clouds

The use of whips by the *Perchten* has also drawn comparison to ritual battles waged for the fertility of the fields. Historian Carlo Ginzburg does so in his previously cited study of the 16th- and 17th-century *benandanti* cult in Italy's Friuli region on the Austrian border. In these nocturnal battles, which Ginzburg regards as visionary experiences, the *benandanti* were said to brandish bundles of dry fennel stalks, while the witches (*malandanti*) they opposed were armed with bundled broom sorghum. Briefly comparing this phenomenon to the *Perchten* activities, Ginzburg declares the latter *to be* "undoubtedly a remnant of the ancient ritual battles," going on to offer a historically inaccurate description of the *Perchtenlauf* as a "ceremony" in which good and bad *Perchten* "square off against one another … brandishing wooden canes and sticks." Especially damaging to the theory is the fact that the opposing *Schönperchten* and *Schiachperchten* duality is one we don't find mentioned until the mid-19th century.

While the *benandanti* believed they fought battles on a spiritual plane, the goal of combat was the welfare of a very specific real-world community and its crops. In this sense, their battles were territorial. The turf wars of Gastein's traditional *Rempler* and stories of the early Krampus-*Perchten Passen* from rival areas brawling do suggest territorialism, or perhaps even point to an underlying combative disposition of these troupes. On this alone, can we conclude their mission, as they understood it, was somehow essentially a "battle"? Common sense here would seem to favor prosaic local rivalries and alcohol over magical intent as motivating factor.

The idea of battles waged on a nonphysical plane is not peculiar to the mythology of the *benandanti*. Looking back several centuries to Burchard of Worms' 1023 *Decretum*, in which he condemns belief in Diana or Herodias, "whom the ignorant call Holda," the German bishop describes something similar: "Have you believed … you have crossed in the silence of the quiet night through closed doors to fly into the clouds where you have waged battle on others, both inflicting and receiving wounds?"

Ginzburg provides a large and surprising catalog of ritual battles elsewhere said to be fought in a visionary state, including an example from Livonia, a historic Baltic region under German influence, where in 1692, a man accused of transforming himself into a werewolf testified that on certain nights (including Christmas and St. Lucy's), he and an army of werewolves armed with "iron whips" battled sorcerers and devils wielding "broomsticks wrapped in horse tails." At stake again was the fertility of the fields.

Suggestive as this is of certain aspects of *Perchten* practice, without more specific historical references to *Perchten* fighting other supernatural beings, it does not seem worth pursuing.

A Swiss Connection?

Just south of the Austrian Tyrol in the Swiss canton of Graubünden (French: Grisons), however, we may have some support connecting the *Perchten* with the notion of ritual battle. From 1538, only a few decades before the *benandanti* trials, we have an account from scholar Gilg Tschudi describing an Alpine tradition involving masked ritual battles said to promote fertility. These battles occurring annually on "certain religious feasts" in the villages of Ilanz, Lungnez, and others, were waged by the *Stopfer* (literally, "piercers"). Masked *Stopfer* marched in troupes to rival towns for fights waged with clubs. They also engaged in a form of stylized combat involving midair collision during remarkably high leaps made with the aid of poles. The purpose of these rites, dismissed as foolish superstition by the scholarly author, was to ensure an abundant wheat crop. The name *Stopfer* is believed to refer to the "piercing" spike at the tip of the staffs used for the pole-vaulting.

Flying Leaps

A possible connection between the Swiss *Stopfer* and the *Perchten* is a common practice of pole-assisted leaps. Until the last decades of the 20th century, this custom was still part of the *Percht's* repetoire. A 1960s issue of the *Tiroler Heimatblätter* quotes a farmer from St. Ulrich am Pillersee, who points out a hole in the floor of his home, saying it was made by a spiked pole used by the *Tresterer* during an prodigious leaping performance. "Unless the soles of the feet touched the ceiling," he explains, "the *Percht* was worth nothing."

Similar stories reference footprints mysteriously left on ceilings where *Perchten* have exhibited their preternatural leaping skills.

Such spiked staffs have been mentioned as an aid in the *Perchten*'s flights over difficult terrain during the days when bans were in effect. Long staffs—perhaps nearly as frequently as bells or masks—are a defining feature in most early accounts of the *Percht*'s equipment, and the mention of *Perchten* leaping is a near constant in these same descriptions. In fact, in the earliest accounts, the word *Perchtenspringen* ("*Perchten* leaping") is used nearly as frequently as *Perchtenlauf* to describe *Perchten* activities. Though these athletic displays have now vanished, the old proverb "the higher the Percht jumps, the higher grows the grain" is still widely known and hints at a connection to the *Stopfer*'s leaping game and its magical aim.

While the value of these acrobatics as pure "Carnival amusements" should not be disregarded, they also partake in a supernatural, even diabolical, quality in associated folklore. In some versions of the "Thirteenth Percht" tale told of the *Percht* grave and elsewhere, the sinister entity hidden under the thirteenth costume sometimes surprises the other members of the troupe by leaping to heights no human could attain.

Here is a tale from Gastein that illustrates this diabolical involvement:

> In Gastein, the son of a dear, old Mother once overheard a wicked man declare that one could experience more joy in the Perchtenlauf if he went 14 days neither praying one word nor crossing himself.
>
> The lad thought, "One should leave no stone unturned. It's worth a try if more joy can truly be had. Neglecting prayers won't be hard as I've never enjoyed it anyway."
>
> When the Perchtenlauf came, everywhere there was great happiness and merriment. Amidst all this, a Percht leapt up balancing upon the top of the village fountain. From there, he suddenly leapt to a roof, and from there he flew up over the tops of the pines in the nearby forest.
>
> The spectators were first impressed but then became afraid and rushed to quickly fetch the clergy. From the village square the vicar offered blessings in all directions, north, south, east, and west. Then from a distance, the people witnessed the Percht fall from the sky. They ran hence to make a horrible discovery—it was the son of the dear, old mother who had followed such evil advice.
>
> One said, "He's almost gone, but at least he has enjoyed this Perchtenlauf he so eagerly awaited. Now he must answer for himself."
>
> Then the lad spoke "The vicar might have spared himself the blessing! To dance about in thin air; what a joy this is! You cannot begin to imagine! But as the vicar comes, the Devil has left me." And with these words the unfortunate lad gave up the ghost.

The Monsters Between the Years

This story makes clear that the *Perchtenlauf* was a recreational activity, but not one free of supernatural associations. Falling midway between the amusements of Carnival (usually in February) and the terrors of a haunted season beginning on St. Martin's day (November 11), the *Perchten* customs of the Twelve Nights drew something from both.

It seems doubtful to me such activities were ever conducted purely in the spirit of magic ritual. However, they probably stirred even in adults the sort of half-belief we still entertain when we enjoy a good ghost story. This sort of balancing act seems particularly well suited to children who inhabit more fully a world of the supernatural while still engaging with the world of the adult. The tradition of the Krampus, who was never a figure truly feared by adults, but created as a pious game and bit of parental pedagogy for children, probably preserves best this mix of play with fearful of supernatural beings. In the Krampus, descendant of the *Percht*, we have something of the wandering ghosts of the *Rauhnächte*, its devils and witches, and especially the image of Frau Perchta with her sickle.

Perhaps all this begins in the New Year Kalends of the Late Roman Empire, in some collective memory of men wandering from house to house disguised with the dried heads and leathery hides of horned beasts. The underlying folklore and exact details of those ancient celebrations remain largely unknown, but to me, their meaning seems somehow intuitive. These creatures are monsters in the old Latin sense—strange marvels portending some great or terrible event of the future. They embody the sense of wonder and fearful anticipation universally experienced when confronting an unknown future. Contemplating a new year always brings me monsters like this.

Conclusion

WHY THE KRAMPUS MUST COME

What Europeans I have talked to seem to fear most about America's adaptation of the tradition is that it will be removed from its context, that purely as a horror figure, the Krampus will lose his connection to Nicholas and his purpose. If we look at the creature's portrayal in the 2015 film *Krampus*, or examine the majority of American Krampus runs or costumed appearances where the devil runs unsupervised by any saint, this seems pretty well-founded.

The fear the Krampus produces has but one traditional purpose, and that is the betterment of children's behavior. This decidedly old-fashioned mission is often downplayed in favor of other aspects of the character more attractive to the hip and progressive. For the rebellious, the Krampus becomes more devilish, more of a free agent of hell than servant to a saint. Neopagans treat the Krampus more as a *Percht*, removing Nicholas and his correctives altogether. For more gentle and progressive souls, he lays down his switches and becomes what the German call the "cuddle Krampus."

But the Krampus' stern old-fashioned ways are also receiving new appraisal. Here and there, and perhaps moreso every day, there is discussion about what good a little toughness might contribute in a child's upbringing. A recent "Op-doc" from the *New York Times* entitled "Christmas Icon Reform" asked, "What do Iceland, Germany, and Japan all have in common? All got higher scores than the

Krampus, Alt Gnigler Pass, Salzburg. *Photo ©Martin Zehentner.*

U.S. in core school subjects," explaining this in terms of the menacing influence of the Krampus, Iceland's Christmas ogress Grýla, and Japan's New Year demon Namahage. Though tongue here may have been cautiously in cheek, the attitude is not that different from many recent—and more earnest—articles and editorials citing damages done by "helicopter parents," the meager life skills of over-indulged millennials, or the benefits of unsupervised play in "adventure playgrounds" rich with old junk, sharp edges, and splinters.

Rising dissatisfaction with the notion of trivializing "participant awards" should also strengthen enthusiasm for the Krampus' tradition. Instead of the rather meaningless generosity of gifts distributed by the American Santa Claus, the theatrics of the Nicholas house visit are geared toward creating a dramatic character-building game of higher stakes. Even in largely secular Europe where St. Nicholas now more often judges children on performances of songs and poetic recitations rather than catechism, his judicious positive comments and small gifts still engender the same sense of accomplishment and self-worth. The fear the child may experience in the face of hovering Krampuses, condemned by critics as mere cruelty, can also be regarded as an opportunity to display bravery and a valuable rehearsal for later real-world encounters.

Those who view the whole production in terms of harsh adult discipline overlook how intimately the house visit is attuned to the child's world of imagination. The encounter is made uniquely childlike and meaningful as it is played out by larger-than-life figures. Success in the encounter banishes ravening horned monsters to the frozen outdoors and brings a small gift and gentle words from a regal man with whiskers like clouds and hat like a church. The child's small trial is envisioned from his perspective, made huge as the child experiences it. He not only becomes the center of this living room drama, but the center of an epic battle pitched between the powers of heaven and hell. That such a drama would be staged in the home, with elaborate, expensive costumes, secret preparations and care to ensure its success in every detail—all the trouble, work and love devoted to this child-centered production seems very touching to me. And in the scene's playful staging, the adults at some level surely also experience and enjoy some of that same childlike grandiosity of imagination.

Even a small taste of fear can itself be a treat, as described in a December 1900 article from *The Lutheran*, in which the author recalls memories of the Belsnickel in the area around Philadelphia, and how children would "find a sort of delight and exhilaration in the very fright they experienced when the ominous birch of the 'Pelznickel' brushed against the window panes or shutters." This remembered feeling is timeless, having little to do with prevailing values or moral instruction. A child's delight in a certain measure of fear never goes out of style. A quick look at popular fantasy media consumed by children today will confirm this.

Beyond the Krampus' potential for inspiring the best in children, his current popularity also suggests a resurgence of a raw appetite for horror that once characterized the Christmas season. From medieval plays re-enacting the Massacre of the Innocents with blood-filled dolls to grisly legends of Frau Perchta and her knife, we've seen how the seasonal imagination has historically reveled in the darker side, and I would speculate that there is something perversely eternal in how the human imagination, once free of the unpleasantries of the workaday world, conjures unpleasantries of a more fanciful scale.

In old, agricultural societies, it was winter that drove laborers indoors and provided those leisure hours during which the mind spun dark fantasies. Today we are richer in leisure than ever before, and our idle craving for this peculiar stimulation ever stronger. Where a few handed-down ghost stories once did the trick, today's longing for those thrills is fed by endlessly renewed streams of horror, sci-fi, and fantasy stories provided on every conceivable entertainment platform.

Digitally delivered media, however, can never provide what an in-the-flesh encounter can. We crave somehow to get inside these stories and images, to walk among the characters that fascinate us, even to become them. Evidence of this is amply provided by San Diego's phenomenally popular sci-fi and fantasy convention, Comic-Con and its thriving cosplay culture, by the thousands of visitors who choose to assume the appearance and identity of fantasy figures and the thousands more who relish the opportunity to interact with them.

Unlike these Comi-Con characters born on screens or within graphic novels, and later embodied by costumed fans, the Krampus is not a media creation. He is not from a comic book, or a comic turned into a movie, a sequel, reboot or television series inspired by the film based on the comic. He is a folktale that bypassed all this to become a costumed figure. He is the real thing, not encountered in a digitally encoded storyline, but in a million unpredictable living interactions. It is precisely those living horns-and-fur encounters that make the figure so compelling.

The Alpine devil is visceral and physical in a way that few figures are. Smelling of animal hides and wet snow, he pushes forward assaulting your ears with his bells, shoving through spectators with a force unknown in polite society, and then, of all things—*he hits you!*

What better stimulant could there be for a leisure-numbed society passing its days moving from one glow-screen representation of the world to another? The devil hits us, and whether we laugh or scream, at least we are now truly awake, experiencing the real world fully, and standing before a myth.

INDEX

ACKNOWLEDGMENTS

Especially helpful in writing this book were my discussions on Krampus customs with Matthäus Rest and Wolfgang Böhm, as well as contact with Krampus troupes recently visiting Los Angeles—namely, Martin Zehentner with members of Salzburg's Alt Gnigler Pass, and Mike Kratzer with members of the Moorpass from Maishofen, Austria.

I'd also like to thank Vern Evans Photo, Gerhard Michel of Gasteinertal.com, Roland Käfer of Barmstoana Perchten, and Wolfgang Böhm as especially generous providers of imagery used in this book.

Critical to my understanding of contemporary practice were questionnaires I directed to various European groups and enterprises associated with Krampus, *Perchten*, and *Rauhnacht* customs. Helpful answers and photos were provided in response by: Alexander Haslauer of Krampusimperium, Alpen Teifen, Bad Mitterndorf Nikologruppe, Bixx'n Bartl, Christoph Haubner of *Krampuszeit* magazine, Claudia Nedwed of Molochs brut, Edi Pauliner of Klausenverein Sonthofen, the Goasbergpass, the Grödiger Krampusse, the Gruabtoifi Saalfelden, Günther Gollner, Hannes Brugger of Alt Gnigler Pass, Inmortuus Pass, Jung Alpenland, the Krampusverein Kappl, the Krampusverein Tisen, Michi Simpson, Miguel Walch Holzmasken, Mike Werger the Hexenschnitzer, the Oberpfälzer Schlossteufeln, the Perschtenbund Soj Kirchseeon, the Rifer Acheteifen, the Rumer Murteufel, Simon Wegleiter of Krampusgruppe Haiming, the Stechla.Pass, Stefan Hable, Stør Sven Dah, and Wolfgang Naumann of Ceteria Satanas.

Institutions kindly providing illustrations for this book were: Harvard Art Museums/Fogg Museum, Stadt- und Universitätsbibliothek at Goethe Universität,

Frankfurt, Tiroler Landesmuseen/Volkskunstmuseum, Tourismusbüro Waldkirchen, Tourismusverband Ostbayern e.V., TVB Rauris, and the Vienna Volkskundemuseum.

Finally, I'm grateful for the invaluable personal support and encouragement I received in researching, writing, and rewriting this book from Lauren Church, Eric Ridenour, and Margaret Cho, as well as Al Guerrero, Christian Pitt, and my comrades in Krampus Los Angeles (www.krampuslosangeles.com), and Stefan Kloo, Daniel Chaffey, and Fareed Majari of the Goethe Institut Los Angeles.

Treu dem guten alten Brauch!

Al Ridenour